I can't think of a better title or subject fc
the midst of disruption and desperately no
thankful for this book.

DANIELLE STRICKLAND, FOUNDER, WOMEN SPEAKERS COLLECTIVE
AND INFINITUM; AUTHOR OF NUMEROUS BOOKS ON MISSION,
SPIRITUALITY AND LEADERSHIP

A well-researched, biblically-based and Jesus-centred book – such a gift
as we seek the church's restoration to the shape Jesus intended. Cath
authentically operates in the prophetic and teaching gifts, making this a
truly exciting contribution.

PAUL HARCOURT, NATIONAL LEADER, NEW WINE ENGLAND;
AUTHOR, *WALKING ON WATER* AND *GROWING IN CIRCLES*

Holy Disruption is one of the most important and timely books for the
global church this year. Cath gives us an exceptionally comprehensive,
biblical understanding of the prophetic that calls the church back into
alignment with the person of Jesus and the true purpose of the prophetic.
She not only gives formative, practical instruction but also paints an
inspiring picture of a prophetically mature church whose feet are firmly
planted in both the presence of God and a life of justice.

CRYSTAL CRYER, NATIONAL COORDINATOR, 24-7 PRAYER SCOTLAND

This is a book the church needs at this unprecedented time of change. It
offers a map of the territory God is inviting his church into and will fill
you with hope and vision for the future. *Holy Disruption* will equip you
to climb the mountain and walk the road of all the prophetic ministry
involves; and with others it will help you establish the culture God always
intended for his church.

REVD CANON JOHN MCGINLEY, EXECUTIVE DIRECTOR,
MYRIAD, THE GREGORY CENTRE FOR MULTIPLICATION; AUTHOR,
MISSION SHAPED LIVING

Holy Disruption is what our churches need right now: a clear, comprehensive and convincing call to prophetic maturity in order to become all
we are called to be as the body of Christ. Our church leaders need to hear

this call and respond. Cath provides powerful, practical and scriptural support to help us understand what is at stake in this call and, importantly, to shape our response. The invitation of *Holy Disruption* is clear: to love and serve the world like Jesus and to live in the loving intimacy of the Trinity. I have been personally blessed by Cath's ministry and seen the transformative impact her teaching and leadership can have when it is embraced by churches and Christian communities. *Holy Disruption* brings together Cath's years of experience and wisdom and is a genuine gift from God to our world!

RT REV DR ELEANOR SANDERSON,
BISHOP OF HULL

Cath Livesey introduces readers to a broad-ranging overview of biblical prophecy and church practice that will help anyone seeking to engage in prophetic ministry today. Livesey bridges common divides between contemplative, charismatic and justice perspectives, showing how prophecy equips the body of Christ in sync with apostle, teacher, pastor and evangelist functions. This comprehensive book – rooted in years of on-the-ground engagement in Sheffield and extensive teaching and consulting on prophetic ministry – effectively closes the gap between worship and action, between hearing God and following Jesus concretely as a disciple. *Holy Disruption* equips us to become individuals and communities of discernment, presence and justice.

BOB EKBLAD, CO-FOUNDER, TIERRA NUEVA & THE PEOPLE'S SEMINARY;
AUTHOR, *READING THE BIBLE WITH THE DAMNED* AND *A NEW CHRISTIAN MANIFESTO: PLEDGING ALLEGIANCE TO THE KINGDOM OF GOD*

Holy Disruption wholly disrupts the pre-conceived ideas, myths, falsehoods and misunderstandings of the prophetic by exploring the depths of this gift in Scripture and considering its role within the fivefold gift mix. Through this book, Cath helps to restore trust in the prophets and calls not only for the lone prophetic voice but also for the whole prophetic church to speak out God's heart.

ANDREW AND ANDREA VERTIGAN, NATIONAL PIONEER AND
FRESH EXPRESSIONS LEADERS, SALVATION ARMY UK

In this day of volatility, uncertainty, complexity and ambiguity, the value of the prophetic cannot be overstated as it serves as a voice of divine guidance. Cath has done a wonderful job of demystifying and clarifying what this gift is and isn't. Timely words in this season.

TAMMY DUNAHOO, DIRECTOR, LEADER HEALTH AND DEVELOPMENT, THE FOURSQUARE CHURCH, US

Through stories, personal example and key biblical principles, Cath Livesey encourages us along a journey of prophetic discovery desperately needed in the Western church today.

NORM DYCK, MISSION MINISTER, MENNONITE CHURCH EASTERN CANADA; TEAM LEADER, INNOVATE, LISTOWEL, ONTARIO, CANADA

Cath Livesey has given us a special gift in *Holy Disruption*. With a clear focus on obedience to Jesus and a commitment to help the local church experience and live into the fullness of Christ, Livesey offers a helpful guide to the reality and riches of the prophetic. Don't be afraid of the holy disruption Jesus wants to bring to your life and ministry! This book paints a beautiful picture of what's possible when the local church steps more fully into all of the gifts available.

LANCE FINLEY, EXECUTIVE DIRECTOR, CHURCHES OF GOD, GENERAL CONFERENCE, FINDLAY, OHIO, US

Holy Disruption is a vital contribution to our understanding of prophecy, prophets and the prophetic. Whether we are approaching it from a charismatic or social justice perspective, Cath's balanced and in-depth biblical analysis helps ground us in this vital contribution to the body of Christ, the world at large and the coming kingdom. With much practical wisdom, Cath helpfully unpacks the need to identify our heart's motivations for pursuing the 'presence' and 'activism' dimensions of the prophetic and highlights the importance of finding the right balance between charismatic and social justice expressions. This book may bring a holy disruption to our lives and churches, but it is one that is much needed!

NIC HARDING, DIRECTOR, KAIROS CONNEXION; FOUNDING PASTOR, FRONTLINE CHURCH, LIVERPOOL, UK

A beautifully challenging and refreshingly practical guide for igniting a prophetic culture in God's people and the church. Releasing the prophetic in the church is paramount for breaking through the noise of our day and communicating who God is and what he's really like to a world that desperately needs him. I found myself praying the Spirit's disruptive presence and voice into my neighbourhood, my community and the churches around me as I read.

GINA MUELLER, DIRECTOR, 3DM NORTH AMERICA

This insightful and exciting book had me hooked from the first page. *Holy Disruption* will equip church leaders and individuals who long to see the church alive and impactful. Cath helps us not only understand the prophetic call on our lives but also how to activate the prophetic function as a church. We can do this!

RON HUNTLEY, LEADERSHIP COACH, PODCAST HOST AND SPEAKER; AUTHOR, *UNLOCKING YOUR PARISH: MAKING DISCIPLES, RAISING UP LEADERS WITH ALPHA*

In *Holy Disruption*, Cath Livesey grounds the prophetic gifting and calling in the person of Jesus. There is no better lens than Jesus through which to gain a holistic vision of the prophetic – one that is faithful to our covenantal relationship with God and committed to pressing out towards the margins. *Holy Disruption* is one of those rare books that melds both solid teaching and practical tools to equip yourself, others and the church. I highly recommend that you read it and put it to use!

JOSHUA JOHNSON, EXECUTIVE DIRECTOR, ALL NATIONS KANSAS CITY, US; HOST, *SHIFTING CULTURE* PODCAST; AUTHOR, *THE POCKET GUIDE TO HEALTHY CHURCH*

HOLY DIS- RUP- TION

CATH LIVESEY

HOLY DIS- RUP- TION

Harnessing the Prophetic to
Shape a More Christlike Church

100
MOVEMENTS
PUBLISHING

ISBN 978-1-955142-19-9 (print)
ISBN 978-1-955142-20-5 (ebook)

Cover image: Nik Merkulov/Shutterstock.com

Cover design: Revo Creative Ltd.

100 Movements Publishing
An imprint of Movement Leaders Collective
Cody, Wyoming

www.movementleaderscollective.com
www.catalysechange.org

To my husband, St.John
With all my love

CONTENTS

FOREWORD

ALAN HIRSCH

In your hands is a serious exploration of the nature and purposes of the prophetic. It is aptly called *Holy Disruption,* in that it disrupts prevailing understandings of this ministry, as well as addressing a church facing not only political unrest but also the significant disruption of a global pandemic. I believe we need God's guidance now more than any other point in my lifetime. The powers in the heavens are being shaken; idols are being exposed; our frailties, and even our sins, are being laid bare; and the US church, in particular, finds itself in an ideological cold war that shows no sign of abating. What does God require of us in these apocalyptic times? How can we discern our way through the maze of swirling ideologies that call for our loyalties and allegiance? How does God guide, equip and empower us to faithfully negotiate the crises we currently face? Into this milieu comes *Holy Disruption.*

Cath's book is arriving at the perfect time – just as the church is taking stock of so much that goes under the rubric of the prophetic ministry. For instance, a recent document signed by hundreds of senior leaders and theologians within the charismatic church has called for greater accountability for the prophetic in the aftermath of numerous inaccurate prophecies concerning the US elections.[1] The signatories of the document proposed that the election debacle was not an isolated occurrence but rather exposed prevailing problems in the global movement, concluding that 'unaccountable prophecy has been a bane on the modern Pentecostal-charismatic movement for decades.'[2] I believe that *Holy Disruption* will provide a much-needed, practical corrective for churches seeking to exercise authentic prophetic ministry.

Having written extensively on the dynamics of the fivefold biblical functions and callings, I believe there are a number of significant explorations in this book that set it apart from the many other books on prophetic ministry. In particular, Cath highlights two aspects I have long felt enrich our perspectives on what God does through genuine expressions of the church's prophetic ministry. These alone will render us a more faithful church.

First, in *5Q* I suggested a dual expression of the prophetic found in any authentic and mature prophetic ministry.[3] I refer to these expressions as *Vertical* and *Horizontal*. The *Vertical* prophetic incorporates the somewhat more 'God-oriented and directed' functions, including, among other things, the maintaining of an active covenant relationship between God and his people; the removal of all that gets in the way of this relationship (the renunciation of idolatry); the call to genuine prayer and true worship; and the distinctive orientation to the supernatural along with the ministry of the discernment of spirits. This dimension can readily be seen in the various mystical as well as Holy Spirit movements that have been part of the church from the very beginning. The *Horizontal* function, on the other hand, includes the calling to be something of a prefigurative community that embodies true witness, a commitment to social forms of holiness, an unrelenting commitment to God's justice (his love distributed), and the like. And, as far as I can tell, apart from the remarkable ministry and writings of Bob Ekblad of Tierra Nueva,[4] I am not aware of any other books that bring the charismatic-mystical (Vertical) and the activist (Horizontal) together. Cath explores both of these aspects in great detail, and for this I am grateful.

The second issue I have long felt requires theological clarity is the differentiation between the *personality/characteristics* of the prophetic person with that of the Spirit-energised manifestation of the prophetic *gift* of prophecy available to all; in other words, the distinction between the prophetic person and the prophetic gift as two separate dimensions of the same function. Clarifying this distinction between person and gifting will enable us to gain a significantly profound insight into the particular *mindset* and orientation – the unique 'take' on reality – that characterises the biblical prophet. This alone is very promising, but Cath combines newfound clarity on the prophetic personality with a clearer understanding of the gift of prophecy as a manifestation of the Holy Spirit's active presence in and through his people. I have no doubt that this will bring much needed revitalisation to the church's prophetic ministry and impact in the world.

There are many other wonderful aspects of the nature and function of the prophetic covered in this well-researched book. In bequeathing us this volume, one which I know has cost her much time in study and writing, Cath does what she always does so well – she helps all of God's people to better understand the knowledge just learnt and to apply it, so that we might live a faithful life in the name of Jesus. *Holy Disruption* is, in the end, an eminently practical book, and I heartily recommend it to you.

INTRODUCTION

OFF THE MAP?

*Call to me and I will answer you and tell you great and
unsearchable things you do not know.*

JEREMIAH 33:3

On a wall of the Beinecke Rare Book and Manuscript Library at Yale
University hangs a scuffed and faded map. Created around 1490 by German
cartographer Henricus Martellus, this detailed document represents the very
best of European geographical knowledge at that time. It was a huge technical
achievement for the late fifteenth century and a wonder of the age. But despite
its presence today in a North American university, this world map is lacking
something very significant: *the Americas*.

At the dawn of the Age of Exploration, the Europeans had no concept
of the American continents. European discoverers believed that if they
sailed west from Spain they would run straight into China. A vast landmass – 8,700 miles long and 5,800 miles wide – was missing from their
perception of the world. A land that would eventually become home to
millions of Europeans was absent from their geography. In 1490, the
Americas were literally 'off the map'.

Imagine travelling back to 1490 with an aeroplane and taking the
cartographer Martellus on a flight over the length and breadth of the
Americas. Picture him seeing the abundance and beauty of the land he
knew nothing of: the glittering lakes and rivers, the vast mountain ranges,
the incredible wildlife, the richness of the human societies already calling
this land home. And then imagine showing Martellus a modern globe so

that he can observe where the Americas fit in relation to the other continents. Consider the seismic shift in understanding that would need to take place for him to absorb this new information.

It took a long time for the rest of the world to get their heads around the concept of the Americas. Europe was to have a complicated relationship with the 'new world' for the next few centuries. Even today, those of us who are Europeans may view the place with a mixture of fascination and perplexity. But at least it's on our maps now.

PUTTING THE PROPHETIC ON THE MAP

For many contemporary churches, the prophetic is a similarly intriguing and puzzling concept, often unseen or unrealised. Perhaps, like Martellus, the prophetic is completely outside our frame of reference and remains undiscovered territory. Or perhaps we are aware of it, but like the sixteenth-century-European perception of the Americas, we are overly wary of the imagined monsters and perils it contains and so prefer to keep our distance. Maybe, like the seventeenth-century Pilgrim Fathers, we have fled to this continent for refuge, but as yet have little understanding of its sheer size and inherent potential.

Even for those of us who love the prophetic land and delight in its many wonders, there is still much to explore. Like our imaginary plane ride with Martellus, my aim is to take the reader on a flight of discovery that will open up the breadth and depth of the prophetic terrain. I want to dispel fears and awaken minds to the possibilities this ministry offers for every expression of the body of Christ. Rather than focusing on the technical aspects of prophecy (the equivalent of being able to name all the tributaries of the Amazon River), we are going to explore together the tone and texture – the contours – of the prophetic landscape. We will observe how it is shaped around the ministry of Jesus and why it is essential for the health and maturity of the church.

I also want us to consider what it means for the church *community* to inhabit this land. For far too long the prophetic has attracted the individual but failed to win over the church. We have focused on the role of the prophet and neglected our *corporate* prophetic identity. I believe it's only when we get the big picture of the prophetic – the view from our imaginary aeroplane

– that we can be the kind of prophetic body Jesus always intended us to be. My aim is to provide a framework for leaders, churches and ministries from many different backgrounds to faithfully engage with the important question of what is means to be an authentic and mature prophetic church.

So, what is this perplexing terrain we call the *prophetic*? And why do we need it on our spiritual and ecclesial maps? Like the vast landmass of the Americas, the prophetic exists, and we can't ignore it.

The word *prophetic* itself is subject to many different interpretations. Perhaps you're a leader in a charismatic church where the gift of prophecy is practised and valued. Maybe your approach to the prophetic centres around a concern for social justice and speaking truth to power. Or perhaps you are from a more conservative background where the prophetic is barely discussed, but you'd like to explore why it is biblical and important for the body of Christ … and even how you might apply it in your own context.

Whatever your starting point, we need a comprehensive understanding of prophetic ministry – one that enables us to welcome and define the prophetic call on the church.

Throughout this book, we will explore a biblical interpretation of the word *prophetic*, and along the way we will take a close look at the words *prophet* and *prophecy* as well. My hope is that this book gives you a fuller realisation of this fascinating ministry and why it plays such a vital role in fulfilling the vision Jesus has for his church.

So, where do we begin? In order to grasp the concept of the prophetic, we need to gain a thirty thousand-foot perspective. Most of us would agree that the prophetic has something to do with God speaking (or at least an alignment with God's heart, intention and future purposes), so let's step back for a few moments to consider the scriptural framework.

A BIBLICAL OVERVIEW

Scripture clearly shows us a God who is not silent. From the start, his voice resounded throughout the creation narrative. God spoke, and stars appeared in the night sky, fish swarmed in the sea, and birds took flight. There are very few books in the Bible without at least some reference to

God speaking. The Bible reveals a God who is intent on communicating with the people he has created; a God with a voice that ranges from 'roaring waters'[1] to a 'gentle whisper'.[2]

We also see a God of covenantal love, who invites us into relationship with himself, and who is absolutely committed to the restoration of relationship with humanity. This is a personal God who has emotions and doesn't hold back from expressing them; a God who speaks of his deep love and affection for those he's in covenant with;[3] a God who is jealous for his people.[4]

This deeply relational aspect of God's nature sits alongside the fact that he is utterly holy.[5] God is pure radiant light and is eternally worthy of reverence and worship. Crucially, his communication calls his people to holiness, righteousness and faithfulness.[6] God is in the business of transformation, never satisfied with leaving people as they are but always drawing them into greater levels of godliness.

God regularly appoints individuals to speak on his behalf.[7] Moses, the prototype prophet, received a weighty commission to convey God's words to Pharaoh and lead an enslaved people into freedom. Speaking on God's behalf might involve standing before pagan kings or communicating God's words to God's people.

Later Old Testament prophets had the hard task of being God's mouthpiece, as well as the privilege of dramatic encounters with God himself.[8] Their stories offer tantalising glimpses into standing in the very presence of God and being party to his plans.[9] These old covenant prophets saw and understood their historical context from God's perspective. Their role involved both calling God's people to repentance and holding out hope. They spoke powerfully and urgently against idolatry and injustice. There was a *fore*telling dimension to their ministry (when prophesying future events); but there was also a *forth*telling aspect. In fact, the vast majority of Old Testament prophecy addressed Israel's immediate or imminent situation.[10] Communicating God's message through both words and actions, the prophets often used startling and bewildering imagery and persuasive rhetoric. They emphasised covenant faithfulness and a vision for the transformation of God's people. Their particular personalities brought a unique flavour to their prophetic utterances. They openly longed for a time when God would intervene and bring restoration to Israel – and indeed to all of his creation.[11]

Moving on to the New Testament, we see the Word of God himself come to this world. Jesus, the ultimate prophetic revelation, shows us exactly what God is like.[12] In Jesus, we see the perfect model of a prophet – the one who sees God, speaks life, and challenges the status quo like no one else. Jesus is the Spirit-filled, justice-focused, end-times-prophesying Son of Man. His is a ministry that prophetically speaks to the past, present and future. And with him comes the gospel of grace, and a shift in emphasis from judgement to reconciliation.

And finally, Scripture records the outpouring of God's Spirit upon the church, making the gift of prophecy available to every believer.[13] The church is a prophetic community, made up of Spirit-filled followers of Jesus. The promise for the new covenant people of God is unrestricted access to the Father's presence through the work of the Holy Spirit – the Spirit of Truth who searches out the deep things of God and makes them known to us.[14]

The theme of God speaking – and how humanity responds to these words – is present from Genesis to Revelation. Scripture itself highlights the significance of the prophetic.

NOT AN OPTIONAL EXTRA

I've spent decades practising, teaching, training, coaching and writing about the prophetic. I love this land! I love seeing the kingdom-impact a mature prophetic culture has among the churches I work with. I love seeing hearts healed through encounters with God's voice. I love seeing wrongs righted, as God's people respond to the prophetic call to restore their neighbourhoods. I love seeing prophetic individuals make sense of the gifts God has given them and multiply them into their churches. And I'm convinced that an authentic Jesus-shaped prophetic ministry is needed now more than ever.

The twenty-first century moved us into an age of misinformation.[15] Objective truth seems increasingly hard to find, and this post-truth reality can leave us fearful and confused. We are in desperate need of the Spirit of Truth, the One given to the church to 'teach us all things'[16] and 'guide us into all truth.'[17] A healthy prophetic ministry, faithfully channelling the Spirit's revelation and submitted to his work of conviction,[18] helps to ensure we are aligned with God's Word. A mature prophetic ministry that complements sound biblical teaching ensures that Jesus' voice is the one we are attending to and following.[19] When a healthy prophetic expression is missing from the church, we become more vulnerable to being 'tossed back and forth by the waves, and blown here and there by every wind of teaching and by the cunning and craftiness of people in their deceitful scheming' (Ephesians 4:14). These ancient words seem particularly pertinent to the times we find ourselves in. When the church and the world are vulnerable to 'fake news', a mature prophetic culture helps us keep our eyes on God's ultimate truth.

We are also living in a world that longs for God. In a post-Christian society we may have lost our sense of the divine, but people are still yearning and searching for transcendence. They are hungry for an authentic spiritual experience, particularly one that speaks to their sense of identity. An essential function of the prophetic is to show us *who God truly is* and then, in light of this, to show us *who we truly are.* The prophetic church can speak to people's true identity and facilitate an encounter with the God who knows and loves them.

When the church is fully engaged with the prophetic, it is equipped not only to call souls back to God but also to tangibly express God's concerns in society and to fight injustice. Without the prophetic, our ability to challenge the status quo is diminished. If we want to be a church that can care for the marginalised, speak truth to power and stand up to tyranny, then we need to adopt a holistic prophetic culture.

As we fully embrace the prophetic, we can increasingly become an *empowered* church: a church that can stay faithful to God's purposes and be a positive force for change in his world. If we want to know more of who we are as children of God, if we want to know and share God's concern for his body and the broken world around us, the church needs to rediscover its prophetic identity and voice.

HOLY DISRUPTION

The prophetic is a land of abundance and treasure; but to fully occupy its breadth and depth, it's important to take stock of what it may demand of us.

The more we cast our gaze over the extent of the prophetic landscape, the more it becomes clear that God speaks for the purpose of *transformation*. He speaks in order that he might reshape us and thus conform us to the image of his Son; he speaks in order to transform our neighbourhoods for the sake of his justice and righteousness. We cannot avoid the disruptive nature of the prophetic. Once we start listening to God's voice, we realise that God is a holy Disruptor, and no part of our lives is exempt from his activity. Mindsets are challenged, agendas surrendered, indifferences shattered, behaviours changed, powers opposed, chains broken and strongholds demolished. The wind blows wherever it pleases,[20] so the Spirit of truth requires 'access all areas'. If we are serious about exploring this land of wonders, we need to ask ourselves whether we are prepared to leave behind our settled existence and be blown by the wind of the Spirit wherever he determines.

The title of this book acknowledges the unsettling and interruptive nature of the prophetic and its role in bringing about necessary change to hearts and society. The prophetic church is one that readily yields to the holy and creative process of divine transformation.

OPENING UP THE MAP

In the pages that follow, I'll address four key issues:

- *Putting the prophetic on the map.* There is plenty of confusion and controversy surrounding prophetic ministry, and the temptation for many church leaders is to ignore it – as if it's not on the map. We will explore why the prophetic needs to be on the map, what the Bible has to say about it, and why it should be an integral part of every church.
- *Broadening our perspective.* In today's polarised culture, different segments of the church claim different elements of the prophetic for themselves. However, very few demonstrate a holistic, multi-dimensional and authentically Jesus-shaped perspective. Few

churches have the whole picture. Like a Texan who has never been to Patagonia or a Costa Rican who has never been to Hudson Bay, it is all too easy to limit our understanding of the prophetic to what is local and familiar. And too often, discussion around the prophetic brings further division rather than greater unity. We'll look at how a fuller understanding of the prophetic can draw the disparate tribes together.

- *Having our feet on the ground.* We can have a theological understanding of the prophetic, but if that is not combined with *application,* we won't grow into the maturity God has planned for us; we won't actualise the full potential of this land of wonders. As disciples of Jesus, the call is always to hear *and* obey; to not only have theological comprehension but also to embody those truths, both personally and corporately. If we don't steward the gifts and tools God gives us, they lie dormant and unrealised.

- *Adventuring together.* Though many churches have grasped hold of *individual* prophetic gifting, there is often a lack of understanding when it comes to the concept of *shared* identity as a prophetic body of people. And so, the fourth key issue to address is how we can help the *whole* church find a home in this remarkable landscape. When a prophetic ministry is centred on certain 'anointed' individuals, the prophetic becomes vulnerable to a lack of accountability and is seen as an exclusive and mysterious pursuit. It's only when the church can fully grasp its identity as a prophetic community that the prophetic becomes truly accessible, normalised and demystified.

Whether we view the prophetic as an unexplored continent or as familiar as our own backyard, I would like to gently challenge all of us to step back far enough to get the big-picture perspective. Let me open up the map – one that will enable us to grasp what we are called to be as a Jesus-shaped prophetic community.

Come with me, and let's explore together.

PART 1
REALITY CHECK

GETTING OUR BEARINGS AND FIXING OUR COORDINATES

*As we set off, we need to fix our coordinates around the person and minis-
try of Jesus. The history of the prophetic down the ages is littered with its
fair share of controversy and disagreement but, as we will discover, Jesus
provides us with the perfect model and rationale for making sense of this
intriguing landscape.*

*In Part 1, we will begin with the theological foundations needed in
order to understand the prophetic. We will track the prophetic as firstly
rooted in the nature and purposes of God, then flawlessly expressed in Jesus'
own ministry, and finally given to the church by Christ himself. We will see
how the prophetic role of God's people deepens as we move from the Old to
the New Testament, and how God speaking through the Hebrew prophets is
a prelude to him speaking through his Son. An in-depth look at the biblical
role of prophet, in chapters three and four, will provide a framework for
understanding how the church itself can embrace its own prophetic identity.*

*This big-picture overview will enable us to start examining what it
means to be a prophetic community of people – a church that faithfully
holds out God's reality to the world. We will need this communal lens in
order to view the full extent of the prophetic landscape.*

1

THE BIGGER PICTURE

Jesus … was a prophet, powerful in word and deed before God and all the people.

LUKE 24:19

What comes to mind when we consider the word *prophetic*? Fiery Pentecostal preachers? Predictions of the end of the world? Political activism? New Age crystals?

As we start exploring the vast landscape of prophetic ministry, we need to pay careful attention to vocabulary. Since words are powerful, especially in their ability to shape and define culture, we need to be confident in our definitions and wise in how we put our lexicon to use.

The words *prophet* and *prophecy* are thoroughly biblical, but in the twenty-first century they have the capacity to ruffle feathers and provoke disquiet in many corners of the church. These words seem weighed down by preconceptions and stereotypes. They generate anxiety in the hearts of many pastors. They have led to arguments, fall-out and alienation. In some quarters they are bandied about in careless fashion, while in many others they hardly dare be whispered.

I'm personally very aware of the complex factors that influence my use of these two words. I lead an international prophetic ministry, but I would rarely introduce myself to people as a *prophet*. I yearn for a profoundly prophetic lifestyle and have prophesied over many hundreds of people, and yet how often do I claim to be uttering *prophecy*?

Another variation of the term – *prophetic* – is an adjective, but it often gets used as a noun. I've already referred to *the prophetic* as a concept in and of itself. The word has a whole host of interpretations, depending on where in the body of Christ you make your camp. Unlike the words *prophet* and *prophecy*, the word *prophetic* rarely occurs in Scripture (in some Bible translations it doesn't occur at all); but in contemporary Christendom it has numerous associations. As a *concept*, the prophetic is thoroughly biblical and extremely useful – provided we have worked out what it actually means.

As we seek clarity in our definitions, we also need to pay attention to how these three words relate to each other. In some church contexts, the words *prophet* and *prophecy* are used almost interchangeably, but it's important to separate them out as two distinct biblical themes and carefully consider their individual semantics. They are not synonymous, and the one does not automatically follow the other. On the other hand, it can be helpful to use the phrase *the prophetic* as something of an umbrella term to collectively refer to many things connected to the other two words.

So, how are we to take hold of the words *prophet*, *prophecy* and *prophetic*? How can we use them wisely?

These three words don't belong exclusively to the Christian church and are certainly not confined to the genre of biblical literature. They are found in ancient texts as well as modern speech. In a secular context, the label *prophecy* is employed to describe a prediction of the future – foretelling events yet to unfold. We can talk about a prophetic *type* found in society – a cultural shorthand for a person who is an artist, seer, mystic, iconoclast or activist. We can also look around us and identify what we might call *prophetic intelligence* – a disposition that is ethical, authentic, challenging and truth-speaking.[1]

While it's helpful to recognise how secular culture uses these words, our primary source of interpretation has to be the Bible. It is Scripture that will enable us to decipher the map legend and thus make sense of the terrain in front of us.

DIFFERENT APPROACHES TO THE PROPHETIC

Within the church there are many different approaches, paradigms, theologies and traditions. There isn't space within these pages to consider all of them, but we do need to recognise and lay aside our own biases and name our specific echo chambers. We've all been influenced by many different factors and experiences, including our particular church background.

In 1986, the *Guardian* newspaper ran what became an iconic TV advertisement,[2] which opens with a skinhead running down a street. At first sight he seems to be fleeing from something; then it appears he's about to mug a businessman; finally, with a different camera angle, it becomes apparent that the skinhead is trying to save the businessman from a pile of falling bricks. As the voice-over explains, 'An event, seen from one point of view gives one impression. Seen from another point of view it gives quite a different impression. But it's only when you get the whole picture, you can fully understand what's going on.' We are all susceptible to bias, to only seeing things from a personal perspective, which is why the widest camera angle – or the thirty-thousand-foot view – is so important.

I'm well aware that within my own tribe – the British mainstream charismatic church – we have a particular take on *prophecy* and *prophet*, and our understanding and application of these words is different from many other contexts around the world. When I talk about 'prophetic ministry' here in the UK, I can be reasonably confident that my listeners will be on the same page as me. But if I visit friends in the United States, the Netherlands or New Zealand, or if I cross denominational borders to be with friends in the Catholic, Mennonite or Methodist traditions, perspectives are going to vary. Nuances need to be attended to.

As we begin to unpack the words *prophetic*, *prophet* and *prophecy* and seek a comprehensive understanding of them, we can start by recognising that there are at least two main approaches to the prophetic found in the global church, both of which have a strong biblical basis.[3]

A ***social justice*** understanding of the prophetic is one in which *prophecy* is mainly understood as social action, with a primary goal of bringing about godly change in society. Within this approach there is more reference to prophetic *actions* or someone having a prophetic *voice* rather than to prophecy itself. When spoken prophecy *is* referenced, it is usually understood as boldly speaking truth to power on behalf of the oppressed. From this perspective, a *prophet* would be a social reformer – someone like Martin Luther King, Jr. – and the focus tends to be much more on the present rather than the distant future. Within this tradition, the Old Testament prophets are viewed as early advocates of social justice and defenders of the downtrodden and marginalised.

A *charismatic* understanding of the prophetic emphasises *prophecy* as a gift of the Spirit and is defined as the supernatural experience of hearing God's voice and then speaking it out. The word *prophetic* is therefore applied to a person or context where this experience is regularly happening, and a *prophet* is someone who frequently and accurately delivers prophecy. This approach particularly emphasises the personal and individualistic side of faith, with prophecy being used to cultivate a deeper relationship with God and to discern his guidance. With this perspective comes an invitation to not only study the likes of Elijah and Ezekiel but also to imitate their prophetic ministry – 'if they can do it, then so can we!'

To get the big picture of the prophetic – and to properly comprehend what it means to be a prophetic church – we have to take both of these schools of thought seriously. Much of this book is focused on broadening perspectives on the prophetic so that we can embrace a more holistic viewpoint.

We also need to be aware of a third approach to the prophetic, which may resonate with some readers and brings something else to the conversation.

A *conservative* understanding tends to be future-focused and eschatological. Within this approach, *prophecy* is found mainly in the pages of Scripture and is seen as something that encourages and strengthens the people of God by pointing them to God's kingdom, his eschatological promises and his cosmic judgements. Words of prophecy are seen as universal rather than personal and specific. From this perspective the *prophets* of the Bible are understood to provide detailed descriptions of events associated with the end times. Under the conservative umbrella would lie the cessationist position: that all revelatory gifts of the Spirit died out once the canon of the New Testament was established. Cessationists contend that God's revelation is complete and all-sufficient within the Bible itself.

The conservative approach to the prophetic is not an explicit focus of this book. Due to its primary emphasis on prophecies contained within the pages of Scripture, it is less applicable to the practical outworking of being a prophetic church. But it is important to recognise that many people hold this theological viewpoint, and when we look at the prophetic ministry of Jesus, we observe significant eschatological elements. I very much want to invite conservative readers to come on the flight of discovery with me.

You may already be able to place yourself within one of the three camps I've outlined above. I hope you can recognise how a particular church background can strongly influence the relationship each of us has with the prophetic.

As followers of Christ today, I believe we need to aim for a holistic attitude in which we are able to hold different perspectives in tension. We need a definition of the prophetic that is biblically based, that creates some common ground, and that provides a safe environment for every Christian to explore this ministry in a healthy manner.

THEOLOGICAL ROOTS

All three approaches highlighted above have something to offer as we seek to refine our vocabulary and develop our understanding. It's helpful to appreciate how the words *prophet*, *prophecy* and *prophetic* are utilised in each camp. But to truly comprehend the prophetic, we have to start with the character and nature of God. In fact, we have to start with the *theology* of the prophetic in its literal sense. Theology is the study of God, and the prophetic is first and foremost rooted in *who God is*. Understanding the nature of God is the foundation for all our thinking on the prophetic.

Prophetic consciousness and experience are essentially a reflection of God himself. The prophetic originates with God; it is grounded and sourced in him. We will get the fullest understanding of the prophetic role and ministry if we are able to pull back and look at God himself, to see how the roots of the prophetic are found in his nature and purposes.

The God who chooses to be known. Scripture shows us a God who wants to be known. He is the *Deus revelatus*, with the pinnacle of divine revelation being Christ's life, death and resurrection.[4] Self-revelation is inherent in the very nature of God and is at the heart of the Godhead.[5]

Despite the seemingly unbridgeable gulf between the infinite, uncreated God and his creation, he takes the initiative and breaks into the finite created realm to reveal himself to us in love, so that knowing him is possible.[6] Self-disclosure is an aspect of his divine nature. Although God can never be completely known – he will never become predictable, packaged or controllable – he tells us his name,[7] he speaks forth his character,[8] and he allows us to know his emotions.[9] We love him because we know him. He holds out the promise that he can be found by those who truly seek him.[10]

The God of relationship. God desires to be known by us because he loves us. He created humanity in his own image so that he could be in committed relationship with us. At the very heart of God's being is the triune relationship of Father, Son and Spirit; the ultimate relationship, and one that we are all invited into.[11] The God we worship is not a distant, unemotional, unconcerned deity, satisfied with burnt offerings. The Bible speaks profoundly of God's heart and reveals the God of love. And this God is our heavenly Father – the type of Father who hikes up his robes and runs towards his prodigal children, ready to kiss and embrace them.[12]

The God of communication. It follows that the God who chooses to be known, the God of relationship, is also the God who speaks. Ongoing communication is a vital part of any relationship, and when we look at the Bible, we find that God is the One who freely initiates communication with people. It is God who speaks first.[13] Throughout the biblical narrative, God readily communicates: through dreams, visions, angelic visitations, but primarily through his voice. A recurring phrase in the Old Testament is the *dabar-Yahweh* – 'the word of the Lord.' It was this word that Abraham first encountered in Genesis 15:1 and that many prophets experienced as a transformational event.[14] Such encounters give a foretaste of the greatest *dabar-Yahweh* – the definitive divine communication – when the Word became flesh in the person of Jesus Christ.

The God of restoration. *Shalom* – meaning peace, wholeness, completeness and well-being – is rooted deep in Scripture and in the nature of God. This rich, beautiful word reflects God's intention that all things shall be restored and made new. Despite humanity's best efforts to rebel and destroy, to sow division and wage war, God and his kingdom bring wholeness, healing and peace. His desire is that all of creation will be reconciled and realigned back to him; that broken relationships will be restored; and he frequently uses his voice to communicate this intention. The *dabar-Yahweh* carries with it inherent restorative potential. When Isaiah prophesied the coming Messiah, he declared that this King would be called the 'Prince of *Shalom*' and that his reign would bring '*shalom* without end'.[15]

God is the Great Communicator: the God of revelation, relationship and restoration. This is the *why* of the prophetic. The most loving, kind and generous being imaginable chooses to reach out to the people he has made in order to reveal his heart and his thoughts, to proclaim his very nature, and to restore all things unto himself. To know God is to be alive to the prophetic nature of God.

The theologian Walter Brueggemann expresses it like this: 'The prophetic alternative is rooted in the character of God himself ... . He is one whose person is presented as passion and pathos, the power to care, the capacity to weep, the energy to grieve and then to rejoice.'[16]

The prophetic ministry of Christ brings this theology into sharp relief, and later on in this chapter we will look at Jesus as the archetypal prophet; but at this stage we are ready for a definition of the prophetic.

THE PROPHETIC: A DEFINITION

In seeking a truly holistic approach, one that aligns with the biblical narrative and prophetic tradition, here is my definition of *the prophetic* (an umbrella term which encompasses both prophet and prophecy):

> The prophetic is about the faithful holding out of God's reality, so that it can be clearly seen and responded to, so that transformation can take place and so that relationship can be restored.

Let's now unpack this definition.

The prophetic is so much more than delivering God's words or projecting his plans onto the future; it's about revealing the living God and his incomparable reality – his utterly 'other' reality. The prophetic is about bringing the huge searchlight of God's truth to our frail and insufficient attempts to make sense of ourselves and the world around us.

God's reality is not something that can be empirically measured and quantified, but it is a reality far superior to any human construct. God's reality is the divine perspective, the *divine interpretation* of any human situation. This is not something we can work out using our human reasoning; we are completely dependent on the grace and power of God's Spirit in order to perceive it. The great Jewish scholar Abraham Heschel puts it well when he writes, 'Prophecy is not simply the application of timeless standards to particular human situations, but rather an interpretation of a particular moment in history, a divine understanding of a human situation. Prophecy, then, may be described as *exegesis of existence from a divine perspective*.'[17] This helps us understand the key difference between the written words of Scripture, with their timeless truths, and the 'now' word of the prophetic that speaks into specific circumstances.

As God's reality is held out to us, his thoughts are revealed. When we stop and think about it, it is extraordinary that we might have any kind of access to the mind of Almighty God. As he declares through the prophet Isaiah, 'As the heavens are higher than the earth, so are my ways higher than your ways and my thoughts than your thoughts' (Isaiah 55:9).

Yet despite the huge gulf between the mind of the Creator and the human mind, the Bible makes it clear that God readily chooses to disclose his thoughts to people. Prophetic revelation is the unveiling of God's truth to us, the point at which the vastness of God's thoughts touches our limited human consciousness. To quote Heschel again, 'Prophecy is a crossing point of God and man.'[18]

We can understand prophetic revelation as a connection point between the physical world and the kingdom of God: a point in space and time when we get a *glimpse of the realm of glory*. So, when we receive revelation from God, it's as if the curtains draw back for a few moments, and we can gaze through a window onto a greater and eternal reality. Just as the wardrobe opened up the world of Narnia for the Pevensie children, so the prophetic opens up the astonishing vista of God's reality for us.[19]

God's reality is preexistent, coming before any other reality. All other perspectives, understandings and ideas must submit to the overwhelming superiority of his reality and his thoughts. God's reality challenges every idol, every empire and every ungodly stronghold. It is sometimes uncomfortable and often inconvenient. It challenges, unsettles, provokes and dismantles. We may spend a lifetime trying to avoid God's reality, but we will all come face-to-face with it one day.

Contained within God's reality is *God's true identity* – God's self-declaration of who he truly is. As Walter Brueggemann writes, 'Prophecy begins in discerning how genuinely alternative Yahweh is.'[20] Encountering the reality of the Great I Am is quite unlike any other reality we will ever find, and we need reminding of just how iconoclastic this may turn out to be. C. S. Lewis observes that, 'My idea of God is not a divine idea. It has to be shattered time after time. He shatters it himself. He is the great iconoclast. Could we not almost say that this shattering is one of the marks of his presence?'[21] The validity of the prophetic word or action is shown by the Presence that is revealed through it. Anything that is genuinely prophetic will always reveal God's reality and allows the invisible God to become seen and heard.

In holding out God's reality, the prophetic not only shows us who God is but also reveals *our own true identity*. We will look more at Moses in chapter three, but it's fascinating that in the moment the prototype prophet meets God for the first time, we see both a startling disclosure of God's name and a clear revelation of Moses' identity as one known[22] and called by God.[23] A fundamental element of the prophetic is God saying, 'This is who I am, and this is who you are.'

But, paradoxically, when confronted with God's reality, we cannot stay as we are. At the heart of the prophetic message or action is the call to transformation: to change; to repent; to turn away from the way of sin, death, hopelessness; to turn back to God, love and life. The prophetic causes us to look honestly, in the blazing light of God's reality, at our current situation and then to embrace the newness he offers us. Sometimes God's reality is held out in order to bring profound challenge to society; sometimes it's so we can be personally transformed; and sometimes it's to hold out the promise of future hope to all people. But the holding out of God's reality will always nourish an alternative consciousness,[24] will always challenge our current perception of reality and will always insist on a changed way of thinking.

When we encounter God's reality, there are only two responses: yield or resist. Resistance takes many complex forms, including indifference, distraction, complacency, disobedience, denial, insolence and defiance. Yielding – a wholehearted and submitted yes to God – is relatively simple, but we have to be prepared for it to cost us everything.

Whether through word or action, whether referencing our past, present or future, the prophetic brings God's reality front and centre and demands all else fade to the periphery.

CARRIERS OF THE REVELATION OF GOD

Holding out God's reality is a key aspect of our calling as God's people. We could even say that this is our defining role: being a people who carry and demonstrate God's reality to the world around us. And so, in a fundamental way, the people of God have always been a prophetic body. This is something we need to pay close attention to as we go on to consider what a prophetic church or organisation is.

Our core purpose – carrying the revelation of God – is central to the biblical narrative. The Israelites, God's people under the old covenant, received the *revelation of the One True God, Yahweh* – which was inconceivably radical for that time. The countries of the world were full of false gods and the abominations associated with them. Thus, the revelation of monotheism – speaking of a God of love, of covenant, the Great I Am – was a startling light in the darkness. The Israelites affirmed a God who was Presence (cloud and fire) and a God who spoke; not a deity as an abstract concept or a detached entity, but a God who was relational and communicative. The God of Israel was truly unique. 'Hear, O Israel: The LORD our God, the LORD is *one*' (Deuteronomy 6:4, italics mine).

The people of Israel were essentially a prophetic community because their primary task was to hold out this revelation to the nations of the world. Theirs was a most holy and prophetic calling: to represent Yahweh on the earth and be the embodiment of a people in covenantal relationship with him. God's original intention for them was that they would be a nation of priests,[25] walking so closely with their God that they would hear his voice and represent him before all other nations. (Sadly, at the critical moment on Mount Sinai, they held back and asked to have Moses as their intermediary.)

The revelation of Yahweh was so revolutionary and countercultural that it's perhaps not surprising that the people group chosen to show it to the world struggled to stay faithful to their call. At times they couldn't resist running to other gods and compromising the covenant relationship. Their identity as a prophetic people was regularly undermined by the lure of idolatry – a tendency that was (and remains) a central concern of the prophets.

As profound as the revelation of Yahweh was, there is a yet richer, fuller and more radical revelation of God for the world to grasp. The shift from Old to New Testament brings a deeper resonance to the prophetic role of God's people. The church of Jesus Christ is now called to carry the *revelation of the Trinity*.

The reality of the triune God is central to the gospel – the truth that within the unity of the Godhead there is a community of three persons:

- Our glorious Father who loves us unconditionally and extravagantly and who invites us into his eternal embrace.
- Jesus our Saviour, the Light of the world, through whom we have redemption, forgiveness of sins and eternal life.
- The Holy Spirit, our ever-present friend and helper, who dwells in our innermost being to constantly bring us wisdom and insight.

A key theme of the New Testament is the unveiling – the making known – of the reality of the Trinity, and through it, God's plan of salvation and restoration. God's three-part personhood is introduced to the world at Jesus' baptism. When Jesus comes up out of the water, Matthew records, 'Heaven was opened, and he saw the Spirit of God descending like a dove and alighting on him. And a voice from heaven said, "This is my Son, whom I love; with him I am well pleased"' (Matthew 3:16–17). The Trinity gives us a picture of a perfect three-way relationship of pure, self-giving and eternal love. This is the reality of the God we worship. And it's our responsibility as Jesus' church to faithfully take this true revelation of God and hold it out for all to see.

The world is desperate for a true understanding of God. The ultimate goal of prophetic ministry is to bring to light who God is; to voice the truth of the nature of God to those who cannot yet see him; to reveal that they have a Father in heaven who loves them; to unveil Jesus their Saviour; and to introduce them to the Holy Spirit who will never leave them.

The prophetically awakened church is a channel of God's beautiful communication to his world. It is the means by which the world can hear the invitation to come back, to find their true identity, and to meet the one who loves them with an everlasting love. The prophetic church, testifying to what we have seen and heard, facilitates the restoration of relationship between God and humanity.

REFINING OUR DEFINITION

Returning to the semantics of *prophecy* and *prophet*, if

> the *prophetic* is about the faithful holding out of God's reality, so that it can be clearly seen and responded to, so that transformation can take place and so that relationship can be restored;

then we can refine the definitions of *prophecy* and *prophets* as follows:

> *Prophecy* is the inspired activity or process of perceiving and then holding out – often speaking out – God's reality. It is the interpretation and application of God's reality to a particular moment or situation.

> *Prophets* are people who are called by God to somehow embody or speak out God's transformative reality and equip the whole body to engage with it. Prophets bring hope to people (both inside and outside the church) by reminding them of God's reality.

When we look at what we might call *prophetic ministry* throughout Scripture, we see many different people in many different ways holding out the reality of God's heart, love, will and purpose.

JESUS: THE PERFECT PROPHET AND
ULTIMATE PROPHECY

At this point, our focus moves to Jesus. In order to gain the fullest understanding of what the prophetic is all about, there's only one destination: the One whose very name is a prophetic declaration of divine intent.

The name *Jesus* is the Greek form of the Hebrew name *Yeshua* (or Joshua), which means *Yahweh saves*. As the angel of the Lord explains to Joseph in Matthew 1:21, 'You are to give him the name Jesus, because he will save his people from their sins.'

That's pretty prophetic as things go! God's profound reality of salvation is held out to the world through this name, reaching far beyond the hopes of restoration for Israel. And then a couple of verses later, Matthew (quoting Isaiah 7), reminds us of another name and another prophetic promise: '"The virgin will conceive and give birth to a son, and they will call him Immanuel" (which means "God with us")' (Matthew 1:23).

As rich with prophetic substance as it is, Jesus' expression of the prophetic is not just through his name. Jesus is the embodiment and the pinnacle of the prophetic across the entire biblical narrative. As we look at the different strands and manifestations of the whole prophetic tradition of the Old Testament, we see that it is magnified, concentrated and redeemed in the person of Jesus. He is the archetypal biblical prophet.

Jesus gives us the best definition of the prophetic and enables us to grasp a healthy, holistic perspective. He is the ultimate expression of the prophetic role, ministry, lifestyle and intelligence. If we want to be prophetic people, and if we want our churches to be prophetic, we need to look at Jesus.

When we observe Jesus' life and ministry, we see that he is uncompromisingly prophetic in a multitude of ways.

Jesus is the revelation of the Father. He flawlessly shows us what God is like. Jesus is perfect theology. He is the exact representation of the invisible God; whoever has seen him has seen the Father.[26] He radiates the brilliance of God and reveals the Father's nature to us.[27] Throughout his earthly ministry, he prophetically enacts the heart of the Father.

Jesus is the Word of God in flesh. He is the supreme *dabar-Yahweh.* He is the eternal and everlasting Word; the one in whom all truth abides.[28]

Jesus is the mediator of the new covenant between God and people. In this way, we can clearly observe how he follows in the tradition of the Old Testament prophets who were guardians of the original covenant. As the mediator of the new covenant, Jesus is primarily concerned with people's relationship with God and their faithfulness to the covenantal relationship. He calls people to return to God and live righteously.[29]

Jesus only does what he sees the Father doing. The basis for his entire earthly ministry is knowing the Father's will and fulfilling it entirely.[30]

Jesus is led by the Spirit and ministers in the power of the Spirit.[31]

Jesus prioritises prayer and worship, spending whole nights in prayer.[32]

Jesus discerns the hearts and minds of people. Wherever he goes, he knows what people are thinking. He has supernatural insight into situations.[33] He regularly uses his prophetic gifts in his ministry to reach the lost, listening to the Father in the midst of personal interactions.[34]

Jesus calls people to repentance in light of the nearness of the kingdom of God, frequently exposing the real heart issues and unmasking hypocrisy. He preaches a message of spiritual health and transformation.[35]

Jesus confronts evil, casting out the demonic and breaking the power of sin.[36]

Jesus speaks truth to power, confronting the hypocrisy evident in both religious and secular institutions.[37]

Jesus challenges injustice and unrighteousness. He regularly calls people to God's high ethical standards and teaches them a new way of interrelating – a habit that threatens the established religious order.[38] His compassion for the downtrodden can 'be understood not simply as a personal emotional reaction but as a public criticism ... of the system, forces, and ideologies that produce the hurt'.[39]

Jesus demonstrates solidarity with marginalised people. The Gospels show Jesus purposefully crossing boundaries and reaching out to people that no respectable first-century Jew would go anywhere near – and making himself vulnerable in the process.[40]

Jesus speaks prophetically of the future.[41] As well as personal prophetic words to individuals, Jesus also speaks larger, universal pronouncements regarding both the imminent and eschatological future.

Jesus exposes ungodly religion, challenging the oppressive religious systems that were promoted through the practices of the Pharisees. His readiness to forgive sin, along with his willingness to heal people on the Sabbath, threatens the control of the religious elite.[42]

Remember our definition of the prophetic: *the faithful holding out of God's reality so that it can be clearly seen and responded to, so that trans-formation can take place and so that relationship can be restored.* Jesus embodies this in many different ways, demonstrating the degree to which he is our perfect and complete Prophet.

Of course, Jesus isn't *just* a prophet. He is the Son of God, the King of kings, the Messiah. But the New Testament writers were in no doubt that Jesus functioned as a prophet. In the Gospel stories, people frequently named him as such.[43] It's one of his many titles.

However, it's not simply that Jesus is our best *prophet*. It's not just that he fulfils Old Testament prophecy. It's not just that Jesus is highly *prophetic* by anyone's standards. It goes even deeper than that. It's that Jesus encapsulates the very essence of what *prophecy* is.

As we look at Jesus, we see the full expression of the Father's Word to his creation, the very pinnacle of prophetic revelation. Jesus shows us who God is and reveals the Father's love to us. He is the definitive revelation of God and the complete articulation of God's reality.

Jesus is the greatest prophecy. There is no better prophetic word to be found anywhere. Jesus is not just the perfect Prophet; he is the ultimate prophecy. All contemporary prophecy must therefore point to him and must simply be a continuation of this one, perfect Word to the world.

A HOLISTIC APPROACH TO THE PROPHETIC

Whatever our background or tradition in relation to the prophetic, each of us needs to reach out beyond our current experience and adopt a multi-faceted, holistic approach to the prophetic – one that encompasses the broad sweep of Scripture and is informed by the life and ministry of Jesus.

For those of us from a charismatic background: yes, we love our worship services and our pursuit of prophetic experiences; we love that we can hear God speaking to us and the impact this has on our devotional lives, but we also need to turn our attention to God's concerns for the world around us. We need to be open to the fact that political confrontation and social action can be an equally valid expression of prophetic ministry. A great deal of the energy we put into our passionate worship can be translated into passionate action towards freedom and justice. If we are serious about modelling our ministry on Jesus, then we need to acknowledge how he expands the concept of being prophetic far beyond a charismatic understanding.

Likewise, those of us who hold a social-justice understanding of the prophetic, or the conservative 'futuring' perspective, will need to move beyond these outlooks. Though these viewpoints bring richness to prophetic understanding, we cannot ignore the fact that Jesus used deeply personal prophetic words to reach out to individuals. We also cannot circumvent the supernatural aspect of prophecy or minimise the reality of divine inspiration. If we are going to follow after Jesus, we have to take seriously the fact that a big portion of his life and ministry was supernatural, and that in John 14 he promises his followers that they will do even greater things than he did.[44] The prophetic is not just righteous indignation and activism; it's engaging with the very voice of God.

We must keep returning to the question that is at the heart of this book: *Do we look like Jesus?* Regardless of our church tradition, being a prophetic church is not an optional extra. If we are not prophetic, we are not imitating Christ. And in our pursuit of the prophetic – prophetic gifts, ministry, expression and action – it is the broad, holistic example given to us by Jesus that we need to guide and shape us.

I've used this chapter to provide a definition of the prophetic, firstly based on who we understand God to be, and then formed around the ministry of Jesus. We can only make sense of the prophetic landscape through the lens of Jesus and his archetypal prophetic ministry. Now that we know what the prophetic is, we can turn our attention to the church and look more closely at our fundamental identity as a prophetic community. In the next chapter we will consider how a vital clue to understanding this identity is found in the book of Ephesians.

2

A JESUS-SHAPED CHURCH

Looking to Jesus the pioneer and perfecter of our faith.

HEBREWS 12:2 NRSV

Can you imagine a world without the potato? Whether your preference is for fries, chips, jacket or mash, we consume vast quantities of them. The story goes that it was the English explorer Sir Walter Raleigh who gifted a potato plant to Queen Elizabeth I, but the royal cooks threw away the tubers and instead served up the boiled stems and leaves.[1] These, being poisonous, made everyone ill, and potatoes were subsequently banned from the royal menu.

Certain historical details may have faded into myth, but at some point in the sixteenth century, the potato arrived in Europe from the Americas. This humble vegetable, a native of the Andes region, would go on to have a major impact on our diets; in fact, some historians argue that it changed the course of European history.[2]

Nowadays, potato products are ubiquitous. They even form one half of Britain's national dish.[3] You can go into a supermarket almost anywhere in the world and find potato-based foodstuffs. But potatoes are actually just one small part of the modern diet that originated in the American continents. Without the Americas there would be no maize, tomatoes, chilli peppers, avocados, peanuts, pecans, beans, pineapples, chocolate, vanilla, squash or yams. The list goes on and on! With today's globalised food market, it's sometimes hard to imagine what it would have been like in Europe before 1492, before the arrival of all these wonderful foods that we enjoy today. We take them for granted now, but our lives would be lacking much flavour and colour without them. We are dependent on the bountiful harvest of the Americas for a significant portion of both culinary delight and nutritional well-being.

WHAT ARE WE MISSING?

The prophetic is a land of similarly abundant harvest. Some of us cannot imagine the church without the prophetic and the benefits it brings. For example, the joy of hearing God's voice has become such a fundamental part of our Christian lives, and such a valuable element of our faith communities, that we shudder along with the prophet Amos at the prospect of 'a famine of hearing the words of the LORD' (Amos 8:11). But the truth is that many expressions of the body of Christ are carrying on with minimal prophetic culture. The prophetic function, with its unique flavour and nourishing qualities, has been absent from the life, leadership and structure of far too many churches and Christian organisations. And it would seem that, similar to Europe before 1492, many parts of the church have *no idea what they are missing*.

If the prophetic is off the map, we are lacking something incredibly significant, something Jesus has intentionally given to the church, something that makes a huge contribution to the vitality and maturity of the body. Imagine having to limit our supermarket trolley to foodstuffs native to the other four inhabited continents; we wouldn't starve, but our diet would be restricted, and we would lack some delightful nourishment. Chocolate, vanilla ice cream and peanut butter, for a start! If we close the door to the prophetic, we can survive; but what are we missing out on?

To understand *why* the prophetic is so important for the health and well-being of the body of Christ, we have to catch hold of Jesus' vision and purpose for his church. This is where the book of Ephesians – especially the first part of chapter four – becomes very helpful. These verses enable us to understand the prophetic as one of *five essential capacities* given to the church, each one of which brings its own unique flavour and enrichment. When these five are operating together, they enable the church to become mature and to fully represent Christ to the world.

Ephesians 4 positions the role of the prophet firmly in the new covenant church of Jesus. Therefore, our retrospective, Old Testament view of prophets needs adjusting. As we will discover, prophets have now been given to the church by Jesus himself. His masterly design for his church includes prophets, and by placing them in the church he is placing his own prophetic ministry in our midst. The text gives us a valuable framework for understanding how this particular role is designed to fit into every expression of the body of Christ.

THE FIVEFOLD MINISTRY

Ephesians, more than any other book in the New Testament, stands out as the one text that brings together Paul's best thinking on the church. It enables us to recapture the essence of who we are as Christ's body here on earth and how, practically, to *be* the church. Ephesians is quite unusual amongst Paul's letters; rather than being situational (written to address specific issues of error, heresy or pastoral need), it covers much more general themes. It was likely written towards the end of Paul's life and was probably intended to be circulated through the many churches in the region of Asia Minor. Paul writes to expand his readers' grasp of God's eternal purposes in Christ and to enable them to comprehend God's great goals for the church and their part in them. What we see in the letter is the big picture of exactly what Jesus has called his church to be: 'For we are God's masterpiece. He has created us anew in Christ Jesus, so we can do the good things he planned for us long ago' (Ephesians 2:10 NLT).

In the first three chapters we are reminded of the glory of the gospel and our new identity in Christ. Our covenantal identity as children of the Father is made clear: we are chosen,[4] adopted,[5] re-created in Christ,[6] members of God's household.[7] In this new identity we have been made alive with Christ and seated with him in the heavenly realms.[8] Our salvation is not only for our personal benefit but also to bring praise and glory to the God who reconciles us to himself and to each other,[9] and who has united us in one body, the church.[10]

And then we come to Ephesians 4, where Paul lays out how we, as the church, are to live out our collective calling to be God's masterpiece. In Ephesians, Paul doesn't prescribe a particular physical expression of church; he isn't telling us that all churches should look a certain way. But he is giving us a fundamental template that works across every denomination and branch of the church of Jesus Christ.

In Ephesians 4:1–16, Paul lays out how, as the church, we are to 'live a life worthy of the calling [we] have received' (Ephesians 4:1) and practically fulfil our shared calling to be the fullness of Jesus in the world. At the heart of his argument is the direct link between a mature, Jesus-shaped church and the embrace of the five roles described in verse 11:

> But to each one of us grace has been given as Christ apportioned it. ... So Christ himself gave the apostles, the prophets, the evangelists, the pastors and teachers, to equip his people for works of service, so that the body of Christ may be built up until we all reach unity in the faith and in the knowledge of the Son of God and become mature, attaining to the whole measure of the fullness of Christ.
>
> EPHESIANS 4:7, 11–13

Paul clearly states that Christ has given certain gifts to *each one of us*, and he implies that this fivefold ministry pattern is central to God's design for the church.[11] If we are at all interested in the church's ability to become healthy, united and mature – if we long to see our faith communities equipped for kingdom impact – then it would seem there is a lot at stake here. So, what are these five roles? What are these five people-gifts that the ascended Christ bestows on his church?

Apostles: the Greek word for *apostle* literally means 'sent one', and the Latin word is *missio*. Central to the role of apostle is the sense of some-one who has been sent on a mission from God. Apostles are wired for change, innovation and progress. They like to be on the move and bring a necessary forward momentum to the church or organisation. Theirs is a pioneering ministry, and we spot them by looking for the people who are forever starting up new projects and extending into new territory.

Prophets: with a passion for God's heart and a desire for everyone to draw closer to Jesus, prophets function as the eyes and ears of the church, as they stay attuned to God's perspective and purposes. They equip the church to hear God's voice and to maintain covenantal faithfulness to him. Prophets have a sensitivity to spiritual warfare and an orientation towards justice, desiring to challenge the status quo and speak out against oppression and unrighteousness.

Evangelists: the role of evangelists is to bring the good news, and their ministry is that of spreading the gospel message and equipping the rest of the church to do the same. As enthusiastic storytellers, evangelists have a natural boldness about sharing their faith and are skilled at making the gospel relevant to people who don't know Jesus. They help to ensure the church is outward-focused, and they tend to be great recruiters and social connectors.

Shepherds: sometimes referred to as pastors,[12] shepherds have a vital role in creating and maintaining strong community. With their watchful eye, they are able to discern the needs of a group and bring the necessary care and protection, so that the entire body is kept healthy. They often act as the 'glue' that holds the community together. Shepherds easily empathise with others and have a great capacity for meaningful friendships and relationships.

Teachers: the primary role of the teacher is to help the church grasp biblical truth, so that people can grow in wisdom and understanding. They help to cultivate a love of Scripture and enable disciples to have God's perspective on the world around them through theological insight. Teachers bring much-needed strength and stability to the church, ensuring that there is grounding in knowledge of the Bible. They are natural researchers and gatherers of information and are gifted in explaining biblical concepts in ways that make it easy for people to grasp.

The purpose of these five callings is made very clear in verses 12–13: all five roles are necessary for the equipping, building up and maturing of the church. Like the five distinct positions in a basketball game, each role brings something unique and necessary. If one is missing, the whole team is compromised. We may think we can carry on just fine without the apostles, for example, but without their particular contribution we will be missing something significant. We will have an 'apostle-shaped hole' that others will struggle to fill.

The word we translate as *equip* in verse 12 is *katartismós*, but, as Alan Hirsch and Jessie Cruickshank point out, this word can also mean *mend what has been broken*, *perfectly join together* and *perfect and complete*.[13] We need the fivefold ministry to heal, restore and perfect the church; without it we'll remain broken or incomplete. And Paul goes on to make an extraordinary claim in verses 12 and 13; he says there is a direct relationship between the fivefold ministry and our capacity as a church to reach the 'fullness of Christ'. Jesus gives these five roles *so that* (verse 12) the body of Christ may be built up, become mature, 'attaining to the whole measure of the fullness of Christ'. To become – together – ever more like Jesus, and for Jesus to live his life in us and through us, we need these five ministries.

The fivefold roles are distributed throughout the entire body, not just to its leaders. Every believer has an inherent potential to mature into one of these five roles. As it says in verse 7, 'to each one of us grace has been given'. *Each one of us* has a calling to be primarily one of five types of people. God has shaped each of us to fit a certain place in the body where we can best serve him. And it's only as we *all* lean into this grace and walk out our particular role that the whole body will be equipped.

I want to emphasise here that Ephesians 4:11 tells us that Christ has given *prophets* to the church, alongside apostles, evangelists, shepherds and teachers. This verse sets the role and ministry of the prophet in a holistic New Testament context. It indicates that we will best understand the prophetic within the bigger picture of understanding the church itself: the unified, diverse and mature church that Paul describes in verses 1–16.

THE MINISTRY OF JESUS

In laying out the five ministries, Paul brings into crystal clear focus the very ministry of Jesus himself. These five roles that Christ has embedded in his church are not a random list of useful, but perhaps optional, functions. Rather, together they encapsulate his very ministry on earth and are given to the church for a glorious purpose: so that the church can actually *be* the body of Jesus in every corner of the globe. They are each necessary and fit together perfectly.

In verse 11, we are, at one crucial level, reading Paul's description of a Person: the ultimate Apostle, Prophet, Evangelist, Shepherd and Teacher. Jesus operated beautifully and seamlessly in all five areas, and the ascended Christ of verse 8 gives this gift to his church – the gift of his very own ministry.

Jesus' five-sided, complete and perfect ministry looks like this:

Jesus is the ultimate Apostle. He is the Sent One, the agent of the

Father's mission to rescue the world, the Founder of the church and the worldwide movement that bears his name.

Jesus is the ultimate Prophet. He is the definitive revelation of God, the One who most perfectly shows us what God is like, the Word of God, who calls people to return to their covenantal relationship with the Father.

Jesus is the ultimate Evangelist. He announces and demonstrates the good news of the kingdom, and he seeks and saves the lost. Every aspect of his life, ministry and nature is the best news we could possibly have.

Jesus is the ultimate Shepherd. He is the Good Shepherd who is prepared to lay down his life for the sheep, full of compassion for the broken and excluded, desiring to gather all into the family of God.

Jesus is the ultimate Teacher. He is *the* Way and *the* Truth, who has the words of eternal life, and in whom are hidden all the treasures of wisdom and knowledge.

The beauty of using the fivefold framework to understand the purposes of the church is that it is centred on Jesus. These five roles are given by Jesus, and they extend the ministry of Jesus. As Alan Hirsch writes in 5Q, 'The ministry of Christ is given to the body of Christ so that it might attain to the fullness of Christ.'[14] It is through the fivefold ministry that the presence and ministry of Jesus is actively expressed in the church and the world. Fivefold thinking enables us to connect our sense of ministry and purpose with that of Jesus himself.

MATURITY

In Ephesians, Paul places a clear emphasis on maturity and paints a wonderful picture of a healthy and unified church. As we, the church, embrace the full measure of the ministry of Christ (yes, that means all five aspects), we attain this maturity and will gain the fullness of Christ that Paul articulates in verse 13.

The dream for any sports coach is a team where each player is fit enough and skilled enough to carry out their specific role to the best of their ability – and in such a way that the *whole team* is strengthened. We could describe the ambition of a coach as unlocking the inherent, synergistic potential of a group of players. In the same way, a truly *Jesus-shaped church* is one where all five ministries are released to work together in harmony and unity of purpose, with each one finding its true value in being part of the whole.

We cannot pick and choose which particular bit of Jesus' ministry we want to cultivate on our 'team'. They are equally vital and important. In order to see the intended outcomes that Paul describes in verses 12–16 (unity, equipping, maturity, growth, strength and knowledge of Jesus), we need the complete, multi-faceted ministry of Jesus in our midst. If Jesus embodied all five, then we need to be very intentional about how we approach Ephesians 4 and invest in all these foundational ministries. To put it simply, we will be less like Jesus if even one is missing.

Maturity on an individual level comes from not only embracing our own fivefold role but also in choosing to be shaped and refined by the other four.[15] Whatever our own particular calling is, we have much to learn from the rest of the fivefold, so we should choose to understand and appreciate each one of these wonderful ministries, welcoming the particular flavour of inspiration (and healthy challenge) they bring.

- Apostles inspire us to pioneer.
- Prophets inspire us to pray.
- Evangelists inspire us to share our faith.
- Shepherds inspire us to care.
- Teachers inspire us to learn.

CULTURE SHAPERS: FROM ROLE TO FUNCTION

Ephesians 4 gives every Christian a powerful framework for understanding how God has shaped and called us as individuals. It should prompt each one of us to explore the specifics of that calling and to see how we can best serve God in this world. We don't have to strive to be something we're not; rather, we can enjoy the fact that we each have a key role to play in ensuring the church reaches unity and maturity. Using the sports analogy again, it's like a basketball team. Each player has a unique role to play – five positions, five necessary jobs, each with its own description.

We have all been built with a beautiful purpose.

Part of that purpose is to *create and shape culture*. Apostles are called to create and shape an apostolic culture around them; prophets are called to create and shape a prophetic culture around them. The same goes for evangelists, shepherds and teachers. Each of the five roles therefore builds a particular type of *capacity* or *intelligence* within the church. And this is where we start to see the fivefold ministry from a deeper and more powerful perspective. Fivefold ministry is not just about individuals; it also relates to the church at a *corporate* level.

When we take hold of our shared calling to imitate Christ and his perfect five-sided ministry, we begin to see how the fivefold gives us a template for envisioning and defining the church *as a whole*. We can take the five nouns in Ephesians 4:11 and turn them into adjectives to describe the five aspects of collective calling on the church, or the *five flavours of culture* we want to see develop.

This is the bigger picture to be grasped, and a critical step to take; one where we move beyond thinking about individual *roles* in order to see how we can embrace these five identities collectively.

When we consider the fivefold in this way, each of the five can be described as a *function* – how we think and act *together* and how our common purposes are embodied. We can understand the apostolic, prophetic, evangelistic, shepherding and teaching as functions of the church itself – implicit purposes embedded in the church's identity and culture.[16] The *church itself* is called to be a mature expression of the five-fold roles, mirroring the perfect and complete ministry of Christ.

This makes perfect sense when we ask ourselves, is the church called to be apostolic? To be prophetic? To be evangelistic? To be a place of shepherding and teaching? The answer to each of these is yes!

When we apply the idea of function to the fivefold, what emerges is our corporate identity:

The apostolic church is a church that is on the move, pioneering and innovating; that extends Christianity into every conceivable culture and is faithful to its missionary calling.

The prophetic church is a church that is focused on ever-deepening relationship with God; that communicates his heart through words and actions; a community prepared to challenge the status quo and expose injustice.

The evangelistic church is a church that compellingly communicates the good news of the gospel, fostering an invitational, inclusive and culturally relevant environment.

The shepherding church is a church that is a caring, life-giving and healing community in which people can safely flourish and reach their full potential.

The teaching church is a church that has deep wisdom, cultivating an impactful engagement with Scripture and rejoicing in biblical truth.

As we move beyond the idea of individual callings and start to think in terms of collective function, we gain a much deeper understanding of what the church is supposed to be. Ephesians 4 gives us a profound key to unlocking a definitive description of the church of Jesus Christ.

The following table summarises the connection between *role* (as individual culture-shapers) and *function* (the impact these people can bring to the church as a whole).

Role	Function
Apostle: wired to catalyse, mobilise and pioneer; motivated to make an impact and extend into new territory.	The *apostolic* church: a community able to be visionary, mobile, innovative and risk-taking.
Prophet: wired for worship and a pursuit of justice; focused on God's voice and God's concerns.	The *prophetic* church: a community able to stay faithful to God, hear his voice and bring God's *shalom* to the neighbourhood.
Evangelist: wired to build connections outside the church and spread the good news.	The *evangelistic* church: a community able to be outward-focused, invitational and culturally relevant.
Shepherd: wired to build a healthy, reconciled community and to protect the vulnerable.	The *shepherding* church: a community able to care, heal, reconcile and disciple.
Teacher: wired to research, study and understand; committed to making complex truth accessible.	The *teaching* church: a community able to learn, understand and apply the truth of Scripture.

DO WE LOOK LIKE JESUS?

One of the most urgent questions for God's people to ask in these turbulent and polarised times is to what extent our churches and ministries truly look like Jesus. Do our words, attitudes and actions mirror those of Christ? Are we speaking as he would speak and acting as he would act? When the world looks at us, do they see an accurate representation of the Light of the world and Friend of sinners? Do they see Jesus in our midst?

He has designed his church to be the tangible expression of his glory and beauty. Our number one goal as his body here on earth should be to imitate Jesus as closely as we possibly can. After all, the fact that we're called his 'body' implies a direct correlation between the life and purpose of the church and the life and ministry of Jesus. We're his hands and feet; we're his voice and touch. We should be the ones radiating his compassion, wisdom and healing presence to our neighbourhoods. Our only role is to be exactly like him.

Ephesians 4 gives us a brilliant perspective on what a Christlike church should look like. We can use fivefold thinking to give us a benchmark for all Christian ministry and church culture: the ministry of Jesus Christ himself. Any and every church should be able to ask itself, *Do we exhibit a healthy and mature expression of each of the fivefold functions that perfectly mirrors that of Jesus?* In other words, *do we look like him?*

Another way to pose the question is this: to what extent do we as a local church or organisation embody the ministry of Jesus the supreme Apostle, the perfect Prophet, the greatest Evangelist, the good Shepherd and the master Teacher?

To get to this place – to 'become mature, attaining to the whole measure of the fullness of Christ' (Ephesians 4:13) – we need to hear afresh the invitation of Jesus to come and learn from him; to walk alongside him and see the world through his eyes. We need to lean a little closer to our Servant King and ensure that our actions reflect the truth of who we are. 'Therefore be imitators of God, as beloved children, and live in love' (Ephesians 5:1–2 NRSV).

Ephesians shows us five ways in which we can imitate Christ; five remarkable ways in which we can represent the heart of Jesus to the world around us.

A PLACE FOR PROPHETS

The fivefold perspective contained in Ephesians 4 gives us an excellent context for understanding who prophets are, what they are called to do, and why the church needs them. This in turn enables us to comprehend what it might mean to be a prophetic church or organisation – because in order to understand what a prophetic community is, we have to look at what fivefold prophets are and how they are wired to build a prophetic culture. Approaching prophetic ministry and the prophetic role through a fivefold lens points us straight to Jesus – which is very good news, because he has to be the primary reference point for any discussion about the prophetic.

In recent centuries the Western church has tended to exclude the apostolic, prophetic and evangelistic frameworks and view ministry exclusively from a shepherd-teacher perspective. This is why most of our churches place such a heavy emphasis on Bible teaching and pastoral care but fail to effectively extend the kingdom and be the fullness of Jesus in the world. It's no wonder we rarely see the level of maturity that Paul describes in verses 12–16 of Ephesians 4. But over the last couple of decades, the Holy Spirit has been reawakening the people of God to what it means to be the church of Jesus from the perspective of the fivefold. There are now many excellent books about the fivefold ministry and the need to embrace all five roles. The focus of this book is on prophets and the prophetic function of the church. But I hope you'll understand why Ephesians 4 is so critical to the conversation. If we're going to study prophets and everything that comes under the umbrella of the prophetic, it's vital to first orientate ourselves around the perspective of the whole body of Christ. We stray into potentially dangerous territory any time we examine prophets outside of the context of the church.

When we truly understand the church – when we understand what it means to *be* the church – we see that our fundamental purpose is to look like Jesus. And, digging deeper, we see that we cannot fulfil this purpose if the prophetic is missing. We need the prophetic in order to fully imitate Christ and represent him to the world. Jesus has given the prophets to the church, and they are part of his ideal design for the church. If we leave the prophetic off the map, we won't look like Jesus. The remedy is to integrate the ministry of the prophets back into every part of the body of Christ, and to do all we can to seek a healthy and mature engagement with the prophetic role, ministry and function. We may not fully understand it, but we'd be very unwise to ignore it.

These days, potatoes, beans, tomatoes and other crops are grown all over Europe (even my own cool, damp Britain has chocolate factories). Living in the twenty-first century, it's hard to imagine a world without chilli peppers, peanuts and all the other wonderful foods native to the Americas. In a similar way, Jesus never intended us to imagine a church without the prophets and the particular flavour of culture and intelligence they bring.

3

THE OLD TESTAMENT TRADITION

Then by a prophet the LORD brought Jacob's descendants out of Egypt; and by that prophet they were protected.

HOSEA 12:13 NLT

Rembrandt's depiction of Jeremiah lamenting the destruction of Jerusalem is a remarkable painting by one of the greatest artists of all time, but it would make a poor recruitment poster.[1] The image powerfully conveys the prophet's isolation and heartache: he sits weeping alone, while the city burns in the background. Jerusalem's destruction is an event he himself had prophesied, but the fulfilment of the prophecy brings him little joy. Slouched in his seat, the old man looks utterly dejected, with sadness and regret emanating from his face. Based on Rembrandt's portrayal, would anyone actively choose Jeremiah's job?

The word *prophet* is certainly an interesting epithet, with its associated stereotype of a wild-eyed, long-bearded, judgement-speaking social outcast. Fortunately, as we have seen, the letter to the Ephesians, alongside Jesus' own prophetic ministry, offers a different perspective.

I love the way fivefold thinking enables us to view prophets as simply 'one of five'.[2] Some people are prophet-shaped – it's their God-given role – and alongside the other fivefold callings, their ultimate aim is to equip and build up the body of Christ to maturity. There is nothing particularly unusual or exceptional about being a prophet. It is not a title or office that denotes rank and authority or one that brings special privileges. It is simply one way in which certain individuals are wired in order to best serve others.

In this chapter and the next we are seeking to understand just who these prophets are and what they do, first by examining the Old Testament expression of their ministry and then by looking at the New Testament perspective. Potentially a fifth of our churches are made up of prophets, but in my experience the prophet is the least understood of the fivefold. Misconceptions about prophets are common in most corners of the church, which historically has led to them being marginalised or heavily controlled. Ephesians 4 makes it clear that Jesus has given prophets to his church, but if we don't understand this particular role, we will deprive ourselves of the incredible contributions they bring and the unique way that prophets shape the culture around them, both inside and outside the church. We need to 'reactivate this latent people-gift'[3] and rediscover a healthy and holistic approach to deploying these individuals effectively.

In order to properly understand prophets, we have to be intentional in separating out *prophet* from *prophecy*. As I've already pointed out, they are not the same thing. Making this distinction is part of the process of moving beyond the somewhat narrow confines of the charismatic tradition. It is a mistake to understand the prophetic *role* (given by Christ) simply through the lens of the prophetic *gift* (given by the Spirit) and thus define a prophet as someone who speaks out prophecy on a regular basis. While it's true that prophets often deliver words of prophecy, not all do. Some prophets rarely utter prophetic words but instead are to be found engaged in prophetic action and challenging societal norms. We need to avoid using the gift of prophecy as the only metric by which we assess whether someone is a prophet. There is a danger that some prophets will disqualify themselves from their fivefold role because they are not regularly exercising the gift. Likewise, it would be an error to label someone a prophet simply because he or she is highly proficient in speaking out prophecy.

It's an interesting exercise to compare Elijah and John the Baptist – two premier prophets in the Bible.[4] Their ministries share common characteristics. (In Luke 1:17 it is written of John that 'he will go on before the Lord in the spirit and power of Elijah.') But whereas Elijah regularly encountered 'the word of the LORD'[5] and was used by God to deliver prophecies,[6] John's prophetic ministry was expressed by preaching a message of repentance. In the Bible a prophet is defined by their role and calling, not by the activity through which this is achieved.

With the perspective that the New Testament brings us, we can differentiate *prophet* from *prophecy* as follows:

	What	Source	Distribution	Purpose
Prophet Role (person)	An individual's identity, calling and way of seeing the world	Given by Jesus	One of five	Developing the overall health of the body
Prophecy Gift (charism)	The experience and process of hearing God for others	Given by the Holy Spirit	Available to all	Strengthening, encouraging, comforting people

If the prophetic role is not primarily about how many prophecies an individual delivers, then we need other methods of identifying and understanding prophets. Going back to the fundamental definition of the prophetic from chapter one, prophets are people who have a particular role in *embodying or speaking out God's reality*, so let's explore how this is played out in the Old Testament and what this can teach us about the ministry of prophets in the present-day church or organisation.

MAKING SENSE OF THE OLD TESTAMENT PROPHETS

The Old Testament prophets are associated with a sizeable chunk of the Bible; indeed, a whole genre of biblical literature is devoted to them. If we include the literary prophets (Isaiah through to Malachi),[7] as well as the additional characters identified as prophets (Moses through to Elisha and Huldah), their ministry spans virtually the whole of the Old Testament. The writers of the New Testament would have been very familiar with the words of the Hebrew prophets and quoted them on plenty of occasions.[8] Thousands of years after they were recorded, the writings and actions of the Old Testament prophets still speak powerfully to the contemporary church and the world around us. But just how closely related are the prophets of old to the fivefold prophets of the church today? To what extent should we consider them as separate entities? How much can we take from the ministry of the Old Testament prophets and apply to our modern context? How much should we model our ministry on theirs?

To become a mature prophetic church, we have to move away, to a certain extent, from an Old Testament perspective and grasp a broader paradigm more influenced by the new covenant within which we now live. The church of Jesus is born into the age of the Spirit and therefore requires new wineskins.[9] At the very least, we should be prepared to reimagine some elements of the Old Testament prophetic tradition. But at the same time, we need to find a way to allow the prophets of Israel to speak into the realities of the church today and learn what we can from their ministry and their experiences of God. When we take time to understand their *context*, they have much to teach us. As Abraham Heschel writes in his classic work on the prophets, the significance of these people lies not only in what they said but also in what they were.[10] To fully appreciate their ministry we must understand their world and their consciousness – what it meant to think, feel, respond and act as a prophet in ancient Israel.

The Hebrew prophets operated in a very different context to that of the new covenant church. In Old Testament times the ability to hear the voice of God was quite rare. In fact, the prophetic gift was concentrated in a small number of individuals. The capacity to discern the validity of a prophetic utterance was very limited, so the onus was on the prophet to deliver the prophetic word faithfully. Under the old covenant, the prophets were commissioned by God to speak his words with divine authority,[11] and the people listening to those words were expected to treat them as the 'very words of God'. There was no room for error, and the punishment for being a false prophet was stoning.[12] Because of their unique connection with God, prophets were sometimes given elevated status and authority in society,[13] though some of them ended up despised and rejected.[14]

Under the new covenant, and with every believer receiving the Holy Spirit, we are no longer dependent on prophets to hear God's voice for us. We each have direct access to God and a responsibility to pursue, discern and respond to his voice – so the way we *relate* to prophets has fundamentally shifted. Fivefold prophets are just as necessary to God's people today as the Hebrew ones were, but we are no longer reliant on prophets as the sole means of hearing God. We have moved on from the days of Samuel and the practice of visiting the seer to enquire of God.[15]

When we read the Old Testament prophets, they appear to be channels for God's discipline and judgement. What are we to make of their stern, chastising words from our modern-day perspective? At the heart of the prophetic there has always been a call to godly transformation, whether personal or societal. But as we move from the Old to the New Testament, we have a new lens through which to view the role of the prophets: that of the gospel of redemption and reconciliation. Pre-Calvary and pre-Pentecost, the prophets' role often included convicting God's people of sin. But under the new covenant we have the Holy Spirit working in each of us to sanctify us and produce his precious fruit in our lives.[16] And rather than individual prophets speaking God's judgements against nations, the Holy Spirit is here to convict the world.[17]

It's also worth noting a further, quite subtle difference between the Old and New Testament prophets: the Hebrew prophets were often *called* by God into ministry (see Isaiah 6, Jeremiah 1, Ezekiel 1–3), whereas five-fold prophets are *given* to the church by Jesus. The Old Testament pattern of a prophet's call involved an encounter with God – sometimes with a spectacular vision of God's glory – followed by a commission to go and speak to a particular audience with a particular message. We don't see this pattern with new covenant prophets. (Bear in mind that John the Baptist was the last of the old covenant prophets.)

It's important to reflect on the key differences between Old and New and see beyond the standard stereotypes of the prophetic role, even if they have been exquisitely portrayed on canvas by Rembrandt. But we can now go on to consider what our ancient friends teach us about prophetic ministry.

MOSES: THE OLD COVENANT PROTOTYPE

The Old Testament character who sheds the greatest light on the role of a prophet is Moses. Indeed, the whole prophetic tradition stems from him. Thousands of years may have passed, but his embodiment of the prophetic role still resonates clearly. Moses heard from God and became the Lord's friend,[18] and it's Moses' ongoing relationship with God that marks him out as the prototype for all other prophets. A great summary of his ministry and significance is found at the end of Deuteronomy:

> Since then, no prophet has risen in Israel like Moses, whom the LORD knew face to face, who did all those signs and wonders the LORD sent him to do in Egypt – to Pharaoh and to all his officials and to his whole land. For no one has ever shown the mighty power or performed the awesome deeds that Moses did in the sight of all Israel.
>
> DEUTERONOMY 34:10–12

What is striking about this valediction is that, in identifying Moses as the preeminent prophet, it highlights first and foremost Moses' deep relationship with God and then the signs and wonders that he performed.

Moses stands as a towering figure over the Old Testament. As we pursue a greater understanding of prophets, we must pay attention to the highly significant parallels between his expression of the prophetic role and that of Jesus. In the book of Acts, Peter and Stephen identify Jesus as the *prophet like Moses*, prophesied by Moses himself: 'The LORD your God will raise up for you a prophet like me … . You must listen to him' (Deuteronomy 18:15). These are the very words that Peter quotes in Acts 3:22 and Stephen references in Acts 7:37.

In a very real sense, Moses, through his own prophetic ministry, gives us a foretaste of Jesus, our perfect and complete Prophet.

Moses is the protagonist of the Exodus narrative – the great archetypal story of an enslaved people becoming free. In Exodus, God raised up Moses as his representative and commissioned him to lead God's people and to confront the evil regime of Pharaoh. Through Moses, God's reality crashed headlong into the dominant imperial culture – into Pharaoh's version of reality – exposing false gods and enabling God's people to break free from oppression and exploitation.[19]

And, of course, the ancient Exodus narrative is a pattern of the ultimate story to come: the salvation story. In establishing the old covenant, Moses acts as a signpost, pointing towards the new covenant. He holds out God's reality of future hope and redemption. In Moses' confrontation with an oppressive empire and a fraudulent religion, in his radical call to faith in the one true God, and in his obedience to God's voice, we get a foretaste of Jesus' own prophetic and redeeming ministry.

But let us also remember that the defining feature of Moses' prophetic identity was in his profound relationship and ongoing encounters with God. From the start – that famous burning-bush experience – God drew Moses into relationship by revealing his very name: Yahweh, the Great 'I Am'.[20] Moses encountered God's reality and presence and therefore stands out in the Old Testament as the one person who knew God face to face.[21] Indeed, he became a friend of God. Moses desired that the people he was called to lead would know God as he knew him; that they would experience the reality of his glory and nature. He longed for the hearts of the Israelites to be connected with God's heart and to hear God's voice in the way he experienced it. We sense this deep longing when Moses says to Joshua, 'I wish that all the LORD's people were prophets and that the LORD would put his Spirit on them!' (Numbers 11:29).

A love of God's presence and voice marked Moses' life. And a passion for God is certainly one of the defining characteristics of the rest of the Old Testament prophets.

LEARNING FROM THE PROPHETS OF ISRAEL

Throughout the Old Testament, God made himself known to his prophets through visions, dreams or encounters. He shared his reality with them and commissioned them to faithfully hold out that reality to his people. They had a particular role as mouthpieces and intermediaries: God's representatives delivering his will, law, direction and judgements. They constantly called people back to covenant faithfulness and spoke sternly against the relentless pull of idolatry.

At the heart of the prophets' message was the reminder to God's people of who they were: a people defined by their covenantal relationship with Yahweh, the one true God. The prophets reminded the people that they were an *alternative* community to every other culture around them, shaped by God's incomparable alternative reality. The prophets of old knew that when we lose our sense of identity, we become especially vulnerable to idolatry.

Idolatry was the perennial sin of the Israelites and the issue that overshadowed the ministry of the Old Testament prophets, especially the literary ones. God had chosen Israel for a unique covenantal relationship with himself, which defined them as a nation and gave them a call to carry the revelation of Yahweh to the world around them. They were invited into a profound relationship with the Creator of the heavens and the earth, the God of Glory. It sounds pretty straightforward, doesn't it? All they had to do was stay faithful to him, especially to the first commandment, 'You shall have no other gods before me' (Exodus 20:3).

But time after time the people failed. Genuine faith in Yahweh was polluted, as the Israelites were seduced by incompatible false religions.

The repeated metaphor that the Hebrew prophets use to describe this unholy crisis is that of an unfaithful wife, and in the words of Jeremiah and Ezekiel we find the raw expression of Israel's devastating unfaithfulness:

> 'I remember the devotion of your youth,
> how as a bride you loved me
> and followed me through the wilderness.
> What fault did your ancestors find in me,
> that they strayed so far from me?
> But my people have exchanged their glorious God
> for worthless idols.
> Does a young woman forget her jewellery,
> a bride her wedding ornaments?
> Yet my people have forgotten me, days without number.
> But like a woman unfaithful to her husband,
> so you, Israel, have been unfaithful to me,' declares the LORD.
>
> JEREMIAH 2:2, 5, 11, 32, 3:20

> 'I gave you my solemn oath and entered into a covenant with you, declares the Sovereign LORD, and you became mine. ... But you trusted in your beauty and used your fame to become a prostitute. You lavished your favours on anyone who passed by and your beauty became his. ... You adulterous wife! You prefer strangers to your own husband!'
>
> EZEKIEL 16:8, 15, 32

The sin of idolatry was the breaking of the sacred covenant, a rejection of the precious relationship. It was Israel turning its back on God and saying, 'You are not enough for us.' In turning to foreign gods, the people defied the true, Living God and the glories of his presence.[22]

The idols they turned to held out a false promise and a quick fix. The prophets knew that these idols appealed to a distorted sense of identity, which still has resonance today: *If I bow to this idol, my life will be better, my social status will be raised, and other people will affirm my value.* In succumbing to idolatry, the Israelites were renouncing their true God-given identity as the beloved people of God and living out of a false one. Jeremiah powerfully conveys this reality:

> 'Be appalled at this, you heavens, and shudder with great horror,' declares the LORD. 'My people have committed two sins: They have forsaken me, the spring of living water, and have dug their own cisterns, broken cisterns that cannot hold water.'
>
> JEREMIAH 2:12–13

This is why the call to holiness was so central to the prophet's message. It was the prophet's job to remind the Israelites of their identity as a people set apart: 'Be holy because I, the LORD your God, am holy' (Leviticus 19:2). The prophets constantly promoted worship of Yahweh because worship is one of the best ways to stay true to the covenant and stay faithful to God. To worship God wholeheartedly in Spirit and truth is to powerfully resist all the other powers at large, and those competing claims on our allegiance.

We can read the ancient words of the prophets today and assume they were preoccupied with sin and Israel's moral failings. But from their perspective, sin was primarily defined in terms of *relationship breakdown* – the rejection of the exclusive relationship with Yahweh.[23] When the prophets delivered God's judgements, their words were not impersonal, factual criticisms but rather were a disclosure of God's agony and disappointment – outbursts of raw emotion over the broken covenant. The prophets' experience was therefore to enter into God's feelings, to fellowship with God in his pathos.[24]

The tragedy of this story is that the people of God forgot who they were. And under the old covenant, the only response the prophets could give to an idolatrous people was judgement and death. This is why reading through the pages of their writings today can be a somewhat depressing experience. But we have to remember that the Hebrew prophets only saw in part, and we can be reassured that there was always a glimpse of future hope somewhere in their declarations.

Even in the midst of relationship breakdown, the prophets held out hope to God's people by reminding them that, at the end of the day, they belonged to Yahweh.

> 'When you pass through the waters, I will be with you; and when you pass through the rivers, they will not sweep over you. When you walk through the fire, you will not be burned; the flames will not set you ablaze. For I am the LORD your God, the Holy One of Israel, your Saviour … . Since you are precious and honoured in my sight, and because I love you, I will give people in exchange for you.'
>
> ISAIAH 43:2–4

Having looked at how the call to covenant faithfulness was at the heart of their message, we can go on to summarise the other key elements of the Old Testament prophets' ministry:

Role of Old Testament Prophets	Examples
Spokesperson for God: God's mouthpiece and messenger, communicating the word of the Lord, usually addressing Israel's immediate or imminent situation. The prophets delivered words of warning, direction, hope and judgement into the social and historical context of their day.	Jeremiah 1:9 Jeremiah 7 Ezekiel 2:3 Haggai 1:13
Intermediary: standing between God and his people. The prophets were sought out in order to discover God's will, or the answer to a question, or to request God's intervention.	Ezekiel 20:1 Isaiah 37:1–7 2 Kings 22:14–20

Role of Old Testament Prophets	Examples
Member of the divine council: invited to stand in the presence of God, to observe and discern God's plans and words.	Jeremiah 23:18 1 Kings 22:19 Amos 3:7
Intercessor: advocating on behalf of others to avert God's wrath.	Exodus 32 1 Samuel 12:19 Jeremiah 37:3 Amos 7:1–6
Watchman: a sentinel/lookout over God's people, warning them of danger.	Jeremiah 6:17 Ezekiel 3:17; 33:7 Hosea 9:8
Miracle worker: not a characteristic of the literary prophets (apart from Isaiah), but true of many of the other Old Testament prophets.	Exodus 17:1–7 1 Kings 18 2 Kings 2:19–22
Political commentator and activist: concerned with challenging empire and society, opposing tyranny, and taking the side of the marginalised and vulnerable. They spoke truth to power and experienced anguish at injustice and oppression.	Exodus Isaiah 1:17 Amos 2:6–7 Amos 7:10–17 Amos 8:4–6 Zechariah 7:9–10
Expression of the Role	**Examples**
Engaged with God's heart: feeling what God feels, participating in divine pathos, experiencing emotions from God's perspective. Many of the prophets felt God's pain, longing, passion and anger.	Jeremiah 6:11 Hosea 11
Reliant on God's Spirit: being, to a certain extent, a foretaste of the Holy Spirit: providing comfort, direction, and acting as mediators between the people and God.	Numbers 11:29 Isaiah 48:16 Ezekiel 3:12
Calling people to repentance: imploring the Israelites to turn from their sins and be reconciled with their God; declaring the consequences of not obeying God but also bringing hope of reconciliation.	Isaiah 45:22 Amos 5:1–17

Expression of the Role	Examples
Acting as a symbol and type: speaking a message through their lives; engaging in symbolic actions that visibly demonstrate God's message.	Jeremiah 13:1–11 Hosea 1:2
Possessing spiritual sight: able to see into the reality of the spiritual realm.	2 Kings 6:17 Ezekiel 1 Daniel 7:9–14
Sensitivity to evil: communicating dismay at injustice, hypocrisy, greed, rebellion and wickedness in the world.	Hosea 4:1–2 Habakkuk 2:6–17
Speaking messianic prophecies: promising deliverance and salvation through the arrival of the future Messiah.	Isaiah 7:14 Isaiah 9:6–7 Isaiah 11 Zechariah 9:9–13
Foretelling: pointing forward to a time when God will intervene and bring restoration to all things; declaring God's plans for individuals and nations. Their messages often started with doom but concluded with hope and redemption.	Jeremiah 33 Ezekiel 38–39 Ezekiel 43:1–12 Daniel 7

In this overview we can see a deep passion for God and for God's concerns in the world. The prophets of old knew both the ecstasy of being caught up with the glory of God and the agony of seeing the broken world from God's perspective.

We can summarise this twin focus as *safeguarding the covenant relationship* and *promoting a just society*. We find a classic example of these two concerns coming together in Jeremiah's famous Temple Sermon.[25] The people of Judah were praising God in Solomon's temple as if everything was fine. They were trusting in rituals and the physical presence of the temple as a guarantee of God's protection and favour. But all was not well. Away from the temple courts there was rampant social injustice, including the oppression of immigrants, orphans and widows. And the people were worshipping other gods. Both of these were violations of the sacred covenant and of the Ten Commandments. Jeremiah had the unenviable task of challenging this toxic situation. God sent the prophet to the temple courts, the place where people gathered for worship, to preach against their idolatry and injustice:

> 'If you really change your ways and your actions and deal with each other justly, if you do not oppress the foreigner, the fatherless or the widow and do not shed innocent blood in this place, and if you do not follow other gods to your own harm, then I will let you live in this place, in the land I gave your ancestors for ever and ever. ...
>
> 'Will you steal and murder, commit adultery and perjury, burn incense to Baal and follow other gods you have not known, and then come and stand before me in this house, which bears my Name, and say, "We are safe"—safe to do all these detestable things? Has this house, which bears my Name, become a den of robbers to you? But I have been watching! declares the LORD.'
>
> JEREMIAH 7:5–7, 9–11

When we read these verses, we can't help but project forward to Jesus' prophetic action of clearing the temple courts. Indeed, he quotes from Jeremiah's sermon in Mark 11:17. And in Jeremiah's words we see how the challenge to injustice and idolatry are so intertwined. In the Old Testament, it was the prophet's job to constantly promote true relationship with God as well as a just society.

EMBODYING THE WORD

As we read through the Old Testament, we see that a call to prophetic ministry meant unquestioning obedience to God. He incarnated his word in his prophets: they had to be so yielded to God that they could *embody* his reality. This was more than simply communicating a message. The prophets had to encounter the very emotions of God's heart and were sometimes expected to live out the message through actions and gestures. Ezekiel had to eat a scroll;[26] Jeremiah had to buy and wear a linen belt;[27] Hosea had to marry a promiscuous woman in order to become a parable of the relationship between God and his people.[28] The prophets' ministry involved standing in solidarity with, and suffering alongside, their own people. In fact, they suffered more, because in personifying the *dabar-Yahweh* they were exposed to the hatred of those opposed to it. Embodying God's word was an all-consuming occupation.

The twentieth-century Catholic theologian Hans Urs von Balthasar observes how, in incarnating his word in Israel's prophets, God is giving us a foretaste of the incarnation of his Son: 'By having them obey and sending them ahead against the battle-front of the sinners, he commits himself to the very hilt. He is already *en route* to the incarnation.'[29] Once more we can trace the pattern of Christ's prophetic ministry in the pages of the Old Testament: it is not only Moses who signposts the One to come, but also all those whose prophetic obedience and embodiment of God's word led to suffering and alienation.

THE CONNECTION WITH CONTEMPORARY MINISTRY

In viewing the breadth of their ministry, as well as their faithfulness and their obedience to Yahweh, there is much we can learn from the prophets of old. Their words echo powerfully down the centuries and their perspectives have validity today. As we study them we find:

- a *prototype* in the person of Moses,
- a *critique* against idolatry and injustice,
- *a taster* of Spirit-empowered prophetic ministry, and
- a *promise* of much more to come.

The Hebrew prophets give us a foretaste of what the coming perfect Prophet will be like. From Moses through to John the Baptist we see elements of Christ's complete prophetic ministry. Jesus takes all these different prophetic threads from the Old Testament tradition and embodies and perfects them.

There is also a connection between the ministry of the Old Testament prophets and the ministry of fivefold prophets in the church today. We can take each of the expressions of the prophetic role we've looked at so far and reflect deeply on how in turn they inform and shape today's prophetic ministry, particularly their concerns for justice and faithfulness. But we also need to be cautious of assuming a direct translation. Remember: their context was different. They only saw in part. The kingdom of God that we see breaking in on humanity in the Gospels was still a long way off. The Hebrew prophets give us a prelude to Jesus, the perfect Prophet, and the Spirit-empowered prophetic function – but they don't give us the full picture. When we encounter the incarnate Word of God, we must rethink everything in the light of Jesus, even the prophetic role.

4

NEW COVENANT PROPHETS

Judas and Silas, who themselves were prophets, said much to encourage and strengthen the believers.

ACTS 15:32

I wonder what Jeremiah would make of contemporary Christendom. I'd love to uproot him from the seventh century BC and chat with him. Imagine inviting Agabus into the conversation as well. (Agabus is one of the prophets named in the New Testament, making his appearance in chapters eleven and twenty-one of the book of Acts.) It would be fascinating to converse with both of these prophets, exploring their differing experiences and reflecting on the seismic changes within the prophetic role post-Calvary and post-Pentecost.

No doubt Jeremiah would soon realise that the Old Testament model of the prophet was never God's ultimate plan for this ministry.[1] The restoration of relationship between God and people, mediated through Jesus, means that every Christian can experience the presence and voice of God. We are no longer reliant on old-school prophets to pass on God's messages to us. We now have a new and greater covenant – one of grace, not judgement. And it's a new age – the age of salvation and the Spirit.

A WORD ABOUT JOHN

We get a sense of the paradigm shift that occurs in the transition from old to new covenant prophetic ministry when we look at Jesus' great friend, John.

In many ways we could say that the New Testament is bookended by two Johns: John the Baptist and John of Revelation – two remarkable prophets. The first had the greatest of prophetic tasks of making the way for Jesus.

The second is one of the most fascinating New Testament characters. The author of Revelation was almost certainly one of the twelve disciples, the son of Zebedee, who as a young man bore witness to the humanity of Jesus and as an old man had a profound vision of the glory of Jesus.[2] The second John offers us a captivating lens through which to view New Testament prophetic ministry and its most obvious trait – all-consuming love.

John the apostle[3] seems to have spent a great deal of his later life meditating on divine love as expressed through Jesus' life and ministry. This is not surprising, considering the deep friendship they shared and how much time John spent with Jesus as part of his inner circle. John was the only one of the Twelve to make his way to the foot of the cross, where he was an eyewitness to the anguish of divine self-giving love. That moment was undoubtedly in John's mind as he penned his letters. God's great love for us and our responding love for him is a theme John continuously returns to: 'God is love, and those who abide in love abide in God, and God abides in them' (1 John 4:16 NRSV).

When we consider the remarkable prophetic vision that ends the New Testament, we need to remember that John saw all that he saw with God's love foremost in his mind and with his first-hand experience of the Son of God etched in his memory.[4]

John the Baptist's vision of Jesus might have begun to fade once he was thrown into prison;[5] but for John the apostle, imprisoned on Patmos, his vision of Jesus burned ever brighter. He saw Jesus in his glory, and this seeing took place from the perspective of the cross and the experience of the incarnation. The whole biblical narrative ends with the revelation of the Father's best Word, seen through the eyes of the Son's best friend.

Adrienne von Speyr puts it brilliantly when she writes,

The prophets of the old covenant did have similar visions, but they saw within the promises. John sees within the fulfilment. He sees with the whole meaning of the Christ he has experienced. His seeing is postincarnational; and the Joannine element in his seeing is the greatness of his love, which can bear seeing such things and including them in his mission, almost in spite of the love that proves itself alive in him. It is no longer a seeing of merely getting to know. It is a seeing founded in the mystery that John has known the Lord as man and friend. In the old covenant the seeing was a premonition; the seeing of John is that of experience. In John the experience covers the premonition in the same way as the fulfilment in the Lord covers the promise.[6]

John the apostle, the clearest example of a new covenant prophet we have in Scripture, knew that at the very centre of God's reality is pure love.

THE SPIRIT

The day of Pentecost birthed the church and changed the world. As noted in chapter three, the coming of the Spirit dramatically changed the *context* in which prophets now operate.

We cannot arrive at a truly holistic understanding of what it means to be a prophetic community – and the subsequent role of prophets within that community – if we omit the Spirit's role. When the Spirit is poured out upon the church at Pentecost, suddenly everyone has access to the voice of God.

Jesus had already told the disciples that, as he returned to the Father, they would be sent the Spirit of truth[7] – a promise that was dramatically realised just a few weeks after the ascension. Young and old, male and female, began to experience what had previously been reserved for a minority. 'I will pour out my Spirit on all people. ... and *they will prophesy*' (Acts 2:17–18, italics mine).

But still, as we read through the rest of the New Testament, it is evident that Pentecost does not negate the need for prophets. Even though revelatory gifts are now flowing through the many church communities that are planted, there are plenty of references to individual prophets, especially in Acts. And of course, Paul makes it clear that Christ has gifted prophets to his church.

But if the Spirit has been poured out on the whole church, then certain elements of the prophet's job description have changed. Their particular role of embodying and speaking out aspects of God's reality now takes place within a Spirit-filled community, where everyone else can learn to hear God's voice. Rather than being the sole conduits of revelation, the prophets' responsibility is more about shaping prophetic culture and curating a fertile environment for listening to and responding to God.

The Spirit's is a beautiful work: the divine holy Fire, closely connected to prophecy throughout the Bible. The prophetic church is one that sets its sails to the winds of the Spirit and follows him wherever he leads. He is the gift-giver, the One who freely distributes the prophetic gifts amongst Jesus' people. And it is in this context that we are to make sense of the prophetic role.

JESUS AS THE BRIDGE

Having been reminded once more of the fundamental shift that occurs post-incarnationally, we can now pursue a deeper understanding of the role and calling of fivefold prophets – this group of people that we find in the New Testament and that possibly make up one fifth of the body of Christ today. As we do this, we are not essentially diverging from the Hebrew prophets, or refuting their influence, but rather building on what we see in the Old Testament and in the life of Jesus and reflecting on the fact that our ministry is now one of reconciliation rather than judgement.[8]

We need to view Jesus' perfect prophetic ministry as the *bridge* between our understanding of the Old Testament (old covenant) prophets and how we perceive the calling and ministry of fivefold (new covenant) prophets.

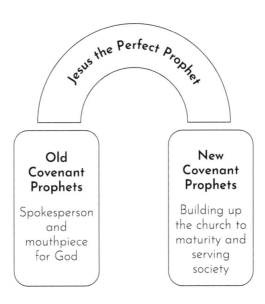

Jesus the Perfect Prophet

Old Covenant Prophets

Spokesperson and mouthpiece for God

New Covenant Prophets

Building up the church to maturity and serving society

Jesus enables us to take all that we can learn from the Old Testament paradigm and apply it to our current church context. He is the means by which we gain the truest perspective on the old covenant tradition. His is a rock-solid foundation on which to build a new covenant prophetic ministry and to reimagine the role of the prophet in this day and age.

Perhaps the most significant light that the incarnation sheds on the prophetic role is this: under the old covenant God is yet to speak his best Word, whereas in the new covenant *God has already spoken his best Word.* This fact defines the parameters of the fivefold prophet and helps ensure that the reality he or she holds out to the world is always Jesus-shaped.

THE WIRING AND ROLE OF FIVEFOLD PROPHETS

In highlighting the key distinctive marks and 'flavour' of the fivefold prophets' role and calling, it's helpful to consider both their internal *wiring,* as well as how this then plays out as they serve the church and society. Prophets (like the rest of the fivefold) have a particular way of viewing the world, and the Old Testament prophets are helpful in illuminating the motivations, attitudes and perspectives of our fivefold prophets. Returning to Abraham Heschel's point about needing to understand the *consciousness* of the prophet, we can consider 'the totality of impressions, thoughts, and feelings which make up the prophet's being'.[9] We find evidence for this consciousness – this characteristic *gaze* – as we spend time immersed in their words and actions depicted throughout Scripture.

Internal: How Prophets Are Wired

More than anything, prophets have a *passion for the heart of God.* This is where their attention constantly returns. They want everyone to experience the glorious nature of God and to be caught up in the wonders of the divine presence. Indifference to God and his concerns is anathema to a prophet.

Most of us know individuals in our local churches who are dedicated to prayer and worship, who are likely to bring the subject of a conversation back to God, and who have a tendency to challenge a lack of holy desire for God. It's these people who are likely to be fivefold prophets, even if they would not describe themselves as such.

Because prophets are focused on God and are very spiritually aware, they are also acutely conscious of 'the gap' – that huge gulf between all that is beautiful, sacred, loving, righteous and life-giving *in* God's presence, and all that is broken, messed-up, unjust, sinful and dying *apart* from God's presence.

The primary impulse of the prophet is to somehow *bridge that gap*. They implore people and society to turn back to God. They look for a place – any place – where they can stand between heaven and earth and facilitate some sort of connection. They long for whatever words, imagery or action will bring the much-needed realignment of created with Creator.

The gap is a place of tension for prophets: tension between the 'now' and the 'not yet', the 'actual' and the 'ideal'. They are simultaneously focused on the glory of God and, at the same time, sensitive to the reality in the world around them, with all its injustice and unfaithfulness. Prophets are therefore people who desire to challenge the current state of affairs and bring an alternative perspective. They are wired to ask questions, to provoke, to confront; to be radical agitators and activists. They have an impulse to go against the grain of popular consensus.

In occupying the gap, prophets are *wired for both worship and warfare*. Their passion for God's heart carries with it an urgency for reverence and devotion. They prioritise prayer and the pursuit of God's presence, but their sensitivity to idolatry, injustice and unrighteousness creates such a holy discontent that they desire to confront the powers that oppress people, whether cultural or spiritual.

Within the tensions of the gap, prophets are *enthusiasts for God*, knowing that he is so much closer and so much better than we can think or imagine. With their eyes turned heavenward, and awake to divine promise, they long for God's *shalom* and the renewal of all things.

Prophets are drawn to *the message of transformation*: 'We have to change! Things have to change!' Remaining 'as we are' is never an option for a prophet. Why stay here when there can be something better? They know that God is on the move and want the rest of the body to catch up.

As they pursue God's heart, they discern the work of the Spirit in refining and purifying his people and speak a message of transformation to the world around them.

Prophets are inherent *truth-tellers*. It's in their nature to simply speak out truth as they discern it. They may fear the consequences, but their love of the truth enables them to overcome such fear. They tend to see everything in black and white: it's either God or it's not; it's either holy or unholy.[10] Navigating shades of grey can be torturous for them. Prophets are often deeply intuitive, alert to the reality of unseen forces and influences that are at work in a situation. Their sensitivity to, and focus on, the spiritual realm means they sometimes struggle against a more pragmatic and less 'spiritual' approach to decision-making and strategy.

In seeking God's truth, prophets are naturally *wired for revelation* – the unveiling of God's thoughts and words. God's spoken word is a source of pure joy for them. In any situation their first question is, 'But what is God saying here?'

External: How Prophets Serve the Church and Society

New covenant prophets have the same fundamental wiring as their Old Testament counterparts, but, as we've seen, operate in a significantly different context. So how is the ministry of fivefold prophets expressed today? What's their unique job description within the body of Christ? We want to avoid having prophets in our churches who are not operating according to their calling, either due to lack of understanding, lack of acceptance, lack of permission or lack of opportunity to grow into a mature expression of the role. We need to do all we can to grasp the big picture of what prophets offer the church and the world – then we can go on to deploy them effectively.

To recap from chapter two, Ephesians 4 tells us that prophets are one of five roles gifted by Jesus to his church, and that all five roles have the purpose of building up the body of Christ to maturity. It is only when all five people-gifts are fully released to equip the body that we will be able to truly reflect the full measure of Christ and express his glory to the world around us.

So, what should prophets be doing?

Gap-consciousness fundamentally shapes and defines the job description of fivefold prophets. The concept of *bridging the gap* provides a lens with which to understand how they are called to serve the church and society. Every aspect of their role is, in one way or another, concerned with building a bridge. They may need to articulate the gap first – lamenting the present order of things – but then, in seeking to bridge it, their job is to communicate the bridge (through words or actions) and rejoice in the hope of the *shalom* it will bring.

The *awareness* of the gap is actually part of what prophets bring to the community. They can see what others cannot see. So, even though the gap is an uncomfortable place for prophets, it's a place they must occupy and embrace because the rest of the church needs them to focus on building the connection between God's reality and the society in which we live. And we can't effectively bridge the gap if we're not gap-aware.

Here are the key ways in which today's prophets function within the church and their important contribution to the maturity of the body.

They listen and perceive. Prophets see and hear with a clarity and precision that helps the church stay attuned and faithful to God's heart. They function as the eyes and ears of the body, alert to the purposes of God and the promptings of his Spirit. With insight and foresight, prophets are able to perceive God's reality when others are a little short-sighted, keeping the channels of communication open between God and his people.

They seek out, and then communicate, God's perspective on current situations. This enables the church to step back from the immediate and consider circumstances from a heavenly viewpoint. They can read the times, helping people understand the here and now through the eyes of God.

Prophets are also able to look ahead – to see clearly with future-focused eyes the 'what could be' of kingdom potential. Because of their keen spiritual sight, they play a vital role in releasing vision and holy imagination. They see the bigger picture of where God is calling us and enable us to lift our eyes and glimpse the future. Prophets help to maintain awareness of God's call on us as a church, keeping the call clear and sharp and preventing our vocation from being too safe and domesticated.

They equip others to hear God. Prophets help people hear God for themselves, so that every follower of Jesus can discern his voice and obey his leading. They build confidence that all his sheep can hear the voice of the Good Shepherd. They don't view prophetic gifts as solely for their personal use, but rather seek to multiply their own gifts into others. Prophets teach the body to hear words for both personal and societal transformation. A mature prophet promotes a culture of active listening and helps to demystify the prophetic so that it is accessible to the whole church, opening the door for others to discover the joy of listening prayer.

Prophets build the church by developing a safe, fertile learning environment and by seeking to equip the whole community with the ability to take hold of God's spoken word. By teaching everyone how to listen to God's voice and perceive God's reality, they can prepare the church to be a responsive and discerning community. They are there to remind the rest of us to pause, to tune in and to listen.

They orientate. Prophets encourage a culture of deep hunger for God and passion for his presence. In the words of Evelyn Underhill, 'they supply, and keep on supplying ... the ever life-giving consciousness of God and his presence in and with man.'[11] They strengthen the church by constantly refocusing attention on God and by calling his people to covenantal faithfulness. They search God's heart for the words or imagery that will draw people back to him. Prophets translate God[12] so that the world can reorient itself towards him and be reconciled.

Prophets are sensitive and alert to compromise and complacency, guarding against idolatry and promoting sincere worship and radical obedience. When we are in danger of being distracted or discouraged, prophets call us back to what our primary focus should be – back to a sense of the holy.

Like John the Baptist, prophets prepare the way for Jesus, helping to usher in his presence. They love to bring a revelation of Jesus. They facilitate divine encounters, helping people experience God and draw closer to him.

They promote spiritual health. Closely linked to the previous point, prophets play a vital role in developing the spiritual health of people, church, organisation and society. Embodying a deep life with God, they focus more on depth than breadth. They easily distinguish between spiritually healthy and unhealthy environments. They guard the community's spiritual immune system, to help build resistance to compromise or any form of idolatry. They aim to prevent faith from becoming lukewarm.

Prophets develop the body's spiritual health by leaning into God's heart and speaking out words of encouragement,[13] as well as by questioning and offering 'holy criticism'. They are sensitive to compromise and complacency, to everything that does not reflect God's heart and kingdom. They discern and challenge underlying satiation and immunity to the refining work of the Holy Spirit. They love to shatter indifference.[14] Like John the Baptist, they will preach for repentance if deemed necessary, knowing this is a vital element of a healthy relationship with God. Prophets provide an essential critical voice that realigns us to the uncompromising call and cost of discipleship. They challenge us when we've lost sight of our mission and calling.

Prophets love to provoke a 'kairos moment'.[15] They interrupt and jolt us out of the routine and challenge us to question our assumptions, to repent and to believe. They help develop an environment that is open and malleable to the leading of God's Spirit rather than one that stubbornly refuses to move. They keep us responsive and call us to change.

Prophets are adept at discerning the slow toxic slide into cultural compromise. They call us to remain true to our core values and confront us as to where our ultimate allegiance lies.

They challenge the status quo. As well as using grace-filled questioning inside the community to build spiritual health, prophets also have a role to play in critiquing the surrounding culture or society. They do this not to cast judgement on the world but in order to realign the world to God's purposes. Prophets are able to stand apart from the dominant cultural consciousness and scrutinise it. They are prepared to question everything that does not seem to honour God and everything that does not reflect the values of God's kingdom. They offer an alternative consciousness to the status quo.

Prophets will also question the institution where it becomes self-protective, compromised or oppressive. They exhort the organisation to return to its fundamental values and are prepared to speak truth to power.

They call people to live differently, to choose God's ways over the ways of the world and to be countercultural.

They maintain sensitivity to spiritual warfare. Prophets are sensitive to the battle going on in the spiritual realm. They are able to discern light from darkness and truth from lies. They function as 'early warning systems' and readily embrace the role of 'watchmen'[16] – protectively standing guard over the church, keenly looking out for any threat from the enemy.[17] They are wired to see beyond the physical and recognise where spiritual strongholds need tearing down.

Not only do they discern enemy activity and shed light on the devil's schemes, they also equip the church to stand in authority in the face of the powers of darkness: mature prophets teach us how to intercede effectively. Their natural tendency to focus on God's heart means they can become advocates for prayer in the church, encouraging others to make prayer and intercession a priority.

They champion social justice. Prophets cause the church to pay attention to God's concerns in the wider society. They enable a passion for God's heart to translate into an urgency to see wrongs righted and societal ills diminished. They prioritise issues of justice and advocate for the poor and marginalised. They speak against the politics of oppression and exploitation, and call society to change. They champion righteousness and a pursuit of God's *shalom* for all. They call for a better and freer society.

They energise God's people. Prophets have a vital role in releasing hope, vision and expectation in the community. They are awake to God's promises and can anticipate the new things God is doing. Their prophetic perspective helps nourish an alternative way of thinking about opportunities in the church and society. They perceive where God is taking us and prepare the church for what God is about to do. Their energising gives us a future when we are struggling to see beyond the trials of the present.[18]

Mature prophets act as catalysts to stir the church into action. They are forerunners, able to facilitate that necessary moment of kingdom breakthrough, so that our earthly context comes into alignment with the kingdom of heaven. They go ahead as pioneers, ploughing up the ground and being instruments of breakthrough.

CLOSING THE GAP

It's clear that prophets have a vital role to play in creating a mature, Jesus-shaped church. Fivefold prophets are necessary if we want to achieve the fullness of Christ and maturity that Paul exhorts us to in Ephesians 4:12–13. We need to promote an understanding of the role of prophets, as well as resourcing and championing their ministry, so that the whole church can have a healthy prophetic culture and consciousness.

Mature prophets have a godly influence on the culture around them by embodying or speaking out God's reality so that relationship with God can be restored and hearts and society can be transformed. Prophets curate the environment so that the church can embrace its prophetic role of carrying the revelation of the Triune God to the world.

For a relatively contemporary example of a prophet calling the church back to God, we can turn to the Lutheran pastor and theologian Dietrich Bonhoeffer. In the shadow of the Nazi regime that would later hang him, and a German church largely incapable of resisting such evil, he preached the following words:

> You have only one master now ... . But with this 'yes' to God belongs just as clear a 'no.' Your 'yes' to God requires your 'no' to all injustice, to all evil, to all lies, to all oppression and violation of the weak and poor, to all ungodliness, and to all mockery of what is holy. Your 'yes' to God requires a 'no' to everything that tries to interfere with your serving God alone, even if that is your job, your possessions, your home, or your honour in the world. Belief means decision.[19]

It's black and white. There is no compromise. This is the uncomfortable but necessary voice of the prophet. In seeking to close the gap between God and his people – calling the church to a yes to God and a no to anything that interferes with that relationship – the prophet knows the true urgency of the message.

5

THE PROPHETIC COMMUNITY

But you are a chosen people, a royal priesthood, a holy nation,
God's special possession, that you may declare the praises of him
who called you out of darkness into his wonderful light.

1 PETER 2:9

Who do you think you are?

That's the name of a popular BBC television series that started in 2004, in which celebrities trace their family tree back through the generations, revealing secrets, surprises and forgotten stories. An underlying theme of the show is the extent to which our ancestors inform our sense of identity and how the past can influence our present.

As human beings, we have a deep desire to understand ourselves and what makes us tick – to discern how we're wired. Whether it's digging into our ancestral heritage, searching for significance and self-worth, or wanting to better understand our interactions with other people, self-awareness is usually an important part of our well-being.

Many frameworks and models of looking at human experience and behaviour can help us define and shape our sense of self. The personality industry alone has churned out myriad tests and analyses, including the Myers-Briggs Type Indicator, the Enneagram, the Hexaco Personality Inventory and more – and is a billion-dollar business.

Some of us resist being put in any kind of box, and it's easy to get cynical about the latest bit of pop-psychology that attempts to explain the complexity of human personality with broad and blunt brushstrokes. But generally speaking, we all want to know who we are. We all want a greater sense of identity and purpose. We all want the personal security that comes from knowing what truly defines us.

As Christians, there are various approaches to understanding our identity. The place most of us start is the new identity given to us at salvation – what we could call our *in-Christ identity*. This knowledge of who we are is based on the profound truth of our adoption as sons and daughters of God.[1] The unbelievably good news is that no matter what we have done in our past, we have a new identity in Christ.[2] We don't have to try to earn God's favour and love. We no longer have to be defined by our achievements (or lack of them), by the jobs we do, by the possessions we own, or by how many 'likes' we have on our Facebook page. We are beloved children of a perfect heavenly Father,[3] and we find our security and significance in the love of God.

This is how Henri Nouwen puts it:

> Our first and most important spiritual task is to claim that unconditional love of God for ourselves. We have to dare to say 'Whether I feel it or not, whether I comprehend it or not, I know with a spiritual knowledge that I am God's beloved child, and nobody can take that divine childhood away from me.'[4]

The journey of discipleship is primarily about becoming more and more rooted in our God-given, Jesus-shaped identity. Being 'in Christ', our focus is on inhabiting and walking out the reality of what we already are: beloved sons and daughters of God. This is our 'divine childhood'. This is our identity, given to us by our heavenly Father. And this is truly where we find our significance and self-worth: through our status as children of God, learning to love like Jesus, think like Jesus and serve like Jesus.

This everlasting identity – as recipients of the Father's unconditional love and grace – is true for every Christian. And it's important to start here. Even Jesus started from this place as he began his earthly ministry.[5]

Once we grasp this foundational truth, we can take a second, more individualised, step in self-discovery. We can begin to explore the specifics of who God has designed each of us to be – what we could describe as our *distinct role and calling*. Each of us has a particular skillset and vocation that God has given us. When we pay close attention to the unique way God has designed us, we gain a clearer idea of who we are – not so we become self-absorbed, but so we know how best to serve him and fully embrace the kingdom purposes he calls each one of us to.

The New Testament makes it clear that we're not Christian clones and that we can genuinely celebrate our God-given differences. Paul's powerful metaphor for the church is a human body: every limb, organ, system is vital, but they all have a different role to play.

> If the whole body were an eye, where would the sense of hearing be? If the whole body were an ear, where would the sense of smell be? But in fact God has placed the parts in the body, every one of them, just as he wanted them to be.
>
> 1 CORINTHIANS 12:17–18

There is beautiful diversity within the people of God. We all need to know what our particular contribution to the body is. We need to embrace the truth that we all have a part to play, that we all have a special gift-mix, and thus we can celebrate God's masterful design in creating each one of us as a unique human being.

As we've already explored, Ephesians 4, with its description of the fivefold ministry, provides us with one very significant framework for understanding ourselves and how we are each shaped and called by God to serve his church and be a blessing to the world.

CORPORATE IDENTITY

There is a third aspect of our identity as Christians that we need to take hold of: our *corporate identity*. Regardless of what our own personal calling might be, a vital part of our identity is that of belonging to something bigger than ourselves. As followers of Jesus Christ, a key element of what defines us is that we are part of God's family. We're in this together!

Going back to Paul's body metaphor, if I'm an eye then I first of all need to embrace the 'eye-ness' of who I am, but I also need to embrace my identity as part of the whole organism with a shared DNA. The body is not just a random collection of organs and systems; it is an intricately connected *whole*. In fact, the eye can only really understand itself from the point of view of the entire body; it makes very little sense by itself.

Being a Christian means I'm not just *part* of a body but that I *share* in the body's corporate identity as the body of Christ.

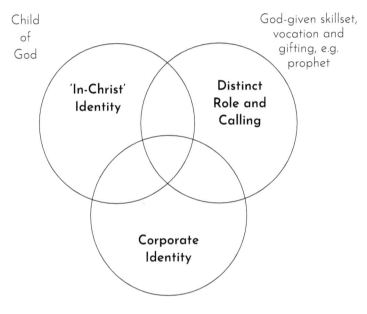

Child of God

God-given skillset, vocation and gifting, e.g. prophet

'In-Christ' Identity

Distinct Role and Calling

Corporate Identity

Collective identity that we all share as the body of Christ, e.g. prophetic church

It's essential that we understand our collective identity and purpose as the body of Christ. We need a clear vision for this 'one body' that is eternally defined by him. Being a follower of Jesus means we're part of something much bigger than our own individual relationships with God and our personal callings. This can be hard to grasp when we live in a society that is primarily focused on the individual, and in which people are increasingly socially isolated.[6] Developing a mindset of corporate identity challenges us on many fronts. But being part of Christ's church on earth has to mean more than just turning up to a building on a Sunday and hanging out with our nice Christian friends. We need to reconnect with exactly what Christ has purposed his church to be and then allow this to speak deeply into our own sense of self.

WHO DO WE THINK WE ARE?

Football (or soccer, to my American friends) is something of a national passion in England, and fans will pay a lot of money week in week out to watch their club play. If you've ever been to a match, you know what happens when you fill a stadium with tens of thousands of supporters all desperate for their team to win. As the anthems are sung, and the cheers and groans echo around the ground, there is an incredible sense of being part of something much bigger. The crowd seems to take on a life of its own. Ask any ardent Liverpool, Arsenal or Sheffield Wednesday supporter, and they will instinctively understand what corporate identity means: a significant part of their identity is defined by being part of that much larger group. They could meet a fellow fan anywhere in the world and have something very meaningful in common – a shared narrative, language, passion and purpose.

When it comes to the church, there are many aspects of our corporate identity and purpose we need to be reminded of. But, as we saw in chapter two, the fivefold thinking that comes out of Ephesians 4 gives us a particular paradigm for understanding our shared identity as fundamentally *apostolic*, *prophetic*, *evangelistic*, *shepherding* and *teaching*. These five functions belong to the *whole* body. These are the team colours we wear.

We are collectively designed to operate as an apostolic church, a prophetic church, an evangelistic church, a shepherding church and a teaching church. This is about having a communal intelligence and purpose. So, it's not that we simply identify a bunch of apostles – 'Look we've got five apostles, so we must be apostolic' – but we recognise that we as a church *together* are called to be apostolic. We don't just find a group of prophets and say, 'That's great, we're prophetic', but instead we recognise that we ourselves as a *whole body* are called to be prophetic.

This way of thinking – this corporate identity – leads us to a genuinely Jesus-shaped church.

OUR IDENTITY AS A PROPHETIC CHURCH

The fivefold pattern in Ephesians 4 certainly points to our corporate prophetic identity, but there are additional biblical themes that also speak into this, and which have been discussed in preceding chapters. What I want to do here is pull them together and suggest how they all contribute something significant to our understanding of why the prophetic is part of our shared identity as God's people.

The nature of God: The roots of the prophetic can be traced right back to the Creator. The very essence of the prophetic is derived from the nature and purposes of God. As we observed in chapter one, prophetic consciousness and intelligence is a reflection of who God himself is. He is the God of covenantal relationship and revelation, the God intent on communication, who speaks so that all may be restored and made whole. Our call to be a prophetic people is grounded in the nature of the God we worship.

Jesus the perfect Prophet: The prophetic is perfectly embodied in Jesus. He is the ultimate expression of the prophetic role. In order to be a Christlike church, we need to embrace the kind of prophetic ministry he models for us. If we claim to be a people following after Jesus then we need to follow in his prophetic footsteps.

The biblical prophetic tradition: The prophetic root that is found in God and embodied by Jesus has been expressed through the ministry of the prophets in the Bible. From the time of Moses onward, God has provided his people with prophets; they have shaped the culture around them by prioritising the covenant relationship and standing up for God's concerns. The prophetic has always been part of the story of God's people. Embracing our shared prophetic identity is simply a continuation of the biblical tradition.

Pentecost: The church born on the day of Pentecost is a prophetic church. The Spirit has been poured out on us. The prophetic is embedded in our DNA, as made clear in Acts 2:17–18. On that momentous day, Peter chose to read from the prophet Joel the promise of young and old prophesying and dreaming dreams. We, as the church, are children of outpouring and prophecy.

The following diagram shows how these different biblical strands speak into our corporate identity as a prophetic church.

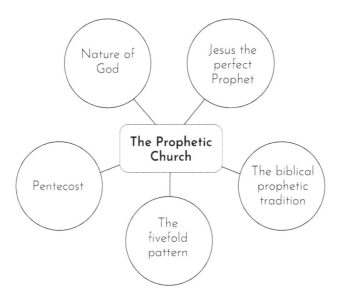

I believe that when we consider all these biblical themes, there can be no doubt that the church of Jesus Christ is called to *be* a prophetic body. This is about how the church itself corporately identifies with, and *embodies*, the ministry of Jesus the perfect Prophet and thus God's prophetic purposes for the church.

At this point it is helpful to be clear about what we are referring to with the word 'church'. Up until now I've been using the word to refer to the concept of the global church: the big, beautiful picture of the body of Christ. But I believe that this sense of corporate identity is equally relevant when we think about local expressions of church – and even other forms of Christian organisation. Wherever followers of Jesus are gathered around a common purpose, we can ask questions of our shared prophetic identity and seek to become an authentic prophetic community. Whether we are talking local or global – whether we are thinking parish, prayer group or Christian non-profit – we need to know who we are. We need to perceive the captivating and holistic vision of a prophetic community that Jesus intends us to be.

The challenge is to be prepared for the shift in mindset that is required to embrace this corporate perspective. A person who is a fivefold prophet is an expression of something much, much bigger. The prophets in the Bible provide us with valuable source material that helps us make sense of the prophetic, but ultimately we need to shift our focus more towards the body. I believe the church has sometimes placed an unhealthy emphasis on the individual prophet. There can be a tendency to celebrate and promote the 'anointed' man or woman of God at the expense of the whole community embracing their shared prophetic calling. The prophetic *church* comes before the prophetic *individual*; the prophetic community – carrying the radical revelation of the Triune God – takes precedence over individual prophets. Indeed, as we have already explored, one of the primary aspects of a fivefold prophet's role is to equip the *whole* body to take hold of its prophetic identity.

Whatever church background we are from, we will need to be prepared to stretch our thinking. This is especially challenging for those of us from the charismatic tradition. We need a broader paradigm than is currently found in many charismatic churches, where prophetic ministry has an overly individualistic emphasis. If all we focus on is delivering prophecies, we miss out on the breadth and depth of prophetic spirituality. If all we focus on is prophets, we miss out on seeing the way the *church itself* can be prophetic in its very nature.

UNDERSTANDING THE PROPHETIC FUNCTION

So, in practice, what does all this mean? This is where revisiting the terminology of the prophetic *function* – the idea of how we think and act *together* – can be extremely helpful. When we talk about the prophetic function, we are talking about a collective prophetic consciousness, intelligence, sensibility and purpose. We are talking about a shared prophetic identity that has been gifted to the church by the ascended Christ.

Let's define a couple of these terms:

Collective consciousness: a set of shared beliefs, ideas, attitudes and knowledge that are common to a social group or society.

Collective intelligence: a group or a team's combined capacity and capability to perform a wide variety of tasks and solve diverse problems.[7] Collective intelligence has been found to be consistently predictive of the future performance of groups and teams.[8]

Our shared prophetic consciousness enables the church to see, understand and love the world through the eyes of Jesus the perfect Prophet; our shared prophetic intelligence gives us the ability to speak and act prophetically in the pattern he has provided for us. The more we intentionally develop these traits, the more likely we are able to imitate Jesus in using them.

Expanding our definition of *the prophetic* from chapter one, the prophetic function can be understood as:

A shared understanding and capability that enables us to corporately hold out God's reality, so that it can be clearly seen and responded to, so that transformation can take place and so that relationship can be restored.

The prophetic function is part of the church's intrinsic identity and purpose – how we are shaped and defined. The church is, by its nature and calling, a prophetic body, appointed to worship, to obey, to bear witness to, and to carry the revelation of the Trinity. This is the global church and the local church. This is every church.

As we consider how the church *in its very nature* can be prophetic, we need to embrace the prophetic pattern we see in the life of Jesus. Our life as a prophetic people must be directly formed around his life, ministry and teaching. He is the quintessential expression of the prophet and so gives us the blueprint for a mature, holistic, multi-faceted way of being the prophetic church. *We need to be prophetic in the way that Jesus was prophetic* – not just as individuals but as a body with a collective prophetic consciousness and intelligence. We want the full measure of Jesus the Prophet in our churches.

Wherever God's people meet in his name, we will find elements of the prophetic function. The church inherently points to the reality of the

Trinity. Calling ourselves the body of Christ, worshipping together, and celebrating the sacraments are all, to some extent, prophetic acts: they demonstrate aspects of God's supreme reality. But it's more than that. The prophetic function is about *every* member sharing in a corporate identity based on Christ's own prophetic ministry. *We are all prophetic* because we are all part of his prophetic body. Each one of us can be a living expression of Jesus the perfect Prophet (just as we can all express his apostolic, evangelistic, shepherding and teaching ministries).

Jesus has designed his church to be a glorious church, with the full measure of prophetic consciousness, intelligence and experience. There is an incredible breadth and depth of prophetic spirituality available to every single local church, every single expression of the body of Christ and every single Christian.

THE TWO DIMENSIONS OF PROPHETIC FUNCTION AND CULTURE

What is the best way to comprehend the full scope of our identity as a prophetic community? What's the best way to imagine the prophetic function in this day and age?

Throughout Scripture we consistently observe a *dual focus* of the prophetic: the Old Testament prophets expressed the twin concerns of safeguarding the people's relationship with God *and* promoting a just society. This was then mirrored in Christ's own prophetic ministry. We see him walking intimately with the Father and calling others to the same depth of relationship; we also see him overturning tables in the temple and defending the cause of the marginalised.

One way to explore this binary pattern is through the lens of 'covenant and kingdom' – two vast themes that wind their way through the whole biblical narrative and find their fullest expression in Jesus. (We will return to these in chapter ten.) The theme of *covenant* refers to our connection with God and expresses God's desire to call people into a committed and loving relationship with himself. The theme of *kingdom* refers to our responsibility to represent God and act on his behalf. Together they provide a perspective that speaks into the clear twofold expression of the prophetic in Scripture.

A fundamental framework that helps us understand the full extent of our identity as a prophetic church can be represented as two primary dimensions: *Vertical* and *Horizontal*. [9]

Vertical Prophetic
- Covenant: loving God
- Attentive to God
- 'We have to change' (heart transformation)
- Challenge idolatry

The Prophetic Church

Horizontal Prophetic
- Kingdom: loving others
- Attentive to God's concerns
- 'Things have to change' (social transformation)
- Challenge injustice

Standing Between Heaven and Earth

The *Vertical* dimension is the God-focused (even God-intoxicated) part of prophetic consciousness and culture. From Moses meeting God face to face, through to Jesus spending whole nights in prayer and Paul being caught up to the third heaven,[10] this is the element of the prophetic that is consumed with God and his immediacy. In this dimension, the priority is loving God, experiencing him, pursuing his presence and maintaining wholehearted devotion to him through worship and prayer. When engaged in the Vertical dimension, we have visions of God and hear his voice, and the veil draws back enough for us to get glimpses of his glory.

When God speaks to us, he speaks for a purpose, and he looks for a response. In the Vertical dimension, God's reality is held out to us so that we can be *personally* transformed. His voice will refine us and change our hearts and minds, both on an individual and a corporate level. Even the simplest words from God have the power to utterly change us if we pause long enough to fully engage with them. Personal, covenantal holiness is developed in the body as we not only listen to God's words but also walk in obedience to them.

The Vertical dimension of the prophetic is also concerned with protecting the covenant relationship God has with his people. When this relationship is threatened, the Vertical prophetic helps to restore and maintain a culture of God-centeredness, so that our hearts remain soft and affectionate towards him.

In this dimension our shared prophetic identity is one of pursuing relational intimacy with God *together*. A church engaged in the Vertical dimension will:

- worship passionately
- pray fervently
- listen intently

The *Horizontal* dimension of the prophetic function, on the other hand, is about attentiveness to God's concerns in the world. The prophets of old make it clear that we cannot hide away in our prayer closets and worship services and neglect what is going on in our neighbourhoods and in society at large:

> 'Is not this the kind of fasting I have chosen: to loose the chains of injustice and untie the cords of the yoke, to set the oppressed free and break every yoke?'
>
> ISAIAH 58:6

The Horizontal dimension of prophetic culture recognises that, to be God's holy people, we have to stand up for his holiness, righteousness and justice in the world around us. God's alternative reality is going to challenge every unjust system, every corrupt government and every unethical corporation; and as a prophetic people we have a responsibility to ensure that this reality is seen and heard. The poor, downtrodden and marginalised need the prophetic church to advocate for them and to take on the powers and principalities that would crush them underfoot.

If the Vertical dimension of the prophetic is about personal and covenantal holiness, then the Horizontal dimension is about *social* holiness. The prophetic church should be able to name cultural, political, institutional and systemic sin, such as oppression or racial injustice.[11] The prophetic voice of the church is one agitating for change and speaking truth to power. 'Things have to change!' In the Horizontal dimension we, the church, are the agents of transformation.

In reflecting on our collective calling, author and missiologist JR Woodward says that,

> Jesus calls us through the power of the Spirit to follow him as the liberator of those who have been oppressed by the system, the lover of those who have been rejected by society and the deliverer of those who have been seduced by consumerism.[12]

In this dimension, our shared prophetic identity is one of pursuing God's righteousness and justice for society *together*. A church engaged in the Horizontal dimension will:

- sit in the place of holy discontent
- defend the poor and oppressed
- challenge the status quo

Both the Horizontal and the Vertical dimensions are ultimately concerned with movement, renovation and transformation. The prophetic function ensures both people and society avoid the perils of stagnation and instead respond to God's promise of newness. The prophetic community knows that God is on the move. He is not content to leave us – or society – where we currently are. The prophetic community is in step with the Spirit, moving forward with intentionality and vision, engaged with God's purposes.

However, the prophetic community also knows that we first have to *recognise the need for transformation*. We have to let God in. We have to confront our own reality and change our way of thinking. We must have our indifference shattered and be prepared to lament the brokenness.

In both dimensions, the prophetic church is making the vital choice not to distance itself from, or become immune to, God's reality. Rather, we are *paying attention*. In the Vertical dimension we are paying attention to God – to his glory, presence and revelation. In the Horizontal dimension we are paying attention to the world – especially God's concerns in the world around us, and opportunities to bring about his justice and righteousness. The prophetic function urges us to pay attention and to beware the perils of getting distracted. Prophetic consciousness requires us to be *fully present* in the moment with God: to stay awake, aware and alert.

Let's go back to our definition of the prophetic – *faithfully holding out God's reality so that it can be clearly seen and responded to, so that transformation can take place, and so that relationship can be restored*. How might this apply to the prophetic community in the Vertical and Horizontal dimensions?

> **Vertical**: As a community, we willingly expose ourselves to the radiant light of God's reality, knowing we must surrender to it and be transformed. We seek God's presence and truth so that he will change us and draw us closer to his heart.

> **Horizontal**: As a community, we then hold out God's reality to the world around us. We carry the revelation of the Father to the orphaned world; we declare his good news and living Word to the poor and broken; we demonstrate the reality of his kingdom by promoting his justice and righteousness.

If we return to the Exodus narrative (that we explored in chapter three), we now see how it can be viewed from a *two-dimensional perspective*. We can observe how, as God's alternative reality collides with Pharaoh's world through Moses' ministry, the twin evils of false gods (idolatry) and empire (unjust society) are exposed and disrupted. Right at the start of biblical prophetic ministry, the Vertical dimension of the prophetic is there to challenge idolatry, and the Horizontal dimension is there to challenge injustice. The contemporary church holds the same two-edged sword in its hand today.

Unfortunately, many churches tend to operate in only one of the two dimensions. As individual Christians we are bound to have personal preferences, but as the body of Christ we need to fully embrace and deeply engage with both dimensions of the prophetic function. We can't limit prophetic culture to either one or the other or choose to focus on only one of the two expressions. We have to find a way to bridge the divide.

Perhaps if we framed the question differently, we would see how compromised and diminished we become through a one-dimensional prophetic culture. Which one of these two commands might you more easily ignore?

- Love the Lord your God with all your heart and with all your soul and with all your strength and with all your mind.
- Love your neighbour as yourself.[13]

If we isolate one from the other, we end up with dysfunction but together they create a holistically mature prophetic body.

The thirty-thousand-foot view of the prophetic helps us overcome the perils of blinkered perspectives and rampant individualism. It enables us to take in the full extent of the prophetic panorama and appreciate that it belongs to every one of us. A vital part of our identity is found in our shared intelligence and consciousness. We're all in this together.

In Part 2, we will explore in depth these two dimensions that together give us a comprehensive understanding of the prophetic identity Jesus has given his church. These dual dimensions are contrasting but complementary terrains to survey and journey through, each rich with tradition and alive with the breath of the Spirit. No matter what spiritual or denominational background we come from, and regardless of our natural preferences and theological slant, each one of us can learn much from this dual approach. My own church background tends to be more focused on the Vertical dimension of the prophetic, so I'm naturally drawn to this space and feel at home here. But over the last few years, as I've intentionally engaged much more with the Horizontal dimension, I've come to appreciate the depth of spirituality found in this domain. My thinking has been stretched, and my engagement with God's beautiful heart has deepened. So, whatever your natural or ecumenical bias, be prepared to meet Jesus the perfect Prophet in some fresh and interesting ways.

PART 2
PRESENCE AND JUSTICE

THE LANDSCAPE COMES INTO FOCUS

In Part 1, we recognised the necessity of certain paradigm shifts: one towards a communal prophetic identity, and another towards a holistic prophetic ministry. We are now ready to study the prophetic landscape in detail. Part 2 takes us to the fundamental elements of this landscape and enables us to carefully chart its contours.

We will first delve deeper into the two perspectives introduced at the end of chapter five. To get a well-rounded appreciation of the Vertical dimension, we will welcome the guidance of two streams of church tradition, learning much from those who have gone before us. To study the Horizontal dimension, we will pay careful attention to some key biblical themes that act as road signs along the way. All these ancient elements of the prophetic are able to profoundly shape our churches today.

As we start to develop an imagination for the prophetic community – where commitment to God's presence and justice become a way of life and part of our communal identity – the challenge is to bring both dimensions of prophetic culture together. And this, in turn, becomes how we define the mature, Jesus-shaped prophetic church. We are first transformed from within so that we can be a people who transform the world around us.

6

THE MOUNTAIN

Now the appearance of the glory of the LORD was like a devouring fire on the top of the mountain in the sight of the people of Israel.

EXODUS 24:17 NRSV

Have you ever noticed the significance of mountains in the Bible? More often than not, they are places connected with a profound experience of God.

In the Old Testament, there is one particular mountain associated with God-encounters and the theophany of Yahweh; in fact, it repeatedly gets called *the mountain of God.*[1] This is Mount Horeb (also called Mount Sinai) – the place where Moses first encountered God through the burning bush experience and then later received the Ten Commandments. This mountain plays a key role in the Exodus narrative. It is the place where the covenant was established and where the Israelites saw the visible manifestation of God's presence.

> You came near and stood at the foot of the mountain while it blazed with fire to the very heavens, with black clouds and deep darkness. Then the LORD spoke to you out of the fire.
>
> DEUTERONOMY 4:11–12

There are two notable encounters on Mount Horeb I want to highlight. The first is in Exodus 33–34, when we see Moses returning to the mountain of God after the golden calf debacle. He comes with a particular request: that he may see God's glory. God's promise to him is still resounding loudly as Moses waits for it to be fulfilled: 'I will cause all my goodness to pass in front of you, and I will proclaim my name, the LORD [Yahweh], in your presence' (Exodus 33:19).

God hides Moses in a cleft in the rock as his glory passes by, allowing him to see God's back but not his face. In this remarkable moment, Moses hears God's voice proclaiming his very name and character.

Centuries pass, and we find Elijah on the same mountain, summoned there by God himself.[2] He may well have found shelter in the same recess or cave from which Moses encountered God's glory. He has been brought to Horeb that he too may experience something of Yahweh's supreme reality and truth: 'Go out and stand on the mountain in the presence of the LORD, for the LORD is about to pass by' (1 Kings 19:11).

As with Moses, Elijah encountered Yahweh's manifest presence and voice on the holy mountain. God allowed both of these prophets to experience a visitation that took the form of the 'passing by' of his presence.

Hundreds of years later, the Bible depicts a third mountaintop epiphany. This time we catch sight of Peter, James and John being led up a mountain by Jesus, in order that they may see him in his glory. We now know this peak as the Mount of Transfiguration.[3] Here again are Moses and Elijah; here again is the cloud of God's presence; once more the voice of God is heard on a mountain. But this time, rather than announcing the momentary 'passing by' of Yahweh, God declares the eternal identity of Immanuel, God with us: 'This is my Son, whom I love; with him I am well pleased. Listen to him!' (Matthew 17:5).

Presence. Glory. Revelation. God's brilliant reality bursting into human experience, revealing his divine name and nature, in order that we may see who he really is.

Today, the prophetic church is summoned to the mountain of God for its own epiphanies, though we don't usually have to go up a physical mountain to perceive God's glory and to hear his voice. Still, in the same way that these three accounts each have a literal Vertical dimension to them, we need to pay attention to the *Vertical dimension of the prophetic* and its role in drawing us to a place of encounter with the Lord's presence and his words to us. This dimension is wholly focused on God and the pursuit of his presence and heart. It centres on our covenantal relationship with him, from which flows our connectedness with him and the ability to tune into his voice.

As we climb this metaphorical mountain and explore its terrain, we want to ensure that our footholds are secure. But we also need to avoid the temptation to play it safe and simply skirt timidly around the foothills. We need to be certain that a 'fear of heights' does not rob us of the opportunity to climb high. It's worth the effort and risk because the view from the top is amazing!

Two church traditions act as mighty guides through this incredible landscape and help us navigate the terrain successfully. Neither is flawless, but both have a rich history of ensuring a firm footing for pilgrims and for significantly shaping church culture. These guides lead us in different ways up the mountain, but their paths cross meaningfully from time to time. To be a prophetic church, we must learn from those who have gone before us. Together these two traditions help us find our way up the mountain, on paths well-trod by many prophets down the years.

MOUNTAIN GUIDE 1: THE CONTEMPLATIVE TRADITION

The contemplative tradition is an undiscovered country for many Western or Protestant Christians. Some are wary of it because of perceived links with Eastern mysticism and the New Age movement; others are unappreciative of the rich contribution it has made to Christian spiritual growth over the centuries; but a careful examination of Scripture reveals this tradition to be deeply biblical.

The roots of the contemplative tradition go back to John the apostle in the first century and the Desert Fathers and Mothers of the fourth century. However, contemplative practices are not merely ancient; they have continued in varying forms throughout church history. Many Christian figures have engaged in contemplative prayer, and we can learn much from the writings of people such as Thomas Aquinas, Thomas à Kempis, Teresa of Avila and Brother Lawrence.

At the heart of the contemplative tradition is a call to focus our loving attention on God – to set our minds and hearts on him and attend to his presence. The word *contemplate* means to look at, observe, or gaze at attentively. To put it simply, this tradition is about contemplating God. As Richard Foster describes it, 'the contemplative life is the steady gaze of the soul upon the God who loves us.'[4] Contemplation is utterly theocentric and soaked in divine love. In gazing upon God, we are concentrating all our senses on his majestic beauty and glory.

The contemplative tradition emphasises that God is *already present* with us and that spiritual growth happens as we learn to attend to and practise his presence. At its basic level, contemplative prayer is openness to God, who is always with us. It is an expression of the heart that hungers for God and his sublime reality:

> As the deer pants for streams of water, so my soul pants for you, my God. My soul thirsts for God, for the living God.
>
> PSALM 42:1–2

The contemplative knows it is vital to nurture this desire for God because it is a necessary part of our Christian life. The Christian disciple has to find space and time to be captivated by the beauty of God, to lavish attention on God. There is a keen *seeking* dynamic to contemplative spirituality, as we intentionally draw near to him. It's not enough to understand God intellectually or to meditate on his attributes as interesting concepts; rather, we recognise that we are on a lifelong journey of seeking out his personhood and pursuing his presence. We are constantly called further, deeper and higher in our pursuit of him.

The contemplative tradition encourages practices that enable us to retreat from the busyness of everyday life; to pause and focus our senses, our thoughts and our emotions on God, and on the simple but profound truth that he is present. However, the goal for many is contemplation as a way of life, in which an awareness of the presence of God is maintained ceaselessly. Seeing God's reality in all that we are doing in our day-to-day lives and delighting in his constant presence with us is the fullest expression of contemplative practice.

This is the very essence of the Vertical prophetic: to be so focused on God, to be so caught up in the divine beauty, that we can gaze unhindered on his preeminent and ultimate reality.

The contemplative tradition sees prayer as much more than bringing a list of requests before the Almighty. Rather, it is prayer as beholding the Beloved, as resting in the goodness of God. It is prayer as an intimate meeting place with Jesus. It is prayer as the place where we are found, cherished and held by him. When we start to understand prayer from this perspective, we can join with our contemplative friends and experience the joys of a prayer-soaked, prayer-filled life.

Rooted in Scripture

The contemplative tradition is well-grounded scripturally. We hear the clear call to contemplative practice in the ancient words of the Psalms:

> One thing I ask from the LORD, this only do I seek: that I may dwell in the house of the LORD all the days of my life, to gaze on the beauty of the LORD and to seek him in his temple.
>
> PSALM 27:4

> You, God, are my God, earnestly I seek you; I thirst for you, my whole being longs for you … . On my bed I remember you; I think of you through the watches of the night.
>
> PSALM 63:1, 6

In the New Testament, Paul exhorts us to focus our attention on God; to set our hearts and minds on the unseen reality and person of God. It is as we gaze on him that we are spiritually formed to his likeness.

> Set your hearts on things above, where Christ is, seated at the right hand of God. Set your minds on things above, not on earthly things.
>
> COLOSSIANS 3:1–2

> So we fix our eyes not on what is seen, but on what is unseen, since what is seen is temporary, but what is unseen is eternal.
>
> 2 CORINTHIANS 4:18

Finally, brothers and sisters, whatever is true, whatever is noble, whatever is right, whatever is pure, whatever is lovely, whatever is admi-
rable – if anything is excellent or praiseworthy – think about such
things.

PHILIPPIANS 4:8

Perhaps the simplest and most profound call to the contemplative way of
life is encapsulated in the image of Mary, seated at Jesus' feet.[5] While her
sister, Martha, is rushing around, 'distracted by all the preparations that
had to be made', Mary discovers the 'one thing necessary'. She chooses
humble attentiveness, listening to all Jesus says. And Jesus is clear that this
is the better way.

A Closer Look

There are three particular emphases associated with this tradition, which
help us navigate the mountain and are relevant for shaping the Vertical
dimension in our communities: stillness, wholehearted love for God and
surrender.

Stillness. It sounds so simple, doesn't it – to be still? But for a great
many of us, stillness is an elusive posture. It's become a cliché, but the
pace of modern life is extraordinary: instant communication around the
world, homes full of the latest technology, 24/7 everything. To grow in
our ability to hear God's voice, and to develop a God-conscious existence,
we have to be ruthless about taking on the discipline of stillness. I know
in my own life that I have many days when I rush from activity to activity,
and it is only when I get to bedtime that I realise I haven't been present
to God and attentive to his voice that day. When we're going too fast,
our spiritual well-being is jeopardised by a shallow engagement with the
'unforced rhythms of grace' (Matthew 11:29 MSG). We lose the ability to
still our hearts and minds and fully encounter God's presence.[6] We lose
our ability to focus on his face.

When Elijah encountered God on Mount Horeb, it was in the whis-
pering of the soft breeze rather than the wind, earthquake or fire. Most
of the time God doesn't shout revelation; rather, he chooses to speak in
a still, small voice and in fleeting impressions. He speaks in the kind of

voice we can only hear by leaning in, getting close and paying attention. His is the voice of the tender Father rather than a sergeant major; a voice that is easy to miss if we're going too fast. But if we slow down enough, we discover a voice of clarity, kindness and breathtaking beauty.

The contemplative tradition points us to stillness as an absolute priority in order that we can be truly present to God and open to the presence of the Holy Spirit. Stillness helps us develop a slowed-down spirituality, modelled much more on the unhurried pace of Jesus' life rather than the frenetic pace of our own lives. We first curate an *external* stillness, where we simplify our environment – often through the disciplines of silence and solitude. Contemplatives view solitude as an essential spiritual practice that increases our ability to be attentive to God and enables us to offer him our undivided attention. Contemplative prayer often uses silence as a way to empty the heart and mind of unnecessary distractions and so be open to the person and work of the Holy Spirit. When we've beheld God and his holiness, there comes a time when mere words lose their ability to express our love and awe of him. As Angelus Silesius puts it, 'God far exceeds all words that we can here express. In silence he is heard, in silence worshipped best.'[7]

For many of us, silence and solitude are challenging concepts. Richard Foster reminds us of the enemy's tactics: 'In contemporary society our adversary majors in three things: noise, hurry and crowds. If he can keep us engaged in "muchness" and "manyness," he will rest satisfied.'[8]

But both silence and solitude are key to awakening our souls to God's presence. They need to be embraced. In our prophetic communities we need to find a way to be comfortable with quiet and to be satisfied with waiting, and thus nurture the unhurried.

As well as helping us to develop external stillness, the contemplative tradition teaches us the path of *internal* stillness – the ability to still our souls that David celebrates in Psalm 131.

> But I have calmed and quieted my soul,
> like a weaned child with its mother;
> my soul is like the weaned child that is with me.
>
> PSALM 131:2 NRSV

The path to internal stillness involves clearing away the inner clutter and chaos, recognising that distracting thoughts, temptations and agendas can get in the way of focusing on the pursuit of God. We put all our attention on God so that we can perceive and experience him. This requires a willingness to wait and rest in God's presence and his loving embrace – which is actually more of an active process than we might first assume. It requires concentration and effort, so that an attentive beholding and watchfulness takes place in the interior silence.

> For God alone my soul waits in silence.
> PSALM 62:1 NRSV

Stillness, both external and internal, has to be cultivated and nurtured with great intentionality; it must be viewed as a skill to be practised and learnt. But the rewards are bountiful, as we begin to 'experience and embrace the reality of God in a way that sets us free and changes us to be like him.'[9]

Here's the wisdom of Henri Nouwen:

> Many voices ask for our attention. There is a voice that says, 'Prove that you are a good person.' Another voice says, 'You'd better be ashamed of yourself.' There also is a voice that says, 'Nobody really cares about you,' and one that says, 'Be sure to become successful, popular, and powerful.' But underneath all these often very noisy voices is a still, small voice that says, 'You are my Beloved, my favour rests on you.' That's the voice we need most of all to hear. To hear that voice, however, requires special effort; it requires solitude, silence, and a strong determination to listen. That's what prayer is. It is listening to the voice that calls us 'my Beloved.'[10]

To navigate the mountain of God, we have to change our pace. We have to embrace a lifestyle of going slow enough to hear, of reordering our priorities, of staying attuned and in synch. And this is a way of life for the whole church to pursue.

Wholehearted love for God. Divine love is at the heart of the contemplative life – being entirely caught up in God's great love for us, and our answering love towards him. The primary focus and aspiration is on loving the One who first loved us; on ever-growing intimacy with God; on letting him become the realised centre of our lives.

Contemplative prayer is living fully into the first great commandment, to love God with every part of our being. Instead of being satisfied by an abstract love, we learn to steadily and meaningfully deepen our love for him. This is about gazing upon God in adoration as we are enveloped in his love for us.

The contemplative knows that the love of God is a vast country to be explored. We can never reach the bottom or find the end of it. But, like John the apostle (by far the most contemplative of the New Testament writers), we too can lean our heads on the chest of Jesus[11] and know ourselves deeply loved.

Human beings have a natural tendency to devote time and focused attention to that which we love. The contemplative community is deeply satisfied by pouring out continuous adoration to God.

Surrender. With divine love comes purifying fire and an awareness that we are fully seen by God. There is nowhere to hide! Contemplative spirituality embraces the fact that, as we gaze steadily on God and encounter his love, we are going to be changed. Contemplating God must lead to transformation: the process of becoming more and more Christlike. A vital element of this tradition, then, is the art of letting go and letting God; of putting aside any temptation to 'live according to the flesh' (Romans 8:5); and of allowing God to prune away all that entangles us.[12]

There is much to be surrendered: worldly distractions and desires; busyness and hurry; everything that would choke or quench our desire for God; anything else that is claiming our adoration. We have to surrender all that keeps us at a distance from him, including behaviours and defence mechanisms we use to avoid his presence and protect ourselves from change. For many of us, simply choosing a depth of quietness and solitude is a huge act of surrender. Contemplative prayer teaches us the necessity of letting go of our sense of importance and of having to be productive and accomplishing more. It is challenging to put aside the more activist elements of our faith and be content with a dimension of spirituality that emphasises rest.

Surrender requires a posture of radical openness to God. We have to ask ourselves whether we are prepared to be overwhelmed by him. This is not a safe, tame spirituality. As we approach him, we choose to be unequivocally open to him, to yield ourselves fully to the fiery brilliance of his presence. We partner with the Holy Spirit in the necessity of the refining process so that he can lovingly reorder us.

A Trustworthy Guide

The contemplative tradition is a great guide up the mountain because it gives us the rigour and discipline to strip away every distraction. It slows us down sufficiently so that we can reorient ourselves upon the heart of God. The best of the tradition sees contemplation as a gift and therefore dependent on God's grace. It's not an exclusive experience for the very holy and deeply spiritual, but rather something we can all partake in as we cooperate with the gracious gift of his presence.

Contemplative spirituality speaks to us of what is truly important: our love for God. It allows the fiery light of divine Love to saturate every part of our hearts and minds and burn up every pocket of resistance. It is an expression of spirituality that we can embrace as a whole faith community, not merely as a lone pursuit. The prophetic function of the church grows out of hearts and minds attuned to God in loving faithfulness, and many of us need the contemplatives to show us how to rest in God and deeply enjoy him in order to prevent our lives becoming dry, distant and indifferent.

MOUNTAIN GUIDE 2: THE CHARISMATIC TRADITION

If the contemplative tradition is associated with quiet and solitude, the charismatic tradition tends to be associated with fervent worship and intense, corporate expressions of spirituality. This is definitely the noisier of the two mountain paths, and some contemplatives would prefer to stick their fingers in their ears rather than go anywhere near a charismatic worship service. However, once we move past initial assumptions, we find that these traditions have a lot in common. Both are built upon a theology of manifest presence and the desire to experience God.

We may tend to assume that the charismatic tradition is not really a tradition at all, but rather a recent phenomenon – notably a development of the Pentecostal movement in the early twentieth century and more recent renewal movements. But its roots go back to the early church. Charismatic spirituality has been a part of Christianity from its earliest days; and though it has ebbed and flowed, we can trace charismatic movements throughout church history, including the Franciscans from the thirteenth century onward, as well as ecstatic and miraculous experiences among the medieval mystics, such as Hildegard of Bingen. Charismatic phenomena were an accepted part of Methodism under John Wesley and were foundational for the Quakers.

The particular focus of the charismatic tradition is on the empowering presence of the Holy Spirit and the special gifts he brings. We are not meant to work out the Christian life through our own effort and limited abilities but in partnership and cooperation with the 'other Helper' that Jesus promised.[13] Every Christian can joyfully partake in the 'life to the full'[14] that is life in and through the Spirit of God. In fact, we can participate with God as his co-workers to bring his kingdom of healing, wholeness and deliverance to those around us. The charismatic tradition pays special attention to the call on all our lives to 'be filled with the Spirit'[15] and be completely reliant on his guidance, instruction, comfort and power. This Spirit-empowered way of living enables us to minister to others in love and power as Jesus did.

Charismatics strongly believe in God's involvement in every aspect of life. God is close, active and at work in the world around us. Charismatic spirituality fosters an expectation that God will intervene through answered prayer and miraculous events, as well as by speaking directly through dreams, visions and prophecy. A supernatural lifestyle is available to all expectant Christians as the Holy Spirit distributes his grace-gifts, the *charismata*, through the body: miracles, healings, signs and wonders, revelations and visions.[16] The contemporary charismatic movement has done much to encourage everyday believers to take hold of the supernatural gifts of the Spirit.

Rooted in Scripture

The charismatic tradition is thoroughly biblical. It's almost impossible to read the New Testament without getting excited about the world-changing potential that is to be found in our relationship with the Holy Spirit. The apostle Paul shows us what this can look like in the life of a Christian: he stands out as someone who wrestled with both the theology and practice of the Spirit-empowered life.

Paul writes about both the gifts and the fruit of the Spirit. He inspires his readers to 'eagerly desire gifts of the Spirit' (1 Corinthians 14:1) and is keen to remind them that 'I speak in tongues more than all of you' (1 Corinthians 14:18). In his first letter to the Corinthians, he points out that 'my message and my preaching were not with wise and persuasive words, but with a demonstration of the Spirit's power, so that your faith might not rest on human wisdom, but on God's power' (1 Corinthians 2:4–5). He then goes on to provide the church with a practical, in-depth guide to the use of spiritual gifts.

However, the book of Acts gives us the best picture of Paul's dependence on the Holy Spirit's power and presence. As a missionary in the first-century Mediterranean world, we observe Paul being commissioned, led and empowered by the Spirit as he faithfully responds to Jesus' unequivocal call on his life.

In summing up his extraordinary ministry, Paul makes clear his reliance on the Spirit's power:

> Therefore I glory in Christ Jesus in my service to God. I will not venture to speak of anything except what Christ has accomplished through me in leading the Gentiles to obey God by what I have said and done – by the power of signs and wonders, through the power of the Spirit of God.
>
> ROMANS 15:17–19

A Closer Look

I'm all too aware of the various criticisms that can be levelled at the charismatic tradition. After all, this is my tribe, and I know its weaknesses very well. I have many concerns about its more extreme wings; but I also know how much this tradition has helped to make the prophetic accessible to ordinary Christians. So, as we consider the Vertical dimension of prophetic culture, we can pay attention to three aspects of the best of this tradition that, in turn, point us up the mountain of God: passion; friendship and fellowship with the Spirit; and expectancy.

Passion. The charismatic movement is well known for its enthusiasm and celebration, with lively and passionate expressions of spirituality. It's hard to be a mere observer in charismatic worship; you have to throw yourself in and fully commit. This is where we really celebrate God with voice and body. Turn the music up, please!

In 2 Samuel 6, we find the story of the Ark of the Covenant being brought up to Jerusalem. Verse 14 presents us with the image of King David 'dancing before the LORD with all his might.' This didn't go down well with his wife, Michal. A few verses later we read that, when she saw David's exuberant worship, 'she despised him in her heart' (v. 16). When David returned home later that day, his explanation was adamant: 'I will celebrate before the LORD. I will become even more undignified than this' (vv. 21–22).

David's example is challenging for many of us, especially those of us from a Western culture. We know we're supposed to be on David's side and start dancing, but such enthusiasm can be embarrassing. Charismatic spirituality calls into question our restrained, self-controlled and half-hearted expressions of worship. If God is who he says he is, then we should be prepared to worship him with abandon.

The charismatics know that there is much freedom and joy to be had in God's presence. God is here to be experienced, not just didactically understood. The prophetic church is never going to be defined by timid, lukewarm, indifferent spirituality. When charismatics gather to worship, there is a wholehearted offering of themselves to the presence and majesty of God. There is a singularity of desire for God himself – for the heavens to open and his fire to fall. When passion is this heightened, it's not surprising that arms get raised and feet start to dance.

Friendship and fellowship with the Spirit. Oh, how we charismatics love the Holy Spirit! Why would you want to do anything, say anything, pray anything *apart* from his fiery presence and staggering wisdom?

Jesus lays things out pretty clearly in his words to the disciples on the night before he died, as described for us in John's Gospel. The Son is returning to the Father, but they are not going to be left as orphans.[17] They are going to be sent 'another Friend' who will be with them forever. Jesus goes as far to say that it is actually *better* that he goes away because then he can send them this just-as-good-as-Jesus Friend.[18] This is the Friend that allows us to experience the communal dynamic that is at the very centre of God's nature. The Holy Spirit brings the community of heaven right into the lives of every disciple. It's through the Holy Spirit that we get to join the family of the Godhead: 'On that day you will realise that I am in my Father, and you are in me, and I am in you.'[19]

One of the wonders of the new covenant is that God has poured – not drizzled or dripped but *poured* – out his Spirit on his covenant people. He has poured out on us the very essence of who he is. Through his Spirit, the Creator of the heavens and the earth now dwells in the inmost being of every believer.

And this Holy Spirit, this third person of the Trinity, is the Spirit of truth and revelation. He always brings his gifts with him, especially prophecy. Throughout the Bible, we see a repeating pattern of the Spirit being released on people and then prophecy happening. This pattern culminates at Pentecost, as foretold by the prophet Joel and fulfilled at the moment the church was born.[20]

It's as we attend to the presence and reality of the indwelling Spirit that we learn how to recognise God's voice. The Spirit searches out the deep things of God and reveals them to us.[21] He speaks in a language of dazzling beauty and utter simplicity. He is the connection between us and the very heart of the Father.

Those who practice the best expressions of charismatic spirituality know that the Spirit is no mere 'it' – a utility to turn to when we need more power, more heat or more refreshment. Rather, the Holy Spirit is a person to be known and loved, and life in the Spirit is about an ever-deepening walk with this remarkable and surprising Friend. This is someone with whom we can converse; someone whose wisdom we can actively seek throughout the day; someone whose joyful company we can treasure.

Expectancy. Charismatic spirituality fosters expectancy. It takes seriously Paul's statement that God 'is able to do immeasurably more than we ask or imagine, according to his power that is at work within us' (Ephesians 3:20). A healthy and thriving prophetic culture is marked by the confidence that God will speak to us if we ask him.

One of the mindset shifts many of us have to make is to gain a better understanding of God's outrageous generosity towards his children. Our heavenly Father is the most lavish person we can ever imagine. To experience a Spirit-filled, Spirit-empowered lifestyle, we have to develop a mindset of the Father's abundance. He is good and generous with his gifts.

> 'Which of you fathers, if your son asks for a fish, will give him a snake instead? Or if he asks for an egg, will give him a scorpion? If you then, though you are evil, know how to give good gifts to your children, how much more will your Father in heaven give the Holy Spirit to those who ask him!'
>
> LUKE 11:11–13

The charismatic tradition teaches us to have faith for the supernatural, for the realities of the kingdom of God breaking out around us with signs and wonders. Too often the reason we're not seeing these things occur is because we're not actually expecting God to do very much. We even succumb to the temptation to control our lives to the extent that we don't actually *need* him to do anything (or so we think).

Expectancy helps cultivate a culture where everyone knows they can join in with ministry. The gifts of the Spirit are freely distributed through the body,[22] so, regardless of age, role or experience, we can all seek to be channels of God's tremendous blessing as we minister to each other and anticipate that lives will be transformed by the touch of the King.

The charismatic's expectancy fits right alongside the contemplative's gazing upon God; faith and love converge so that the kingdom can break out. It's as we gaze upon God, meditating on the wonders of his love, kindness and generosity, that we grow faith that his kingdom is indeed 'at hand'[23] and anything becomes possible.

A Valuable Guide

The charismatic tradition is a great guide up the mountain because it fosters confidence that God speaks today and that through the Holy Spirit *every* Christian can hear the *dabar-Yahweh* – the word of the Lord. There is a radical egalitarianism in the Spirit because *all* of God's people can receive his revelation. As we seek for eyes to see and ears to hear, our charismatic friends provide a faith-filled, worshipful environment in which to experiment and grow in spiritual gifts. The best expressions of charismatic spirituality promote a Christ-centred, Spirit-empowered, outward-focused discipleship – where *charismata* are used for the benefit of all and where gifts of prophecy are taken into the neighbourhood. To be a prophetic church, there is much we can learn from the charismatics. They don't necessarily have the complete expression of the prophetic function, but they can teach us a great deal about equipping the whole church to hear God's voice.

And they know a thing or two about power – the world-shaking power of the Holy Spirit. Of course, it gets abused from time to time, but lives can be profoundly transformed through a timely, accurate prophetic word; through divine revelation breaking into hungry hearts. A humble, discerning, grace-drenched charismatic spirituality provides a safe path up the mountain and is worthy of our attention.

JESUS AND THE MOUNTAIN

These two traditions – the contemplative and the charismatic – beautifully demonstrate a way for every believer and every church to explore the riches of the Vertical dimension. There are untapped resources in both traditions for many of us seeking an authentic engagement with the prophetic. And even though the focus within the contemplative tradition tends to be more on the individual, both our mountain guides have relevance for how we explore the Vertical dimension as a community.

There is no hierarchy in either tradition; the mountain of God is open for all to discover. There is also a useful tension in choosing both as guides, since they complement and balance each other, offering a safer, more inclusive and more accessible path.

But as the mountain comes into focus, how does Jesus speak to the Vertical dimension of the prophetic? How can we understand the mountain from a christological perspective? First, it is important to note that, in the Gospels, we see Jesus demonstrating many facets of both the contemplative and charismatic traditions. He lived a prayer-filled life and prioritised time alone with his heavenly Father; he also lived and moved in the power of the Spirit, as Luke repeatedly reminds us.[24] But Jesus not only modelled a life focused on prayer and the presence of God, Jesus *is* Presence. And this is where the biblical theme of the tabernacle and temple shed some important light.

In the ancient world, the temple was understood as a place where heaven and earth came together – a symbolic dwelling place of God with humanity.[25] For the Israelites, it was first the tabernacle of the desert journey and then Solomon's temple that represented the place where Yahweh dwelt. These structures were signs of God's presence in the midst of God's people. And when each was completed, the Bible records that the *glory of the Lord* was seen to come and fill them.[26]

No wonder, then, that for the psalmists the existence of the temple in Jerusalem symbolised their deep desire for God's presence. The writer of Psalm 27 expresses his longing to 'gaze on the beauty of the LORD and to seek him in his temple' (v.4). The writer of Psalm 48 declares that 'Within your temple, O God, we meditate on your unfailing love' (v.9).

By the time we come to the New Testament, Solomon's temple had been destroyed and then rebuilt. But at the beginning of his Gospel, John reveals a remarkable truth about Jesus: that the Son of God is the *new temple*, and with him comes a new revelation of the glory of the Lord.

> The Word became flesh and made his dwelling [literally *tabernacled*] among us. We have seen his glory, the glory of the one and only Son, who came from the Father, full of grace and truth.
>
> JOHN 1:14

In fact, we can best understand the old Hebrew tabernacle and temple as foretastes and prototypes that point towards Jesus as the ultimate temple: Immanuel, God with us. In Jesus, heaven touches earth, and the kingdom of God breaks out. Jesus is our new and living temple who provides the way back to God's presence. Jesus is the living, breathing in-dwelling of God with humanity; a 'temple' that could walk around ancient Palestine and bring the rest and reign of God into broken lives and communities; a 'temple' through which everyone could reconnect with God.

Jesus not only models a perfect example of the Vertical dimension, but he is the very essence of it. And so any pursuit of prophetic gifts and ministry, any seeking of God's heart and presence, must be utterly Jesus-shaped.

7

CLIMBING THE MOUNTAIN TOGETHER

When you come together, each of you has a hymn, or a word of instruction, a revelation, a tongue or an interpretation.

1 CORINTHIANS 14:26

In the days before 'health and safety', and when youth leaders had never heard of risk-assessment forms, I attended a wonderful Christian youth camp in Wales. Each year, it was the tradition for the whole camp to spend a day climbing Snowdon, the highest mountain in England and Wales. Different groups would take various routes up the mountain, but we'd meet at the top and eat our sandwiches together in celebration. One year, a group of us were led up via the Crib Goch knife-edged arête – one of the most dangerous mountain walks in Britain. It was an adrenaline-fueled, and at times terrifying, climb; a near-impossibility for a lone, inexperienced teen. But tackling it as a group made it possible and gave us all a marvellous shared sense of achievement.

When it comes to the Vertical dimension of the prophetic, there are plenty of people who would prefer to go it alone – to leave the rest of the church behind and focus on a solo pursuit of God's presence and voice. And I get that. My own prophetic wiring can easily pull me towards my private prayer closet. But even the most introverted contemplative would do well to remember that the mountain of God is to be climbed *together*.

The two guides we considered in the last chapter have given us a much clearer sense of the topography of the mountain. The next step is to consider how to allow the contemplative and charismatic mindsets to shape the culture of our churches so that we can scale the heights as a *community*.

What follows are four foundational elements that an authentic prophetic community needs to attend to as it seeks to live out the Vertical dimension. Together, these elements give us the language and perspective we require in order to create a prophetic culture. They describe the type of place we want our churches to be – the particular *flavour* of a community with a healthy and mature Vertical dimension.

COVENANT FAITHFULNESS

We are to be a people who love God with all our hearts, souls and minds. This is the primary call on our lives and a key part of our corporate identity: to nurture and protect a deep, authentic faith in God and a sincere love for him; to worship him and him only.

As the Israelites were encamped around the mountain of God all those years ago, they were given this remarkable revelation of God's intention via Moses:

> 'You yourselves have seen what I did to Egypt, and how I carried you on eagles' wings and brought you to myself. Now if you obey me fully and keep my covenant, then out of all nations you will be my treasured possession. Although the whole earth is mine, you will be for me a kingdom of priests and a holy nation.'
>
> EXODUS 19:4–6

God's desire was to have a people who were his special treasure; a people who would enjoy deep relationship and friendship with him. God made a covenant with the Israelites that, as long as they stayed faithful to him, they alone would be the people who could draw close to him and know his favour.

Unfortunately, as the Old Testament makes very clear, God's people didn't have a great track record of staying faithful to the covenant. Their eyes wandered. They got distracted. They failed to pay attention. They forgot their fundamental identity as a people set apart for Yahweh.

The Israelites turned away from their true and living God and looked for other gods to satisfy them. Idolatry became their perpetual sin – the shadow Israel could never escape from – which is why so much of the

Bible's prophetic literature is taken up with confronting the issue. As we explored in chapter three, it became a central part of the prophet's role to warn, to chastise, to plead on God's behalf: stay away from foreign gods, 'the vile images you have set your eyes on' (Ezekiel 20:7).

What does covenant faithfulness mean for the church today? How do we keep our love for God pure, untarnished and unadulterated? In Old Testament times, the lure of foreign cults was the big problem; these days idols are perhaps more subtle but they are equally dangerous. Today's prophets know that there is a war going on for the soul of the church. Will we succumb to the lure of consumerism and individualism, to the lust for power and status? Will we be satisfied with a lukewarm, compromised, ineffective faith that is vulnerable to ungodly distractions? Or will we follow the narrow path of Jesus-shaped discipleship and stay faithful to him alone?

The prophetic community takes the dangers of idolatry very seriously and ensures that faithfulness to God is our highest value. It vigilantly guards the covenant relationship and our identity as children of God. In promoting a culture of covenant faithfulness, the prophetic church chooses to be satisfied with God alone.

The contemplative's devotion to God and the charismatic's passion for God combine to create a culture of sheer delight in God, where the dangers of wandering hearts are minimised. Both contemplative and charismatic spirituality help us live fully into a depth of blissful intimacy with the Lover of our souls.

When we make covenant faithfulness a priority for our life together as a church, worship will be at the heart of community life and will play a big part in our corporate activities. Whether it's Sunday services or mid-week fellowship groups, there will be a natural emphasis on keeping our 'first love' alive[1] and every part of our church culture will be marked by love and passion for God.

The *faithfulness* culture we want to see developed in our churches can be described as follows:

- A community where people can come and be spiritually renewed; where we encourage and enhance each other's covenantal relationship with God.

- A community that takes the first of Jesus' two great command-ments seriously.
- A community where authentic worship is a priority, where profound and meaningful worship is made accessible to all.
- A community where people can develop a life of intimacy with God.

PRESENCE OF GOD

Fundamental to prophetic culture and consciousness is a focus on the presence of God. As we explored in the previous chapter, both the contemplative and charismatic traditions emphasise the fact that God's presence is to be sought and enjoyed. We have all been created with a capacity to encounter the living God and to experience the joys of togetherness with him. The prophetic community is a place where we delight in God's presence together.

There is something of a tension in Scripture between the ideas of God's omnipresence (his manifestation within the whole of creation) and his special, perceptible presence at a particular time and place. In the Old Testament there are descriptions of the divine presence making a dramatic appearance – when the glory of God was made manifest at a significant moment. We've already noted the descriptions of Yahweh's visible presence on the mountain of God, as Israel gathered around Mount Sinai; and then, as the people set out from the mountain, the presence of God was visible as the accompanying pillar of cloud by day and fire by night.[2] These Old Testament episodes remind us that God is unspeakably holy – as seen in the consuming fire of Exodus 24:17 and Hebrews 12:29 – but also a presence we can encounter and be led by. The narratives ultimately point us to Jesus and the new covenant reality of the indwelling Spirit. The transcendent One (far beyond our reach) becomes the fully immanent One (God with us).

The Bible also makes it clear that God takes the initiative in being present with us. At the moment of creation, God chose to send his Spirit. He entered into the world even as it was being formed,[3] as an expression of his desire to be present with his creation. The fact that humanity is made in his image is a sign that he purposes to be present with us. From all eternity, he has been moving towards us and finding us, and he sent his Son to restore our relationship with him. He has promised to never leave us;[4] we are deeply connected to him;[5] indeed we are one with him;[6] and our life is now hidden with Christ in God.[7] 'Where can I go from your Spirit? Where can I flee from your presence?' exclaims the Psalmist (Psalm 139:7). The contemplative tradition is particularly helpful in reminding us, as the body of Christ, that God is much closer than we realise. As Martin Laird says in *Into the Silent Land*,

> God does not know how to be absent. The fact that most of us experience throughout most of our lives a sense of absence or distance from God is the great illusion that we are caught up in; it is the human condition. The sense of separation from God is real, but the meeting of stillness reveals that this perceived separation does not have the last word. This illusion of separation is generated by the mind and is sustained by the riveting of our attention to the interior soap opera, the constant chatter of the cocktail party going on in our heads. For most of us this is what normal is, and we are good at coming up with ways of coping with this perceived separation (our consumer-driven entertainment culture takes care of much of it).[8]

The sense of separation or alienation from God is one that the prophetic community is there to dispel. The problem is not that God is not with us; the problem is a lack of *awareness* of his presence. It is a failure to perceive what is truly there in front of us. Any sense of isolation or separation from God can be overcome as we awaken to the greater reality of his nearness to us.

Whether it is through quiet contemplative prayer, corporate worship in our fellowship groups and Sunday services, or some other devotional pathway, there are patterns of church life that draw us back to the reality of being immersed in the sacred presence of God's light and love. The prophetic church chooses to meditate on and celebrate God's nearness and the fact that he loves being with us as a good Father rather than keeping himself at a distance.

Brother Lawrence is a significant figure in contemplative spirituality, and the church has learnt a great deal from this humble saint about how to practise the presence of God in our regular, day-to-day lives. Even when washing pots and pans, we can delight in meeting him. 'I do nothing else,' says Lawrence, 'but abide in his holy presence, and I do this by simple attentiveness and a habitual, loving turning of my eyes on him.'[9]

Prioritising the presence of God means emphasising the *experiential* aspect of our relationship with him, which is deeply rooted in both the contemplative and charismatic traditions. The emphasis is not on what we know but on *Whom* we experience. This is not about leaving our brains behind; it's about recognising that we can enjoy God and the vibrant pleasure of his company as well as study theology. There is something of a radical audacity in delighting in his perceptible presence as he pours out his love upon us. Ecstatic spiritual experiences are not just for a few strange medieval mystics but can be part of every church's journey as we learn to take wonder and delight in God-encounters.

What could be better than pursuing the joys of God's presence, and doing this as a community? But, if we're honest, many of us would prefer to keep God at arm's length and thus maintain our independence. God's presence is acutely challenging as well as delightfully invitational, and a lot of the time our fallen hearts and our flesh don't want the holy disruption that comes with it. Yes, the presence of God is accessible, but that is not to say that it is safe or controllable or containable. We cannot in any way determine what God is going to do or say when we start paying attention to him. We are utterly defenceless before him.

In 1 Thessalonians 5:19, Paul exhorts us 'not to quench the Spirit'. We can't confine him, manipulate him or domesticate him. All we can do is surrender to him. We all have a choice: God's fully available presence can be received or resisted. We can be a church that lets him 'access all areas', or we can be defensive and hang on to our deeply embedded aversion.

This brings us back to the prophetic call to covenant faithfulness and the importance of maintaining a culture of God-ward movement. We need soft hearts that thirst for his presence rather than rebellious hearts that keep their distance. We need to create communities centred on the presence of God as exemplified by our charismatic and contemplative friends – creating 'pause' in our gatherings and then being expectant of what God-with-us will do in our midst.

As we seek to make presence a priority for our life together as a church, we need to implement simple, accessible practices in our community life that enable everyone to engage with God. We might do something as straightforward as having '12 o'clock prayers' – when everyone sets a reminder on their phones to pause and pray at the same time every day. Or we might build time into every Sunday service to quietly contemplate God's presence together.

This is the kind of *presence* culture we want to develop:

- A community where all who seek him can find God and his manifest presence.
- A community that actively chooses to be present with God whenever we meet together.
- A community where we are expectant for an encounter with God.
- A community of friendship and fellowship with the Holy Spirit.

REVELATORY GIFTS

The mountain of God is the place where we hear God and come face-to-face with his reality, and of course hearing God's voice is a central feature of the Vertical dimension of prophetic culture. Both the contemplative and the charismatic traditions emphasise a posture of receptivity to God's voice. Contemplative practice helps create the focus and stillness that opens up our spiritual senses to discern the Spirit's whispers; charismatic spirituality fosters the expectation that our good Father wants to speak to us.

They may seem a very obvious part of the prophetic function, but revelatory gifts need to be carefully nurtured and attended to. As we've noted previously, having a few highly prophetic people in our midst who easily hear God's voice does not equate to being a *listening church*. Instead, we need to consider how we develop a culture where *everyone* has confidence they can hear God, both for themselves and for the whole body.

In chapter eleven, we will look in detail at how we can create a church culture of listening to and responding to God's voice. But at this stage we can use a few broad brushstrokes to start describing what this *revelatory* culture might look like:

- A community that makes space for intentional and expectant listening in all parts of church life.
- A community that prophetically reveals the Father's heart in the way we love each other.
- A community where we help each other connect with God's heart so that together we are strengthened, encouraged and comforted.[10]
- A community where the Spirit's presence is manifested through his revelatory gifts as we meet together, and gifts of discernment and prophecy are received to guide the life of the church.

PERSONAL HOLINESS

With God's presence comes God's holiness and, as we've already noted, to meet with God means to be changed by him. The prophetic community takes seriously the call to holiness and obedience, and a vital aspect of the Vertical dimension is the commitment to transformation through ongoing repentance. Our contemplation and worship of God must always lead to this. The call to holiness is both individual and communal, and the question for us as a body is how we promote the sort of culture that readily embraces repentance and transformation, so that we can be cheering each other on towards a holy lifestyle.

For the disciple of Jesus, the Christian life is about progressive sanctification and spiritual formation in order to reflect God's glory and goodness and be conformed more and more to the image of his Son.[11] The pursuit of holiness is not about being perfect, but it is about taking our commitment to Christ very seriously and understanding the rebellious nature of our fallen human condition. As we encounter God and welcome his Spirit, we cannot remain as we are. A healthy prophetic culture welcomes the purifying fire of God's love as it burns up the dross and causes us to face our selfishness and pride.

A culture of personal holiness is not about thinking we are better than other people or following a long list of rules. It's not about a 'them and us' mentality, where we try to distance ourselves from anyone we consider less than pure. It's definitely not about judging others. But it is about being surrendered to the majesty of God and the untameable Spirit. It's about choosing to open our hearts to God and allowing him to speak into every area of our lives. It's about being accountable to each other and welcoming godly challenges from our Christian friends. In a healthy prophetic culture, we desire to both hear *and* obey.

The prophetic church takes holiness seriously because when the Holy Spirit does his work and makes us more like Jesus, we are better able to hold out God's reality to the world and see his kingdom come in our neighbourhoods. To carry and reflect God's revelation, we must be prepared to lay every competing claim on the altar. The prophetic church is not perfect, but it is obedient. It is the church that is willing to be transformed.

As we make personal holiness a priority in our churches, we give each other permission to speak into our lives, to call us onwards and upwards in Christ. It may look like everyone having an accountability partner; it may look like creating space for confession and repentance in our Sunday services. There will be an expectation that worship, prophecy and the presence of God will always have a transformative effect on our lives.

This is the kind of *holiness* culture we want to see develop:

- A community that cultivates a hunger for holiness and obedience, and pursuit of lives consecrated to God.
- A community that welcomes accountable relationships and transformative discipleship.
- A community where we know how to faithfully respond to God when he speaks to us.
- A community where we encourage each other to live lives wholly dependent on the Spirit.

COMING FACE TO FACE WITH IDOLATRY

These four fundamental elements – covenant faithfulness, presence of God, revelatory gifts and personal holiness – describe how the prophetic church can live vertically into its prophetic identity. They provide us with a multi-faceted vision for how every expression of the body of Christ can orient itself upon the mountain of God. But as we finish this chapter, it's important to pause and once more consider the issue of idolatry, because each of the four elements has its own way of challenging – and being challenged by – this perennial threat. A holistic pursuit of the Vertical dimension will always be about protecting the community from idolatry.

An idol is anything other than God that we worship, anything that claims too much of our time and attention, anything that absorbs our hearts and imaginations more than God. Idols may be things, people, constructs or attitudes, but they always replace God as the focus of our affection and attention. As we already noted, guarding covenant faithfulness involves guarding against idolatry. But idolatry is a primary danger in the other three as well.

We can summarise it like this:

Covenant faithfulness. Idolatry violates the sacred covenant relationship between us and God. In succumbing to idolatry, we are scorning our God-given identity and allowing our idols to define us. Idolatry compromises the worship life of the church.

Presence of God. Idolatry pulls us away from the glories of God's presence and makes us think we can be satisfied elsewhere. Idols limit our attention span and distract us from our focus on God. The church struggles to be fully attentive to God's presence when idolatry is luring us somewhere else.

Revelatory gifts. Idolatry keeps us from hearing God's voice. We mistake the demanding and insistent voices of our idols for the voice of God, and our prophetic vision becomes distorted and corrupted by them. Our corporate listening is much less effective when idols are present.

Personal holiness. Idolatry makes us unholy and hinders us from faithfully demonstrating God's reality in the world. Idols prevent the church from wholehearted obedience to God.

As we seek to create healthy and holistic prophetic communities, we need to help the whole church understand idolatry and why it is such a vital issue. We can also remind our prophets that part of their role involves challenging idolatry wherever they see it. We would do well to take note of these words from Travis Kroeker's and Bruce Ward's book on Dostoevsky:

Prophecy, as an unveiling of the truth about God, is also an unveiling (and judgment) of idols – false images of divine purpose and truth, and a false naming of reality. Indeed, as both John of Patmos and Dostoevsky emphasize, demonic powers of darkness often perform their mysterious and seductive arts through concealment. The proclamation of the prophetic word seeks to reveal the 'god of this world' who has blinded the minds of people and deceived the nations, in the light of Christ who is 'the likeness of God'.[12]

The prophets of the Old Testament knew that if we remain faithful to the true God, we keep centred in our identity as being made in his image. But the creeping poison of idolatry undermines our identity, and we lose the ability to discern in whose image we have been made. When we've forgotten who we are, our vision becomes domesticated, tame and de-energised; and we are no longer able to anticipate future hope. It is always the task of prophetic ministry to remind God's people of who they really are; to enable the truth of our God-given identity to shape our field of perception and to challenge the false identities invited by the surrounding culture.

We can summarise the Vertical dimension of prophetic culture like this:

Covenant Faithfulness

Presence of God

Revelatory Gifts

Personal Holiness

**Challenge
Idolatry**

The
Prophetic
Community

As we climb the mountain together, we find ourselves in a very special place; a place where we are completely focused on who God is – his name, his glory and his utterly different reality. We will of course find Jesus on this mountain, and we continue to follow in his footsteps in becoming an authentic prophetic community.

8

THE ROAD

*The Spirit of the Lord is on me, because he has anointed me to
proclaim good news to the poor.*

LUKE 4:18

Some of us find it very hard to leave the mountain of God, but there is another dimension to attend to, another terrain to explore. This is a landscape of tables upturned; of highways made straight; of an alternative kingdom ready to break out. A place where things get somewhat (and perhaps uncomfortably) political. This is where the prophetic call to love God passionately hits the road, and our upwards gaze translates into a love for humanity and a desire for God's *shalom* in his creation. As the prophets of old remind us, faithful worshippers cannot stay in the temple; we have a responsibility for the world and its restoration. The prophetic is as much about desiring a just society as it is about desiring God's presence. A holistic prophetic culture can be consumed with the presence of God while *at the same time* being committed to the physical, practical, down-to-earth aspect of paying attention to God's concerns in our neighbourhood and wider society. This is about getting our hands dirty and confronting the hard realities of human trafficking, poverty, racism and environmental catastrophe. In fact, the prophetic community knows that God's presence is found just as much in the slums as it is on the mountaintop.

> 'I was hungry and you gave me something to eat, I was thirsty and you gave me something to drink, I was a stranger and you invited me in, I needed clothes and you clothed me, I was ill and you looked after me, I was in prison and you came to visit me.'
>
> MATTHEW 25:35–36

The road before us is dirty, dusty and inevitably less travelled. It's marked by inconveniences and interruptions. It's a rather narrow road and not popular with the crowds – though we find some interesting people along the way. But we can see Jesus' footprints in the dust as we dare to follow him. These footprints speak prophetically to the times and seasons we find ourselves in. They lead us to the edges of society and show us what love actually looks like.

In this chapter and the next we explore the *Horizontal dimension* of prophetic community and culture and consider how the church needs to shape itself in order to hold out God's transformative reality to the world around us. The prophetic impulse in this dimension is to bring a godly critique and ethic wherever a lack of true justice is perceived, and to respond with empathy, lament, solidarity and hope to those on the margins.

There are many questions we can ask ourselves as we get on this dusty old road, but I believe there are two that need highlighting:

- How do we as a church follow in the footsteps of Jesus the perfect Prophet as he speaks prophetically to society?
- How do we ensure we are hearing God clearly about his concerns for the world we live in?

In asking these two questions, we recognise the *twofold prophetic hearing and speaking* that are necessary to walk the road to social justice. We need to hear God that we may speak prophetically *to* society, and we need to hear God that we may speak prophetically to the church *about* society (and thus discern what he would have us do to change things for the better). We can never guarantee that society will hear our prophetic voice, as the Hebrew prophets knew only too well; but it is vital that the body of Christ can hear what the Spirit is saying about the issues that grieve the Father's heart. A healthy prophetic culture is one in which the church is properly equipped to hear and speak well.

The prophetic voice is key in shaping culture and society, and we can be thankful that, over the preceding decades and centuries, many voices (both inside and outside the church) have spoken clearly and urgently to the need to bring change. The world would be a darker place without

William Wilberforce, Dietrich Bonhoeffer, Dorothy Day, Martin Luther King Jr, Mother Teresa and many, many others.

God desires to see justice and restoration on the earth, and he very often uses prophets to call for change and to challenge the status quo. The prophetic is frequently expressed through a deep engagement with social transformation, and this reflects a clear pattern observable in Scripture and throughout church history. From Moses onwards, God's prophets have not only communicated his heart to his people but have also carried a *transformational message to society*. A significant part of the prophetic tradition is the impetus to seek justice and *shalom* for all people and all social structures. Prophetic consciousness, with its passion for God's heart, groans with the Spirit at every unjust system and situation. It knows that God cares deeply for a humanity made in his image, and desires that his church exercise its prophetic voice to challenge, agitate and provoke for godly change. Prophets have always been at the heart of finding a Jesus-shaped way of responding to the cultural and political powers that dominate our consciousness and actions, and this should be equally true for the prophetic body of Christ.

SIGNPOSTS ALONG THE ROAD

The Horizontal dimension of the prophetic is not always easy to navigate. To start with, the word *justice* means different things to different people,[1] and concepts such as *social justice* can be controversial and polarising in certain parts of the global church. But we cannot claim to be a prophetic church if we avoid this road due to a discomfort with some of the language. There is a clear invitation in Scripture, as we walk humbly with God, to let him show us what is good, and to prioritise justice and mercy.[2]

In seeking to comprehend what it means for the church to prophetically seek a just society, we can be thankful that the Bible provides us with some clear signposts. These way-markers enable us to make sense of the prophetic call to challenge injustice and liberate the oppressed. They help us take hold of a biblical approach to social justice and release the term from political controversy. Perhaps most importantly, they enable us to grasp that biblical justice is less of an abstract concept but better seen as part of who God is, wrapped up in his person and presence. These signposts – God's *hesed*, justice and righteousness, and *shalom* – are formed out of some profound scriptural themes and will keep us on track as we seek to follow Jesus down the road.

Signpost 1: God's Hesed

The Hebrew word *hesed* is translated as mercy, lovingkindness, steadfast love and goodness in the Old Testament, and is frequently used to refer to these as fundamental elements of God's nature.[3] This is a vital signpost because it reminds us that the concern of the church for societal transformation must be rooted in the very heart and character of God. As we descend the mountain and get on the road, we cannot lose sight of God's *hesed* even for a moment.

Any Spirit-breathed engagement with social justice has to flow out of the reality of God's nature and his unending compassion and mercy. He cares deeply about people, especially the poor and vulnerable. As Moses learnt on the mountain, when we encounter God, we encounter his very goodness. 'I will cause *all my goodness* to pass in front of you … . The LORD, the LORD, the compassionate and gracious God, slow to anger, abounding in love [*hesed*] and faithfulness' (Exodus 33:19 and 34:6, italics mine).

It is God's *hesed* that sends us down the mountain and compels us to do something. This is not a theoretical or sentimental compassion – not simply an emotional response to the injustices present in the world – but compassion as an urgency and compulsion to *see things change*.

When divine lovingkindness sends us out into the broken world to challenge unjust systems and structures, we are representing God's very heart and nature; we are demonstrating all that is good, merciful and compassionate in his kingdom. We care about justice because God cares about justice. The prophetic concern for a just society is birthed in the heart of God, not in the pages of our daily newspaper or social media feed. It is not subject to the political spirit, though we will inevitably need to engage politically as we respond to its call. It is not about left or right, conservative or liberal; but it is very much about the heart of God and being prepared to respond obediently wherever he sends us.

Both dimensions of the prophetic function are equally important, but there is a certain biblical trajectory from Vertical to Horizontal – from the mountain to the road – that we must note. God's call to Moses to challenge the power of empire and lead the Israelites out of slavery started with the burning bush encounter on Mount Horeb. Moses was commissioned out of God's glory, God's compassion ('I have indeed seen the misery of my people ... . I am concerned about their suffering') and the revelation of God's name. *Presence* came before *Justice*.[4] In fact, Moses' earlier attempt at righting wrongs ended in disaster – the murder of an Egyptian and the subsequent flight to Midian.[5] Our passion for justice has to flow out of our love and worship for God, not from a political angst or desire for confrontation for its own sake. As Paul reminds us in 1 Corinthians 13:3, 'If I give all I possess to the poor and give over my body to hardship that I may boast, but do not have love, I gain nothing.' The starting place is always love – our love for God, and then our love for our neighbour – otherwise we end up operating out of ideology, guilt, legalism or our own self-righteousness. We must always be reliant on his grace and strength to confront, challenge and question; reliant on his beautiful Spirit for the courage to take a stand. Love must be our motivation, so that it's not the cause or issue that consumes us but real people who are suffering.

When God's *hesed* is our starting point, our radical, love-soaked prayer life will result in a radical, love-soaked commitment to the world around us. But there is more to *hesed*. As many of the Old Testament prophets found, an authentic connection with the heart of Yahweh means at some point coming face to face with *divine pathos*. Properly engaging with the Horizontal dimension of the prophetic means experiencing the sheer emotion and suffering of God as he looks on the broken world. The prophetic community takes this facet of God's reality seriously and refuses to skirt around its companion call to lament.

God's *pathos* is God's intimate involvement with creation and history to the extent that he is actually affected by and responds to events. He is not just concerned about humanity; he is emotionally *affected* by our conduct and attitudes. Throughout the biblical narrative we see a God who refuses to remain dispassionately at a distance from human history but instead chooses to fully participate. He is personally involved in our state of affairs.

Abraham Heschel, in his development of the theology of *pathos*, writes this:

> To the prophet ... God does not reveal himself in an abstract absoluteness, but in a personal and intimate relation to the world. He does not simply command and expect obedience; he is also moved and affected by what happens in the world, and reacts accordingly. Events and human actions arouse in him joy or sorrow, pleasure or wrath ... . Quite obviously in the biblical view, man's deeds may move him, affect him, grieve him or, on the other hand, gladden and please him. This notion that God can be intimately affected, that he possesses not merely intelligence and will, but also pathos, basically defines the prophetic consciousness of God.[6]

God cares deeply. And he is incapable of turning a blind eye to corruption, oppression and injustice.

God's *pathos* requires something of us. If God is affected by unjust systems and actions, then the prophetic church should be as well. To truly hold out his reality to the world means engaging with the very emotions of God – the depths of his *hesed* – and feeling what he feels. We need to be able to groan with him. The prophets of old knew this only too well. But theirs was an individual encounter with the heart of God; for the post-Pentecost, new covenant church, a *corporate* response is required – not just a few crazy prophets weeping and groaning.

As we as a community engage with God's *pathos* and bravely start to feel what he feels, we will recognise the need for *lament* as part of our prophetic response. Lament is an important spiritual practice in Scripture, and we will talk more about it in chapter eleven. Often the first stage of hearing God for our neighbourhoods is creating space to lament – which is something the Western church has habitually failed to do.

The church that is prepared to lament is a church that acknowledges honestly before God the brokenness and injustice in the world. This is the church that is prepared to sit and groan with the Spirit and to weep with those who weep.[7]

Signpost 2: Justice and Righteousness

The next signpost is a word-pair: two words so intertwined that in the New Testament the Greek word *dikaiosune* is used for both.[8] To comprehend the prophetic call to social justice – and indeed what the Bible means by a just society – we need to understand the fascinating way that Scripture uses these two words.

The Hebrew word that commonly gets translated as *justice* in the Old Testament is *mishpat* and has much broader connotations than justice in a strictly legal sense (retributive justice – where bad deeds get punished). *Mishpat* mostly refers to a *restorative* justice – based on what is ethically right – that seeks to advocate for the vulnerable and provide restoration for those who have been wrongfully hurt. The Hebrew word for *righteousness* is *tsedakah* and refers to right relationships and conduct between people – treating others with dignity, decency and fairness, and recognising the image of God in them. (Notice that the biblical understanding of righteousness is as much social and communal as it is personal and individual.) When these two wonderful words are brought together, as they are repeatedly in the Old Testament, they speak of a way of life that is selfless, community-focused and compassionate; they reflect God's desire that his people treat each other with equity and respect. They are used frequently in Scripture to focus our attention on the needs of the vulnerable.

> Thus says the LORD: Act with *justice* and *righteousness*, and deliver from the hand of the oppressor anyone who has been robbed. And do no wrong or violence to the alien, the orphan, and the widow, or shed innocent blood in this place.
>
> JEREMIAH 22:3 NRSV (italics mine)

Today we tend to talk about 'getting justice', but the Bible speaks of justice and righteousness as something we *do*.[9] Justice is done when wrongs are set right, relationships are restored and when the vulnerable are protected.

But it's more than how we act. To grasp the prophetic significance of justice and righteousness, we need to return to the theological roots of the prophetic and see how these two concepts are grounded in the centre of God's being as essential attributes of his divine nature.

Justice and righteousness follow on from *hesed*, and we observe in Scripture that God is passionate about all three qualities. As he declares in Jeremiah 9:24, 'I am the LORD who exercises kindness [*hesed*], justice [*mishpat*] and righteousness [*tsedakah*] on earth, for in these I delight.' He loves righteousness and justice,[10] not as abstract concepts but because he cares passionately about every single man, woman and child on earth. The psalms tell us that justice and righteousness are the foundation of God's throne,[11] and Isaiah prophesies that the Messiah will establish and uphold his kingdom with justice and righteousness.[12] Any authentic pursuit of God will lead us into an encounter with these essential attributes.

Justice and righteousness are so much a part of God's nature that he requires his people to live by them. In establishing the covenant with Moses, Yahweh put compassionate justice at the centre of community life: the Year of Jubilee and the law of gleaning were examples of God insisting on an ethical way of living that paid attention to the needs of all in society.[13] He cares deeply about how humanity treats the poor, the widows and orphans. His *pathos* reveals his desire to create compassionate relationships of love and justice with and among all people. He desires to see justice established on the earth.

In holding out God's reality to the world around us, we are declaring his heart for justice and righteousness and a refusal to tolerate wrongs done to others. To be a prophetic community means taking on the kingdom responsibility to make right what has gone wrong, to fix what is broken and to restore what has been lost.

Signpost 3: Shalom

Our third signpost is the beautiful Hebrew word that reminds us that God is the God of restoration. The word *shalom* epitomises peace, harmony, completeness, wholeness, unity and well-being. God's *shalom* is present when everyone has the opportunity to flourish and thrive, when true *mishpat* and *tsedakah* are activated, when enemies are reconciled and communities are healed. The writer of Psalm 85 offers a delightful vision of *tsedakah* and *shalom* kissing each other, as the land and people are shown God's favour.[14] Isaiah prophesies that *shalom* will be the outworking of God's justice and righteousness, and that their effect 'will be quietness and confidence forever.'[15] The presence of *shalom* 'means that justice has taken root in the world'.[16]

Shalom is a word that brilliantly encapsulates the biblical vision for a just and whole society and is a theme that leads us through both Old and New Testaments. In God's kingdom, all things are made right and restored. In God's kingdom, all things are reconciled.

Writer and activist Lisa Sharon Harper describes *shalom* like this:

> *Shalom* is the stuff of the kingdom. It's what the kingdom of God looks like in context … it's what the kingdom of God smells like and what Jesus requires of the kingdom's citizens. It's when everyone has enough. It's when families are healed. It's when shame is renounced and inner freedom is laid hold of. It's when human dignity, bestowed by the image of God in all humanity, is cultivated, protected, and served in families, faith communities, and schools, and through public policy. *Shalom* is when the capacity to lead is recognised in every human being and when nations join together to protect the environment.[17]

Understanding *shalom* as something at the heart of God's intention for his world helps us move beyond a purely individualistic gospel. We begin to see that the good news is relevant for society as a whole, including our social and economic systems. Under God's *shalom*, there is no exploitation or oppression, there is no systemic injustice, because all humanity is understood as being made in the image of God. Everyone is cared for and there is peace between people groups, as all are reconciled to God and each other. The ethics of the kingdom of heaven demand that all humans are equal before God and have the right to be treated with dignity and fairness.

Shalom is such a central feature of God's vision for creation that the prophetic church is called to pursue, demonstrate and embody it. This is not simply an abstract concept to be studied; it is a concrete reality to be lived into.

ROOTED IN THE PROPHETIC TRADITION

Our signposts give us a clear indication of God's intention for the world he created, as well as for how he wants his people to live in it. As the prophetic community faithfully holds out God's transformative reality to society, we need to be profoundly shaped by God's *hesed, mishpat, tsedakah* and *shalom.* These four Hebrew words rotate around God's intention to heal our broken world. They are very much rooted in the prophetic tradition of the Old Testament, informing the message of the prophets. As we journey through the Horizontal dimension of prophetic culture, we return to the ancient texts and allow the weight of their message to propel us forward.

Reading through the prophets of old, we see their concern – indeed their demand – for justice and social righteousness. Amos in particular gives us great insight into this aspect of prophetic consciousness. For Amos and others, worship was only of value if it grew out of an ethical way of living. The prophets went as far as to proclaim that when justice is lacking, worship is abhorrent:

'I hate your religious festivals; your assemblies are a stench to me … . Away with the noise of your songs! I will not listen to the music of your harps. But let justice [*mishpat*] roll on like a river, righteousness [*tsedakah*] like a never-failing stream!'

AMOS 5:21, 23–24

'I desire mercy, not sacrifice.'

HOSEA 6:6

With what shall I come before the LORD … ? Shall I come before him with burnt offerings … ? Will the LORD be pleased with thousands of rams … ? He has shown you, O mortal, what is good. And what does the LORD require of you? To act justly [*mishpat*] and to love mercy [*hesed*] and to walk humbly with your God.

MICAH 6:6–8

'The multitude of your sacrifices – what are they to me, says the LORD?
I have more than enough of burnt offerings … . Your New Moon feasts
and your appointed festivals I hate with all my being … . Learn to do
right; seek justice [*mishpat*]. Defend the oppressed. Take up the cause of
the fatherless; plead the case of the widow.'

ISAIAH 1:11, 14, 17

Time and again the Hebrew prophets reminded God's people that deeds
of injustice polluted their worship. Faith in the God of Israel was never a
private belief but was lived out in community and demonstrated in how
others were treated. Abraham Heschel states it succinctly and powerfully
like this: 'Men may not drown the cries of the oppressed with the noise of
hymns, nor buy off the Lord with increased offerings.'[18] We can be devoted
worshippers, but if we are not paying attention to the needs of the poor
and marginalised, we have somehow missed the mark. Our relationship
with God has to impact our relationships with others. The prophets teach
us that oppression of the weak is an insult to God and that true worship
is synonymous with doing good and with the mighty flow of justice and
righteousness.

The Old Testament prophets were acutely aware that justice needed
to be promoted and injustice condemned. They were relentless in their
naming of injustice and oppression, and their exposure of political, social
and religious evil:

The LORD enters into judgment against the elders and leaders of his
people: 'It is you who have ruined my vineyard; the plunder from the
poor is in your houses. What do you mean by crushing my people and
grinding the faces of the poor?' declares the Lord, the LORD Almighty.

ISAIAH 3:14–15

Of all the Hebrew prophets, Amos's message is the most sustained in his
critique of social, political and commercial injustice. Amos was neither
a man of the court like Isaiah nor a priest like Jeremiah; he earned his
living from looking after flocks and sycamore trees.[19] But this humble
shepherd was called to deliver a blistering message against the injustices

prevalent in society at that time. Though he lived in southern Judah, God sent him to northern Israel. At that time (around 760–750 BC), under Jeroboam II's rule, the kingdom was enjoying great economic prosperity and military success. Expansion of territory – and with it, commerce – had brought wealth and power for the elite. From a human perspective, it was Israel's golden age; but idolatry was rife, and the moral soul of the nation was being blighted through indulgence, immorality, corruption and the heartless oppression of the poor.

Amos pulls no punches in describing the gravity of the situation:

> They sell the innocent for silver, and the needy for a pair of sandals. They trample on the heads of the poor as on the dust of the ground and deny justice to the oppressed. Father and son use the same girl and so profane my holy name.
>
> AMOS 2:6–7

> You levy a straw tax on the poor and impose a tax on their grain … . There are those who oppress the innocent and take bribes and deprive the poor of justice in the courts.
>
> AMOS 5:11–12

If we understand social injustice fundamentally as the abuse of power, then Amos sees this abuse everywhere: in the selling of the poor into debt-slavery, in the wealthy exploiting the vulnerable, in the corruption of judicial procedures, in crooked business practices that benefitted the rich and in the sexual violation of defenceless young women:

> Hear this, you who trample the needy and do away with the poor of the land, saying, 'When will the New Moon be over that we may sell grain, and the Sabbath be ended that we may market wheat?' – skimping on the measure, boosting the price and cheating with dishonest scales, buying the poor with silver and the needy for a pair of sandals, selling even the sweepings with wheat.
>
> AMOS 8:4–6

The irony of this, as Amos points out, is that the very people-group God rescued from oppression and slavery in Egypt are now trampling their own poor under foot. They have forgotten their God-given identity, allowing idolatry to pervert their religious practices and injustice to pollute every part of society. The prophet's understanding of who God really was, and who God's people were called to be, fundamentally shaped Amos's message. He knew that the living God cared deeply for people, and he understood God as righteous – indeed that God's central concern was righteousness and justice. Amos knew that Yahweh therefore demanded a social righteousness of his covenant people.

This is a message we still need to hear today – a prophetic awareness that the contemporary church needs to get hold of. The call to social justice must stem from our understanding of God and his inability to tolerate injustice and exploitation. In Amos's shatteringly clear perception of God's reality and the urgency to communicate it – 'The lion has roared – who will not fear? The sovereign LORD has spoken – who can but prophesy?'[20] – there is no Presence without Justice. True worship should always lead to justice, righteousness and love for our neighbour.

JESUS AND THE ROAD

As the road to social justice comes into focus, where is Jesus? What do we see him doing? How does Jesus speak to the Horizontal dimension? The message of Amos is not in any way lost in the pages of the New Testament; indeed, the extraordinary prophetic ministry of Jesus illuminates it and expands it.

Jesus is both following in the long line of Hebrew prophets and at the same time demonstrating an utterly unique prophetic presence as the very Word of God. He prophetically and comprehensively reveals God to the world through his incarnation, ministry, death and resurrection. As we've already seen, he is the greatest prophet and ultimate prophecy; he is the Father's best word. Through his teaching, actions and person, he prophetically demonstrates the wonders of God's reality. This Jesus, as the embodiment of God's divine Word, is the means by which the alternative reality of God's kingdom bursts visibly into this world. His words and works speak not just to individuals but also to wider society and culture. This was never just a private gospel; through Jesus' ministry, the justice and righteousness of God are made evident, and with them God's intention to heal the whole of creation. In Jesus we see the depths of God's compassion for his broken world – the Father's desire to heal, restore and make everything whole.

The primary way Jesus articulates God's reality is through the disruptive language of the *kingdom*. Jesus speaks repeatedly of the kingdom of God, and in doing so holds out the promise of the inbreaking of God's rule and reign in the here and now – a reality marked by *shalom* and sacrificial love.[21] In proclaiming the kingdom, he is unmasking and challenging the powers that oppress people. Throughout his ministry, he is not only focused on restoring the broken communion between God and humanity, but he is also offering a critique of the social, economic and religious systems that grind people down. He challenges each in turn and subverts their legitimacy.

The kingdom of God that Jesus proclaims has clear social implications, which we hear in his declaration in the synagogue at Nazareth:

'The Spirit of the Lord is on me, because he has anointed me to proclaim good news to the poor. He has sent me to proclaim freedom for the prisoners and recovery of sight for the blind, to set the oppressed free, to proclaim the year of the Lord's favour.'

LUKE 4:18–19

The people gathered in the synagogue that day would have recognised that, in quoting Isaiah 61, Jesus was alluding to the Year of Jubilee. Once every fifty years slaves were freed, debts were cancelled and ancestral property was returned to the original owners. At the start of his ministry, Jesus is pretty clear about the ethics of the kingdom.

The promise of good news for the poor is not just an eschatological one but is practically demonstrated in the way Jesus lives his life. He spends a good deal of his time with the poor and ostracised, which was revolutionary for any respectable, first-century Jewish man. His actions testify to the inherent value God places on every single person. Through many aspects of his life and ministry he breaks convention, crosses social boundaries and identifies with the destitute, wronged and oppressed, prioritising time with people on the edges of society. He demonstrates a way of resisting the dominant culture and its assumptions, and calls for a better and freer society – not through violent uprising, but through radical compassion and solidarity with the marginalised. Jesus is incarnating the very *mishpat* and *tsedakah* on which Yahweh's throne is built.

When we are brave enough to take off the blinkers of Western individualistic Christianity and look at the words and works of Jesus from an authentic, Middle-Eastern, community-based perspective, we can't help but notice the revolutionary nature of the Gospels. In Jesus' upside-down kingdom, the poor are blessed and the last come first. And this of course is a huge threat to the established order – whether religious, social or political. It didn't take long for those threatened by this alternative kingdom to sense the challenge to their power and control.

Luke's Gospel in particular emphasises the social nature of the kingdom. In Luke's account of the Sermon on the Mount, Jesus' concern for the poor is made clear. He offers a vision for a radical society that involves loving our enemies, blessing those who curse us, turning the other cheek in response to violence, redistributing wealth, and lending to others without expecting repayment.[22] The Beatitudes represent the heart of Jesus' kingdom message, and in the Lucan Beatitudes, Jesus is quite clear in telling us that the kingdom of God belongs to the poor.

Jesus' kingdom is a countercultural phenomenon; it's certainly not business as usual. His prophetic word is a word of liberation for both those in captivity to sin and for those in captivity to the dominant powers of empire. He comes to set free *all* oppressed people. His freedom is not just spiritual, but economic, social and religious. He restores and heals the whole of our humanity.

Our understanding and experience of Jesus fundamentally shapes our message to the world. *Hesed, mishpat, tsedakah* and *shalom* find their greatest expression in Jesus. It is vital that our theology and Christology are robust enough to stand up to tyranny, oppression and evil, because Jesus *is* Justice.

9

ON THE ROAD TOGETHER

He will not falter or be discouraged till he establishes
justice on earth.

ISAIAH 42:4

Jesus blazes a trail for us as we follow him down the road. But, just as with the Vertical dimension, the challenge is how to do this together as an authentic prophetic community. How does the prophetic call to social justice get worked out in and through the life of the local church?

A healthy prophetic culture is more than just an excited bunch of prophets looking to change the world while the rest of us carry on with our lives, secretly relieved that we don't have to do anything remotely 'prophetic'. A prophetic culture is something for the whole community to fully embrace as we follow in the footsteps of Jesus and cooperate with God's Spirit in standing up for the vulnerable and marginalised.

The work of justice is overwhelming; but, as with all things, God has given the church everything it needs to get the job done. God has called his church to be the primary agent of making change happen – he intends his church to be the main instrument for bringing forth justice, righteousness and *shalom*. The world needs us to take seriously our kingdom responsibility to make our neighbourhoods a better place for all, allowing God's alternative reality to speak to and transform society.

A church with a healthy Horizontal dimension will be marked by four key elements that we share together as we respond in a Christlike way to God's desire for justice and righteousness. Just as with the Vertical dimension, these four foundational features describe the type of place we want our churches to be.

ALTERNATIVE CONSCIOUSNESS

The church that is prepared to think differently is the church best equipped for the road ahead. We are all products of our upbringing and cultural environment, and thus have certain ways of seeing and understanding the world. To be a Jesus-shaped prophetic community requires us to seriously consider where our cultural baggage may cause blind spots as far as the work of justice is concerned. We have to be prepared to *change the way we think*: to surrender our opinions, ideologies and sensibilities to the lordship of Christ. When our societal norms are acting to oppress people, we have to choose a different mindset. When the media is stirring up antagonism against certain minorities, we need the Spirit's help to see such issues from a godly perspective.

Near the start of his classic text *The Prophetic Imagination*, Old Testament theologian Walter Brueggemann writes, 'The task of prophetic ministry is to nurture, nourish, and evoke a consciousness and perception alternative to the consciousness and perception of the dominant culture around us.'[1]

We need the capacity to imagine a world other than the one legitimised by the dominant culture and the powers of consumerism, individualism, and so on. We need the Holy Spirit to interrupt what we think we know – to so unsettle our established paradigms that we can humbly allow something different to emerge.

It's only as we nourish and develop this alternative consciousness that we will be able to perceive God's reality and hold it out to the broken world as the ultimate source of hope and healing. It's as we nurture an alternative consciousness that we will be able to feel what God feels, see others through the eyes of Jesus, discern the cultural strongholds that perpetuate injustice, and dare to dream for something better.

Jenny and Justin Duckworth are the founders of the Urban Vision community in New Zealand, and they have spent many years sharing their lives with the homeless, poor and neglected. In their book *Against the Tide, Towards the Kingdom*, they describe how they have repeatedly embraced an alternative consciousness to that of the society around them. Choosing to think differently has enabled them to jettison the cultural norms of nuclear family, financial security and respectability. As they and their team have engaged with this new way of thinking, it has freed them to pursue a lifestyle centred on justice, opening their home to others and raising their children in inner-city community households of shared resources. Reflecting on their experience, Jenny says,

> Watching some of my peers go up and down emotionally with the market and spend all their spare time doing up houses and selling them, only to buy and start again, I'm so glad that the picket fence of our cultural dream fell down. Our expectation of a good family home, or the equivalent cool-student pad, depending on our age and stage, has to be reviewed. But we are freer of that cultural pressure than we would have been. We're rowing against that tide.[2]

As we long for God's *shalom* and his renewal of all things, the prophetic community needs to reframe the big-picture cultural narrative from the perspective of God's reality, so that we can see the world differently, hope for what is possible and allow justice to flourish.

How do we start doing this as a church? We can begin by asking God to show us where our paradigms need shifting; we can make space for honest conversations to help uncover our cultural blind spots; and we can talk to people from outside our demographic, asking God to help us hear the fresh truths he wants to reveal as we do this.

This is the kind of *alternative* culture we want to develop in our prophetic communities:

- A community of effective discipleship that is open to having our established thought patterns disrupted by God's Spirit.
- A community that allows Jesus to dismantle our cultural biases and birth a prophetic imagination in us, aligning us more to his heart.
- A community that perceives our neighbours through the loving eyes of Jesus.
- A community that encourages people to lament over injustice.

PROPHETIC VOICE

In the words of Abraham Heschel, 'Prophecy is the voice that God has lent to the silent agony, a voice to the plundered poor.'[3] Jesus calls his prophetic church to be a place of brave voices that refuse to sit on the fence of ambiguity; voices that are prepared to speak out as spokespersons for the very heart of God; voices that tell the truth. As we choose to stand apart from the prevailing culture, we are able to speak to it, with eyes to see and ears to hear.

Our prophetic voice is, first of all, one that *speaks on behalf of the poor and marginalised.* As we hear the cries of the oppressed, we can be a powerful voice for the voiceless, speaking for those too weak to plead their own cause. I'm thankful for the work of Tearfund[4] and other similar parachurch organisations that work tirelessly to advocate for the forgotten poor of the world and give them a voice in front of governments and policy makers. However, let's not forget that *every* expression of Jesus' church can speak on behalf of the poor in their own neighbourhood.

Our prophetic voice is, secondly, one that *speaks truth to power.* This is where we address society itself, where we prayerfully discern the words necessary to critique the wrongs inflicted on other people, the words that oppose tyranny. Prophetic criticism is a tradition that goes right back to Moses standing in front of Pharaoh and is expressed through the ministry of many biblical prophets as they criticised the policies of kings and nations. We shouldn't shy away from a Spirit-empowered challenge to the status quo as we stand up for God's justice in hostile environments. At times the prophetic voice comes with a 'bite' – it needs to be confrontational and iconoclastic. As we speak to society, we need a voice that will cause people to sit up and take notice, a voice that shames the sins of indifference, silence, collusion and complicity.

Rather than blindly submitting to the dominant powers of consumerism, racism, empire and everything else that the prevailing culture uses to maintain the status quo, the church of Jesus is required to faithfully speak *against* them. We have to overcome entrenched resistance to change and use prophetic criticism to dismantle the unjust systems that are crushing people.

History is full of people who used their prophetic voice to speak out against the prevailing culture and enact change in society. Most of us are familiar with William Wilberforce and his tireless campaign to end the British slave trade in the late eighteenth and early nineteenth century. In more recent times, British footballer Marcus Rashford became a prophetic voice when he used his social media platform to critique government policy towards impoverished children and lobbied parliament to provide free school meals. Imagine the impact we might have if every local church asked God what issue they were called to speak out on … and did something about it.

A vital element of speaking truth to power is being able to ask the right questions. To do this requires us to be well informed about the world we live in and to be ruthless in seeking the truth about issues. This quote from Dom Helder Camara, the Brazilian archbishop, reminds us of the confrontational nature of godly questioning: 'When I give food to the poor, they call me a saint. When I ask why the poor have no food, they call me a communist.'[5]

The prophetic voice of criticism is vital, but the world also needs to hear the voice of hope. Walter Brueggemann describes this as 'prophetic energizing'. He writes about how criticising and energising need to go hand in hand in order for the prophetic community to truly speak to society:

> I suggest that the dominant culture, now and in every time, is grossly uncritical, cannot tolerate serious and fundamental criticism, and will go to great lengths to stop it. Conversely, the dominant culture is a wearied culture, nearly unable to be seriously energised to new promises from God. We know, of course, that none of us relishes criticism, but we may also recognise that none of us much relishes energising either, for that would demand something of us. The task of prophetic ministry is to hold together criticism and energising.[6]

So, let us remember to sing songs of hope and redemption over our cities and neighbourhoods. We can prophetically call them to something better: to God's vision of *shalom* for all.

The final prophetic voice we must remember is the one that *speaks to the church itself*. We need to be able to hear the clear voice of God and communicate to the body of Christ his 'now' word *about* society. Effective prophetic ministry will stop us from averting our eyes, from switching channels. It is here to ensure we pay attention to what's really going on in the world.

This is the kind of *advocacy* culture we want to develop:

- A community that listens to the stories of the poor and marginalised.
- A community that supports whistle-blowers.
- A community that welcomes questions.
- A community that influences the agenda of local politics so that the concerns of the poor and vulnerable are heard.

INCARNATIONAL PRESENCE

As prophecy and justice come together, the church has an opportunity to be an incarnational witness that demonstrates God's alternative reality through the way we live our day-to-day lives. To do this we must join with the ancient ministry of the biblical prophets and allow God to incarnate his word – his revelation – in us. But rather than doing this as individuals, we do this together.

This is the church as an alternative community, which changes the world by *being* as much as by speaking. This is the church that is a promise, a portent, that God's reality – that glorious, alternative and chain-breaking reality – is just around the corner. This is the church that is so passionate about the kingdom of God that anyone coming across us will experience an authentic foretaste of the kingdom and be swept up in our infectious kingdom culture.

In his book *Becoming a Just Church*, Adam Gustine writes about pastoring a church in Bay Ridge, Brooklyn, a place with more than its fair share of inner-city challenges and racial tension. Gustine encourages us to understand the church as 'a parable of God's intentions' and shares how his local faith community learnt to live in such a way as to offer a compelling alternative to the surrounding culture.[7] He believes every church can become a community of *shalom*, an 'embodiment of God's tomorrow'[8] in this present age; and a 'declarative signpost that God intends to make everything right and new again.'[9] Gustine writes,

> Our church was the Revelation 7 future of God showing up in twenty-first-century New York City. You could understand a bit of what God might be up to in the world by being part of this community of faith. This is true for every church. As a prophetically alternative people, we enact a parable of God's future. This means the church is profoundly eschatological.[10]

To be an incarnational presence means we embrace a way of being and living that stands in stark contrast to the dominant culture that sustains injustice. We pursue a way of living that denounces unjust systems by quietly showing that things can be done differently. We refuse to conform to the pattern of the world[11] – the pattern that is holding humanity hostage; instead, we see our vocation as making the ethics of Jesus incarnate in the kind of life we live. We choose to become a radical embodiment of the Sermon on the Mount.

The prophetic community is a place of reconciliation and transformation; of right living and right relationships; of Jesus-shaped compassion; of nurture, hospitality, acceptance and liberation. It is a quietly subversive place, and a place of radical creativity as the Holy Spirit stirs up the poets and artists to craft beautiful expressions of God's alternative reality.

The prophetic community is a people who have truly learnt to be *present*. Not just present in the divine presence (as wonderful and necessary as that is), but also present in and to the world.

There is a way of being in the world that practitioners call the 'ministry of presence', in which we demonstrate God's love for people by coming alongside them. We get close enough to listen, to empathise and to be a tender Christlike presence for them. It's a simple but necessary way of participating in the lives of others and serving them as we respond to their felt needs. Sometimes holding out God's reality is as simple as sitting quietly and holding someone's hand.

Here's how Henri Nouwen describes it:

> More and more, the desire grows in me simply to walk around, greet people, enter their homes, sit on their doorsteps, play ball, throw water, and be known as someone who wants to live with them. It is a privilege to have the time to practice this simple ministry of presence. Still, it is not as simple as it seems. My own desire to be useful, to do something significant, or to be part of some impressive project is so strong that soon my time is taken up by meetings, conferences, study groups, and workshops that prevent me from walking the streets. It is difficult not to have plans, not to organize people around an urgent cause, and not to feel that you are working directly for social progress. But I wonder more and more if the first thing shouldn't be to know people by name, to eat and drink with them, to listen to their stories and tell your own, and to let them know with words, handshakes, and hugs that you do not simply like them, but truly love them.[12]

Sometimes incarnation is more powerful than words. Sometimes what the world needs most of all is the life-giving presence of Jesus embodied in our prophetic communities.

This is the kind of *incarnational* culture we want to develop:

- A community where kingdom life is expressed through creative arts.
- A community where normal, everyday lives are celebrated as holy spaces to demonstrate God's love.
- A community that slows down enough to be a peaceful, non-anxious presence[13] in our neighbourhoods.
- A community that builds networks and communities of inclusion and healing.

ACTION FOR JUSTICE

Finally, we come to the part where we get to cheer on Jesus causing havoc in the temple, and the prophetic activists get released upon the world. When it comes to justice, the Bible makes things highly practical:

'How long will you defend the unjust and show partiality to the wicked?

Defend the weak and the fatherless; uphold the cause of the poor and oppressed.

Rescue the weak and the needy; deliver them from the hand of the wicked.'

PSALM 82:2–4

'Is not this the kind of fasting I have chosen: to loose the chains of injustice and untie the cords of the yoke, to set the oppressed free and break every yoke?

Is it not to share your food with the hungry and to provide the poor wanderer with shelter – when you see the naked, to clothe them, and not to turn away from your own flesh and blood?'

ISAIAH 58:6–7

Religion that God our Father accepts as pure and faultless is this: to look after orphans and widows in their distress and to keep oneself from being polluted by the world.

JAMES 1:27

There is work to be done. Feeding the hungry, visiting the prisoners, housing the homeless, rescuing the trafficking victims, adopting the orphans, protecting the vulnerable – and mobilising church and society to be actively involved. Engaging prophetically with God's heart for the world means the practical and messy work of loving our neighbour as he or she lies beaten and robbed on the side of the road.

There is also the work of active protest and holy rebellion, as we champion ethical causes – campaigning, lobbying, and influencing governmental and corporate policy. As Richard Foster writes, 'Our task is to envision and work to realize a society where it is easier to do good and harder to do evil; a society with institutions and laws and public policies that provide justice for all and enhanced life for all.'[14]

By corporately listening, the prophetic church needs to be a place where we can clearly *hear* how God wants us to act and then walk in obedience. We will explore the practicalities of hearing God in chapter eleven, but for now we simply note that there are so many issues of injustice we could attend to that it becomes imperative for the prophetic community to clearly discern which ones Jesus is leading us to. Effective, world-changing, Spirit-empowered action comes from the divine spoken word.

This is the kind of *activist* culture we want to develop:

- A community that validates, prays for, and supports prophetic activists.
- A community where we work for justice by how we shop, vote, use our resources and care for the planet.
- A community that together prayerfully discerns which issues God wants us to tackle.
- A community where people are empowered to change society for the better.

COMING FACE TO FACE WITH POLITICS

Having mapped out the four elements of the Horizontal dimension – alternative consciousness, prophetic voice, incarnational presence, and action for justice – I want to draw your attention to two 'hot topics' that need some careful consideration if we're going to faithfully follow Jesus down the road: politics and spiritual warfare.

First, politics.

It's safer and much more comfortable for churches, and especially church leaders, to stay out of politics; but, by choosing to distance ourselves from the political sphere, we effectively ignore a significant chunk of Scripture. Though not explicitly a political book, the Bible has much to say about how God's people should function in the world. Our Christian faith gets lived out in our neighbourhoods, cities and cultures. A passion for justice, righteousness and *shalom* is not tied to any particular political ideology, but it often requires us to be politically discerning and engaged.

Western Christians can get so used to our personal 'quiet times' that we forget that the Bible is a very social, community-focused book. In both

Old Testament and New Testament times, people encountered Scripture in the context of community: they heard it read to them as they gathered. They understood it from a communal and social standpoint. So, when we read Scripture today, we need to primarily hear how it speaks to us in a communal setting, because that's what the original writers had in mind. We need to be cautious of an overly individualised faith, and instead hear Scripture with a mindset of the *polis* – the purposeful community.

Alongside this, we cannot divorce Scripture from the political and social context in which it was written. We understand the Gospels better when we comprehend the realities of living under Roman occupation; we understand Paul's letters better when we appreciate the cultural and political factors influencing life in Asia Minor. Through his divine grace, God inspired many different people to write down the Bible we hold today, but nearly every one of those writers was living in the context of real or threatened colonisation. When we take the Bible seriously, we hear it speaking to the oppressive system of empire over and over again. And things don't get much more political than the theme of imperial domination.

Jesus, like all of us, was born into a political context. Two thousand years later we should pay attention to how even the manner of his death was highly political. As a means of execution, crucifixion was a vicious tool of empire, used to crush rebellion and punish slaves. Christ's death took place because the religious leaders of his day sensed a threat to their power-base, and the Roman occupiers feared an uprising. Jesus was executed because he embodied a politics that threatened both the religious elite and the political authority of Rome. The politics of the cross, and thus the politics of the kingdom of God, offer a radical alternative to that of empire or religious control. The kingdom promotes healing, reconciliation and forgiveness. It stands with the poor, suffers alongside the broken, and refuses to return evil for evil. The politics of Jesus are not an attempt to control the lives of others or hold on to earthly power, but rather to demonstrate revolutionary servant leadership.

The English word *politics* comes from the Greek word *politiká,* which means 'affairs of the cities'; and *The Oxford English Dictionary* defines politics as 'the activities involved in getting and using power in public life, and being able to influence decisions that affect a country or a society'.[15]

Politics therefore relates to how a society is run and organised, which inevitably has huge implications for people's welfare, freedom and prosperity. Ungodly politics perpetuates injustice.

In engaging with politics we are hopefully working towards a vision for the best way for humanity to live together – a way that allows peace, justice and flourishing for everyone. All human systems, constructs and institutions are, to a greater or lesser extent, broken through sin; and there is only one Lord of history, Jesus Christ. But as his kingdom representatives here on earth, we are called to influence the society and culture we find ourselves in and to work for the common good.

If we reject the political aspect of our Christian faith, we will never stand up to tyranny. To deny the political element of our faith is to deny that things have to change and instead be content with the status quo. But, as we pursue God's heart and encounter the divine *pathos*, feeling what he feels, we cannot remain indifferent to issues of injustice. We cannot avert our eyes, otherwise we are complicit in the perpetuation of these evils. Poverty, oppression, slavery, racism and global warming are political issues. Opinions will vary in the church about how best to eliminate them, but distancing ourselves from politics will not make them go away. The prophetic voice is necessary to challenge the status quo and demand change. The prophetic call on the church is about campaigning tirelessly for the eradication of every kind of injustice, which will inevitably mean getting involved politically at some level. The challenge is how we engage with political issues in a prophetic, Jesus-shaped, Spirit-led way, so that it is our love for God and neighbour that compel us to action, rather than any particular political party or ideology.

Hans Urs von Balthasar points out that there was an interesting relationship between the institution of monarchy and role of the prophet in Old Testament times – the latter acting as a counterweight and corrective to the former. The Hebrew prophets had a clear political role:

> From David to the last king of Judah, this painful and yet fruitful dualism will dominate history: the close confrontation between the king, who obeys the political necessities, and the prophet, who relates the whole political sphere to the direct word of God and points to direct obedience.[16]

Once Israel demanded a king and monarchy replaced direct theocracy, there was a need for prophets to keep kingship focused on obedience to God without compromise.

In the following verses in Isaiah, we clearly observe how the prophet speaks to policy makers:

> Woe to those who make unjust laws, to those who issue oppressive decrees,
> to deprive the poor of their rights and withhold justice from the oppressed
> of my people, making widows their prey and robbing the fatherless.
>
> ISAIAH 10:1–2

It may make us uncomfortable, but the prophetic community cannot afford to shy away from politics. And the same is true for spiritual warfare.

COMING FACE TO FACE WITH SPIRITUAL WARFARE

It is not just political systems that oppress people. There is a battle raging in the spiritual realm. Very real powers seek to stand in the way of God's *shalom* being established on earth, so the prophetic church needs to be well equipped to fight on a spiritual level as well as a political one. We need to discern the demonic powers at work across all parts of society, and we need a prophetic, prayer-soaked response to those powers that perpetuate injustice.

So, what are these powers that we take a stand against? Scholars debate about the precise interpretation of New Testament words such as *stoicheia* – 'elemental spiritual forces'[17] – and *ochyrōma* – 'strongholds'[18] – but Paul is quite clear about the nature of the conflict we are in:

> For our struggle is not against flesh and blood, but against the rulers,
> against the authorities, against the powers of this dark world and against
> the spiritual forces of evil in the heavenly realms.
>
> EPHESIANS 6:12

There are powers and principalities that have embedded themselves in ideologies, systems, institutions and political movements throughout society and history. This, in part, explains why our social, political and economic structures are so resistant to change. When we confront societal evil, such as institutional racism or poverty, we do well to remember that we are engaging in an intense spiritual and cosmic struggle, and that reform comes through prayer as much as protest.

In terms of spiritual warfare, the prophetic call to social justice is about exposing, resisting, confronting and dismantling the principalities and powers. Any resistance to injustice is spiritual warfare, but an *effective* warfare, seeped in wisdom and discernment, follows a systematic approach and enables us to become effective agents for healing and transformation. Here's how we come against the powers:

Name them. The prophetic church needs to be able to identify social and collective evil so that the gods of this age can be exposed for what they are in all their inhumanity. We shouldn't be shy of calling out strongholds of

- individualism
- conformity
- empire
- consumerism
- corporate greed
- sectarianism
- systemic racism
- sexual exploitation
- militarism
- passivity
- elitism

Worship. This is a powerful weapon. As we worship, we magnify the name of Jesus in our midst. To worship God is to resist the other powers in the world. As the early church knew too well, to say 'Jesus is Lord' is to say that Caesar is not. Worship centres us on Jesus and helps us focus on his victory over the powers of darkness. Through our worship we declare the truth of the nature and reality of God. Worship changes the atmosphere around us: as we lift up the name of Jesus, the darkness has to retreat.

Repent. The prophetic church embraces repentance, especially where we have been complicit with the powers. Corporate and structural repentance – where we confess and lament together – is very effective at dismantling the powers of darkness. It breaks the hold of guilt and shame and ushers in God's forgiveness.

Intercede. Prayer is a mighty weapon against the powers, especially when we come together as God's people and pray for breakthrough in the name of Jesus. He has taught us to pray to the Father, 'Your kingdom come, your will be done, on earth as it is in heaven',[19] so we can be confident in interceding for the justice of the kingdom to overcome demonic schemes of injustice.

Live in an opposite spirit. Once we have identified the strongholds of darkness, we simply live in a completely different way. For example, to counteract a stronghold of sectarianism, we can actively develop a culture of bridge-building; to counteract a stronghold of consumerism, we can practice a lifestyle of radical generosity.

Every prophetic church should be a threat to the powers and principalities, to the strongholds that would crush the weak and vulnerable.

FOLLOWING JESUS DOWN THE ROAD

Politics is important. Spiritual warfare is important. We are not to be overly consumed with either of them but taking them both seriously helps develop and resource the type of church culture in which we can hear and speak prophetically to see needed societal transformation.

Going back to our four elements, we can summarise the Horizontal dimension of prophetic culture this way:

Challenge Injustice

Alternative Consciousness
Prophetic Voice
Incarnational Presence
Action for Justice

The Prophetic Community

As the prophetic community engages with all four of these elements, we can effectively contribute to the social holiness that God desires to see established on his earth. We are all change agents. We all have responsibility. And we can all welcome the unique creativity of the Holy Spirit as he comes alongside us to help. As we engage in these practices, the prophetic community partners with the Spirit to 'disturb the comfortable' – allowing him to first disturb us, and then being used by him to humbly and sacredly disturb ungodly comfort in society.

Our identity as the people of God and as a prophetic community needs to be one that allows justice to flourish. We need to understand ourselves as a countercultural, Jesus-shaped community that demonstrates the ethics of the kingdom and that is able to speak to the world in which we live. So, let's faithfully follow Jesus down the less-travelled road. He can always be found on the margins.

10

BRINGING THE TWO DIMENSIONS TOGETHER

Maintain love and justice, and wait for your God always.

HOSEA 12:6

Unlike our American cousins, most British people learn to drive in a car with a manual transmission. We therefore have to master the gear stick and clutch pedal in order to change gears. This requires us to understand what the *biting point* is.

A straightforward way to understand a car's clutch is that it is made up of two different metal plates in the engine. Depressing the clutch pedal separates these plates, allowing a change of gears. When the pedal is down, the engine isn't driving the wheels; but as the clutch pedal is raised, the two plates move closer together, and eventually they make contact. This is the biting point – where the engine can start moving the wheels once more. The trick is to learn how to raise the clutch pedal and lower the accelerator pedal so that the car moves forward smoothly. Many a learner driver has stalled at a junction because of their inexperience with the biting point. But over time, good clutch control becomes second nature.

When it comes to mature prophetic culture in our churches, we need to address the specific issue of how we bring the Vertical and Horizontal dimensions together – how to find the 'biting point' of our corporate prophetic identity and move forward effectively – because keeping them separate will deprive the church of an incredible source of strength and energy.

God's prophetic purposes for the church are equally about the Horizontal and Vertical dimensions. But, as we have already observed, there is a great deal of tension in the contemporary church between these two contrasting expressions of prophetic culture and consciousness.

A BALANCING ACT

Though Christian communities may articulate the need for both Vertical and Horizontal dimensions, in reality they are usually focused on only one. Some churches are all about the presence of God – worship, prayer, personal prophetic ministry – and they pay lip service to their responsibility to challenge societal ills. ('We've got a foodbank. Tick.') Other churches are all about justice – advocacy, defending the marginalised, social prophetic ministry – and they pay lip service to the pursuit of God. ('We've got a prayer group. Tick.')

As an individual prophet, it's fine to have a leading beat. Some prophets will be called more to the Horizontal expression, and some to the Vertical. (We see this to a certain extent in Scripture.) But we cannot say the same for the prophetic *community*. What I observe across the church is a dysfunction that stems from the two dimensions being disconnected from, and even opposing, each other.

Because both sides of this divide view each other with suspicion and a fair amount of judgement, we face the following two challenges in our endeavour to establish healthy prophetic communities:

- The need to build bridges between the two camps.
- The need to build dual-perspective churches that can operate well in both dimensions.

One of the things I've sought to do in this book is honour different church traditions and acknowledge the deep work of the Spirit in each of them. I am truly thankful for the contemplative and charismatic traditions, and I praise God for the social justice stream in church history. The church of Jesus Christ is a multi-faceted wonder, and it's understandable that different Christians will be attracted to different expressions of the body. But in order for us to be a *mature* prophetic church, we have to find a way to hold the Vertical and Horizontal dimensions together, so that each and every local church can faithfully embrace both.

We've already noted the fundamental role of the Vertical dimension in challenging idolatry, and the fundamental role of the Horizontal dimension in challenging injustice; but idolatry and injustice are not unrelated. In fact, as Adam Gustine points out, idols are often doorways to injustice.[1] The idol of the British empire perpetuated the injustice of colonialism. The idol of fast fashion props up the injustice of child labour. A functioning Vertical dimension will provide the church with both the ability to discern and the voice to critique such idols, and thus tackle the injustices. Presence and Justice are profoundly interconnected; allowing both dimensions to flourish in our communities releases their full synergistic potential.

A vital and necessary way to define an *immature prophetic culture* is the neglect of one dimension or the other. If we are committed to being a Jesus-shaped church and committed to developing an authentically Jesus-shaped prophetic culture, we must bring the two dimensions into alignment. We cannot build our churches on one expression or the other, as if it were a choice. We have to take seriously the danger of imbalance – the tendency to get pulled towards one or the other – and recognise that it takes effort, humility and strategy to hold the middle ground.

PROPHETIC RESPIRATION

We will find the greatest motivation to pursue both dimensions by searching the heart of God and seeing how they are intricately connected reflections of the divine nature. Our responsibility to faithfully hold out God's reality should lead to a beautiful harmonisation of the two dimensions. The truly worshipping church will love Justice. And the truly just church will love Presence. When we travel deep enough into God's heart, we find that action and prayer are one.

As we endeavour to steer the church towards greater conformity to Jesus' own pattern of prophetic ministry, it's worth noting how Luke in particular highlights the two-dimensional perspective.

Each of the Gospel writers has their own way of illuminating Jesus' role as a prophet. For Matthew, Jesus is the new Moses; and for John,

Jesus is the Son who reveals the Father. But Luke takes things a step further. Not only does he present Jesus as the great Prophet (with many references naming him as such), but he also highlights how Jesus holds the two dimensions of the prophetic together. On the one hand, Luke pays close attention to the role of the Holy Spirit in the incarnation and ministry of Christ;[2] he emphasises Jesus' prayer life and intimate fellowship with the Father, especially before important occasions.[3] In these instances, the Vertical dimension is clearly evident. But on the other hand, Luke points to the Horizontal as he stresses Jesus' special concern for outsiders – for the poor and marginalised, for outcasts, and for women. Many of the parables are based around the theme of reversal, where the humble are commended and the rich and mighty are rebuked or brought down.[4] And, as we've already noted, it is Luke who gives us Jesus' Nazareth Manifesto,[5] with its clear message of good news for the poor.

As we seek to follow Jesus and pursue a truly balanced, Christlike prophetic culture in our faith communities, we would do well to sit for a while with the shattering simplicity of the Beatitudes. In his book on listening prayer, Brad Jersac writes about how, at the heart of Jesus' teaching, we can trace a motif of respiration:

> The Beatitudes show us a type of 'prophetic respiration' in which the disciple inhales the fullness of the Spirit in contemplative prayer then exhales justice and mercy into the community. They step into the meeting place of the heart and then emerge as lights in the darkness of a world-gone-mad. Inhale and be filled. Exhale and be merciful. Inhale and be purified. Exhale and bring justice. Inhale and receive peace. Exhale and be peacemakers. Inhale and be illumined. Exhale and be light … . In the Beatitudes Jesus teaches us how to breathe properly. He shows both inner and outer spirituality – contemplation and social action, mysticism and mercy. Retreat to the mountain, the heart or the throne room. Then return to the city, the crowds, and the lepers. From this discovery emerges the beginning of prophetic maturity.[6]

STANDING BETWEEN HEAVEN AND EARTH

If imbalance is a strong indication of immaturity, and if the two dimensions *together* create an index of maturity, many churches will need to do some significant recalibration. We need to capture a vision for what a mature, balanced prophetic church can look like. It's important to continually remind ourselves of the immense benefits of both aspects of prophetic ministry and culture – what they each bring to the body, and why we can't afford to neglect either.

There is huge potential for good in each dimension. We need both! But there is work to be done in communicating this well and casting a vision for a holistically balanced prophetic culture in which everyone can partake.

One thing we can all do is ask the Holy Spirit to reveal any unconscious cultural biases that may be causing us to lean towards a particular dimension. What is there in our church's history or tradition that might make us prioritise one dimension? Is there anything about our demographic that draws us one way or the other? We also need to be prepared to change our way of thinking so that we actively embrace the dimension we have been neglecting. The community has to be discipled so that new concepts can be legitimised and new patterns of behaviour accepted. With humility and a healthy approach to risk, we must develop fresh practices that embed two-dimensional thinking into the rhythms and habits of the body.

To embrace both dimensions means being able to stand between heaven and earth – a location well known to prophets. As we saw in chapter four, prophets are people of the 'gap' – that place of tension between the glories of God's presence and the injustice and unrighteousness of the world around us. The challenge of living in the gap is of simultaneously being sensitive to both realities.

What is true for prophets must also be true for the mature prophetic community. We are called as a body to occupy that space where we can stand between God's heaven and God's earth, with eyes focused on both – passionate about faithfulness *and* justice; concerned with both God's reality *and* the reality of the world we face daily; attentive to God *and* attentive to what he requires of us. It's a place of tension, a place of experiencing the divine *pathos*, but a place we must inhabit.

Maturity is honestly acknowledging the tension and then choosing to engage well with both dimensions. When we do so, we create a depth and integrity of prophetic culture. We can leverage the strengths in each dimension to bring excellence and challenge to both.

IN THE SHADOWS

We also need to be honest about the pitfalls of prophetic ministry. Any honest discussion about the prophetic will acknowledge the temptations, blind-spots and vulnerabilities that accompany prophets and the prophetic function. In his book on the fivefold ministry, church planter Neil Cole writes about the different 'shadows' cast by each role.[7] Less-than-mature prophets cast a distinct shadow. We can say the same for an immature prophetic culture.

We have so far defined communal immaturity as the neglect of one or other dimension, but it's also important to understand the key dangers specific to each dimension. This is an important step towards a grounded and balanced prophetic culture. Let's look at some examples of how immaturity results in functioning with wrong or imbalanced priorities.

Problems in the Vertical Dimension

In highlighting two potential Vertical problems, we see a deadly irony: the dimension designed to minimise the danger of idolatry in God's people can easily slip into an idolatrous pattern of thought and behaviour.

Spiritual gluttony. As God's covenant people, it's absolutely right that we are passionate about our love for him. But a danger in the Vertical dimension is an over-reliance on (or even an addiction to) spiritual experiences, where we end up seeking experiences for their own sake and somehow take our eyes off Jesus. The strength of the Vertical – passion for God – can easily tip over into an unhealthy ongoing quest for the next spiritual 'high'. We can become so consumed with the spiritual side of life that our walk with Jesus becomes all about experiential euphoria, and we end up idolising the experience rather than worshipping God.

True worship is an act of our will, not an emotional high; but, in a church with a strong Vertical dimension, the lines between 'good worship' and 'good feelings' can get blurred. We can easily confuse the temporary buzz we get from a great worship band with pure worship of God. We also readily get drawn to the sensational. Prophetic culture is very dangerous when we seek the feelings rather than God himself, and we find ourselves worshipping worship. Any tendency towards a consumer culture (focusing on what we personally get out of church, such as comfort, our needs being met, and a feel-good factor) is only going to exaggerate these dangers. It is possible to have a very charismatic church that doesn't look much like Jesus.

An over-emphasis on spiritual experience also devalues an intellectual engagement with faith and can cause a rejection of the rational. We are called to love God with our whole hearts *and* whole minds. Neglecting our God-given ability to reason can lead to prophetic culture becoming very 'wacky' – where we end up losing sight of Jesus and our rootedness in him.

When we are too consumed with experience, we often end up with a shallow engagement with Scripture and the accumulated wisdom of church tradition. There can be a lack of biblical literacy and solid theological foundation. We can become overly influenced by those deemed to be 'anointed' – the latest charismatic celebrities – putting them on man-made pedestals because they seem to be closer to God than we are. We may devour their teachings at the neglect of a serious engagement with the Bible and a commitment to discipleship.

Spiritual pride. It is all too easy for a church with a strong Vertical dimension to succumb to spiritual pride – viewing our vibrant worship and prayer life as a mark of God's special favour and assuming that because prophecies are flowing freely, we are somehow better than others.

When we are paying too much attention to the form rather than the substance of true spirituality, we are vulnerable to the religious spirit: a mindset that says that our behaviour and our beliefs are our righteousness, that we can gain value through our own works. It's incredibly easy to slip into a way of thinking that equates the frequency of our prophecies and the 'success' of our ministry with our spiritual worth. The temptation to grandiosity is real, even though it is the antithesis of the gospel.

If we are spiritually prideful, we can end up with arrogance instead of humble submission to God's will – focusing on performance rather than the deep work of the Holy Spirit. People can get tied up in knots as they try to work out the right way to pray, the right way to worship or the right way to invite the Holy Spirit – striving for the magic formula that will usher in the presence of God.

Spiritual pride also leads to a community that is judgemental towards others and lacking in grace. Such a community struggles to work alongside other churches. In thinking that we are the only ones who've 'got it', we become deaf to criticism and resistant to challenge.

Problems in the Horizontal Dimension

Wrong motives. A key question to ask ourselves in the Horizontal dimension is this: *what is driving us?* Activism needs to flow from our love for God and a passion for his concerns. Our desire to change the world needs to be birthed out of God's righteousness and compassion, but it is very easy for a concern for social justice to be rooted in something else. Our hearts may be burning within us at injustice – but what ignited the fire? It is our worship of God that should lead the prophetic community to the slums, to the foodbanks and to the prisons. If we are reacting out of ideology, belligerence or our own brokenness, yes, we may still be doing good in society, but we cannot necessarily claim it as prophetic. We'll end up exhausted – burnt out on good causes – rather than fulfilled. It is possible to be a very 'activist' church that doesn't look much like Jesus, because the cause has become bigger than him.

It is all too easy to stick the label 'prophetic' on a lot of social justice activity. (It is also easy to stick this label on plenty of activity and phenomena in the Vertical dimension that are clearly not prophetic.) We have to discern whether our Horizontal activity truly arises from an encounter with God's heart, empowered by the Holy Spirit, or if it is rooted in something else. There is 'holy protest', and then there is protest motivated by the political spirit. There is 'holy discontent', and then there is just discontent. We must be careful not to 'reduce prophecy to righteous indignation' as Walter Brueggemann puts it.[8] We have to be wary of angry activism. To quote Brueggemann again: 'If we are to understand prophetic criticism, we must see that its characteristic idiom is anguish not anger.'[9] A mature engagement with the Horizontal dimension is not dependent on a particular temperament.

The prophetic call to social justice is more than just protest and dissent. Shane Claiborne warns us of the peril of defining ourselves by what we are against:

> Protesters are everywhere, but I think the world is desperately in need of prophets, those little voices that can point us towards another future. Some of us have spent so much time fighting what we are against that we can barely remember what we are for … . Protesters are still on the fringes like satellites, revolving around the system. But prophets and poets lead us into a new world, beyond simply yelling at the old one.[10]

We need to guard our hearts carefully and allow God to lead us at his pace and through his grace. If our motives are right, we can leave the results of our actions to God. Action and protest birthed in the prayer room will come with the kingdom power to effect lasting change.

Self-righteousness. When we come face to face with the apathy, indifference and passivity to injustice that exists in many churches, it is easy to be outraged and judgemental and to start thinking we are better than others. The danger of self-righteousness in the Horizontal dimension mirrors the danger of spiritual pride in the Vertical dimension.

It is a sobering thought that the godly impulse to make the world a better place can easily end up becoming legalistic. Those of us who are passionate about social justice and righting society's wrongs can become very black and white about who is living 'right' and quick to judge others about how they spend their money and which causes they support. There can be a lack of love and grace for people who are not as committed and as ethically 'pure' as we are. The prophetic voice can quickly become hypercritical and contemptuous towards different expressions of the body if they are not seen to be in line with our positions. In our drive to be right, and in our rush to be pure, we can disparage and vilify others, and completely miss some valid expressions of the Spirit's work in our community.

Arrogance is as real a problem with Justice as it is with Presence. An elitist mentality of 'We're the only ones who can do this' has echoes of Elijah's attitude in 1 Kings 19:10: 'I have been very zealous for the Lord .... I alone am left' (NRSV). Without an intimate dependence on God, the prophetic community can develop something of a hero syndrome, seeking recognition as the unique solution to the problem.

COVENANT AND KINGDOM

Over the years, as I've worked with many churches and helped them establish a healthy prophetic culture, I have found that one of the most important things we can do is to build the prophetic on a foundation of 'covenant and kingdom'.[11] The great truths of *covenant* – relationship with God – and *kingdom* – the responsibility to represent God – lead us all the way through the Bible. As we develop a thorough understanding of these two great themes, we will find a safe place to let prophets flourish and to allow the dual-perspective prophetic function do the work it is designed to do.

The theme of *covenant* is woven throughout Scripture and has particular resonance for the prophetic community as we remember the call on the Hebrew prophets to safeguard the relationship between God and his people. It's because of our covenant identity in God that we can be confident in hearing his voice. The covenantal side of prophecy draws us to the Father's presence where we are affirmed in his love and conformed ever closer to Jesus. The theology of covenant speaks deeply to the Vertical dimension of prophetic culture.

The theme of *kingdom* is the second essential strand of spiritual DNA that winds its way through the biblical narrative. At its heart, this theme is about our responsibility to act on God's behalf and to extend his kingdom on earth. As his people, we are commissioned to make the world a better place for all. The kingdom perspective brings a necessary outward momentum to prophecy, motivating us to engage with the world around us, to be a voice for the voiceless and to seek the restoration of society. This of course speaks profoundly to the Horizontal dimension of prophetic culture.

These two majestic themes connect powerfully with each other; they are a fundamental warp and weft making up the fabric of Scripture.

We see both covenant and kingdom being established in the life of Moses as God first settles Moses' identity and then commissions him to lead the people out of slavery. We see Jesus flawlessly living out both themes as he reveals the depth of relationship he enjoyed with the Father as well as being the perfect representation and channel of God's kingdom.

'Covenant and kingdom' – being and doing, relationship and responsibility. The prophetic church needs to live in both paradigms.

This is a scriptural framework that enables us to stand between heaven and earth and engage well in both dimensions. It helps us to calibrate our lives and ministry around the biblical narrative and be a Jesus-shaped community. Our pursuit of God – in whose image we are made – must fundamentally affect our perception of what he has made us to do. Applying the framework of 'covenant and kingdom' to prophetic consciousness and function will ensure we can build a culture that is grounded, biblical and healthy.

PRACTICAL STEPS FORWARD

As we go on the journey of becoming a truly mature prophetic community that holds both dimensions together, it is helpful to consider three levels of culture development and how they build on each other:[12]

- *Grounded:* are both dimensions *understood?*
  Ensuring that the Vertical and Horizontal dimensions are understood and valued by the community, using biblical teaching to embed the principles, as well as providing healthy examples of both.
- *Holistic:* are both dimensions *present?*
  Ensuring that both dimensions are present in community life; intentionally pursuing active engagement with both, celebrating the diversity of expression within the community, and ensuring that each dimension has a voice to speak into the culture of the community.

- **Balanced:** are both dimensions *working together*?
  Ensuring that the two dimensions come together, serving each other, equipping each other, and working in partnership to build up the body and extend the kingdom.

In a healthy prophetic culture, all three levels will be present.

At the end of chapter thirteen, there are some practical exercises to help the whole community explore the two dimensions. But here I want to mention the importance of finding a *common language* to help us build bridges between them. As an exercise in bringing the two dimensions together, we can take the four foundational elements of Vertical culture and the four foundational elements of Horizontal culture (from chapters seven and nine) and see how they sit alongside and connect with each other, as well as what common language draws them together. (Note that the order of the Vertical elements is reversed.)

Vertical	*Connection Point*	Horizontal
Personal holiness	Change the way we think	Alternative consciousness
Revelatory gifts	Hear and speak from God's heart	Prophetic voice
Presence of God	Being present	Incarnational presence
Covenant faithfulness	Living faithfully and justly	Action for justice

Set out like this, we can start to see the connections and formulate a language to enable the two dimensions to understand and interact with each other.

The elements of *personal holiness* and *alternative consciousness* are both about being prepared to *change the way we think* – about ourselves and about society. This requires us to surrender our existing mindsets and opinions to Christ and be open to holy disruption and the process of God's reality refining our internal world.

The elements of *revelatory gifts* and a *prophetic voice* are closely connected: we *hear and speak from God's heart*. We listen to God and listen to the voice of the oppressed, speaking the prophetic word and speaking for the voiceless. Both these elements need us to be attentive listeners and bold speakers.

The elements of *presence of God* and *incarnational presence* share, of course, the concept of *being present* to reality, both God's reality and the reality of the world in which we live. We pursue God's presence, and we practise a lifestyle that demonstrates the incarnational presence of Christ in our neighbourhoods.

The elements of *covenant faithfulness* and *action for justice* find a common language when we consider the two greatest commandments: to love God and love our neighbour. In the ever-practical world of the kingdom, we fulfil these commands by *living faithfully and justly*.

Language creates culture. Intentionally shaping our language in order to hold both dimensions together is an important step towards a balanced, Jesus-shaped prophetic community.

FINDING THE BITING POINT

The primary prophetic impulse has always been the pursuit of God's heart; but we cannot just pursue God's heart for his people or just pursue God's heart for the world. For the mature prophetic community, the biting point has become second nature: seeking after the full heart of God so that we can speak hope and transformation to the church and to the world. In the utterly beautiful and alternative kingdom of God, Presence and Justice go hand in hand.

This twofold vision for a balanced church needs the prophets. The task of prophetic ministry is to give people an imagination for what is possible in both dimensions – to hold out God's alternative reality in order that we can first encounter the Living One, and then carry his transformational word to society.

CASE STUDY
ST THOMAS PHILADELPHIA, SHEFFIELD, UK

Perhaps the best example I can present for integrating the Vertical and Horizontal dimensions of the prophetic is that of the church I am part of: St Thomas Philadelphia, Sheffield, UK. We're not perfect and still have a long way to go, but for years we have experienced God calling us to a deeper engagement with both dimensions. Most of the values and principles I've written about in this book flow out of what we have learnt at St Thomas Philadelphia.

We have outworked our prophetic expression over three decades of actively pursuing missional discipleship. This gives us a profoundly solid foundation on which to build a prophetic culture. Accountability and a heart for mission are hard-wired into the system. We eagerly desire the prophetic, but we see it as a means to an end: a greater love for Jesus and a greater impact on the city of Sheffield.

Our primary motivation is to hear God's call and then respond obediently. This has required us to intentionally reject the consumer culture that can lead to 'spiritual gluttony' and to constantly reorient outward to the last, the least and the lost.

The church's fundamental building block for life together has been missional communities. These are groups of twenty to forty people gathered around a clear missional vision, with the aim of sharing the good news of Jesus and extending God's *shalom* in a particular neighbourhood or network of relationships. These lay-led groups form an extended family of people who are on mission together. This way of structuring our church has significantly impacted our prophetic culture. Missional communities, by their very nature, are places of discernment, of paying attention to the work of the Holy Spirit in our city, of disrupting the status quo, and of bridging the gap between the kingdom and the world. They have been vehicles of profound incarnational presence and action for justice. They have also provided a safe space for people to pursue prophetic gifts. The existence of missional communities has counterbalanced any tendency for prophetic ministry to be associated solely with Sunday services and/or professional church leadership.

Our engagement with the prophetic has also been impacted by the way we have developed a healthy fivefold culture. Prophets are understood as fulfilling one of the five roles given to the church, making their own contributions to our community alongside persons expressing the other four roles. The language around prophets has been normalised. This welcoming of the prophetic role has enabled our prophets to shape the culture around them and create an environment conducive to *everyone* hearing God's voice and seeing as God sees.

DEVELOPING THE VERTICAL DIMENSION

Praise and worship have always been at the heart of our community life as a church, and alongside that, we've emphasised enjoying the presence of God and friendship with the Holy Spirit. There has also been an intentional pursuit of revelatory gifts, which have become well-embedded in our culture.

The following table summarises some of the paradigm shifts and practices that have helped us develop a mature engagement with revelatory gifts and listening prayer.

Paradigm Shift	Examples of Practices
We have normalised the gift of prophecy so that it's accepted, expected and a regular part of church life.	• Modelling by our leaders of a healthy engagement with prophetic gifts in their personal walk with Jesus. • Hearing testimonies from church members about the positive impact prophecy has had in their lives. • Engaging in pre-service prayers where we listen to God for prophetic words to share in the service.

	• Encouraging the use of revelatory gifts in our missional communities. • Making it normal, whenever we are gathered (from Sunday services to staff meetings and small groups), to say, 'Let's wait on God for a few minutes and hear what he is saying to us.'
We are committed to teaching all our church members (including children and young people) how to hear God's voice and have provided a wide range of training opportunities.	• Intentionally communicating the message that all followers of Jesus can learn to hear God's voice. • Ensuring that prophetic ministry is not focused around, or perceived to be dependent on, a few 'gifted' individuals. • Providing a variety of courses and training sessions on prophetic ministry, open to everyone. • Creating safe spaces for people to practice hearing God's voice. • Hosting prophetic conferences, providing learning from mature practitioners from around the world. • Equipping our children's team so they are confident to teach our young people how to hear God. • Establishing clearly defined guidelines about the exercise of prophecy which provide a safe context for revelatory gifts to flourish.
We view prophetic gifts as an important way in which we can serve one another. We love 'speak[ing] to people for their strengthening, encouragement and comfort' (1 Corinthians 14:3).	• Organising 'prophetic appointments': giving people the opportunity to come and receive prophetic ministry at a specific time. • Regularly using prophetic gifts in prayer ministry. • Having prophetic teams prophesy over businesses connected with church members.

	• Giving prophetic words to baptism candidates. • Utilising WhatsApp groups so church members can share prophetic encouragements with each other.
We understand that discipleship and the prophetic are closely interlinked.	• Frequently using the questions, 'What is God saying to you? What are you going to do about it?' • Seeing discipleship happen within 'huddles': small groups of people meeting regularly and facilitating the answering of the two questions above. • Encouraging church members to have an accountability partner: someone to help them be responsible for faithfully responding to what God is saying to them. • Understanding that prophetic words involve both 'hear' and 'obey.'
We desire to be a community that can discern God's will together and seek him for vision and direction.	• Being committed to good communication between prophets and the leadership team. • Carefully recording the prophetic words given to the church. • Leaders regularly setting aside time to hear God in the decision-making process. • Encouraging the prophetic to work closely with the apostolic.
We understand that revelatory gifts are not just for church on Sunday but are to be taken into our workplaces and neighbourhoods.	• Intentionally bringing an outward focus to teaching and training on prophecy. • Exploring different ways of taking prophetic gifts to the streets and testing their use as effective tools in evangelism. • Using culturally appropriate language to prophesy over non-Christians. • Birthing missional communities out of prayer and prophecy.

DEVELOPING THE HORIZONTAL DIMENSION

One of the ways that the *Horizontal dimension* has developed at our church is through the work of Restore,* a wonderful ministry that has grown over the last two decades to serve the most vulnerable people in our city. At the heart of Restore is a desire to inspire hope and release potential in every person who comes into contact with us. Restore's vision is to practically support people experiencing poverty and social isolation, whilst giving space and opportunities for them to encounter Jesus, to be welcomed into community and to be discipled. Over the years, Restore has brought together a large number of social action projects that provide holistic support and care to individuals and families – including rough sleepers, ex-offenders, asylum seekers, street sex workers and people experiencing mental health and/or substance misuse problems. Restore's current projects include eleven foodbanks (which advise clients on getting access to the right support as well as providing emergency food supplies); financial and debt advice; a drop-in café; and Streetwise, our informal church service primarily for people using Restore's services.

Our commitment as a church to justice and restoration has meant that resources are constantly channelled away from the centre towards the places of greatest need in our city. We meet in an old factory building that is never warm enough in winter, but we rejoice that just next door we are able to host a foodbank that feeds 1,200 hungry people each week.

The following table summarises some of the key paradigm shifts and practices that have enabled our church to align ourselves with God's heart for the poor and marginalised in Sheffield and to respond effectively.

---

*   See https://ncsheffield.org/church-life/restore/ for details.

Paradigm Shift	Examples of Practices
We have embraced a downwardly mobile mindset, challenging the assumption that we will all automatically climb the career ladder and live in prosperous neighbourhoods.	• Some people opting for part-time work in order to free up days for part-time ministry among the vulnerable of the city. • Some people living in extended households, sharing resources, doing life, and being on mission together.
We recognise the necessity of an incarnational approach to ministry: a mindset of living among the poor in a reciprocal way; not just ministering *to* the poor but being *with* the poor.	• Rejecting the functional/transactional (client/provider) approach to serving others. • Advocating for an organic, long-term commitment to social transformation, with church members buying houses together in some of the poorest areas of the city. • Listening to (and being a part of) people's stories in a way that is impossible if we weren't living alongside them. • Actively choosing to build relationships with people who are different from us; seeking to avoid a 'them and us' mentality; articulating that whatever our background we can all make a contribution to the life of the church. • Empowering everyone (regardless of socio-economic status) to work towards the restoration of their city. • Making our Sunday services as welcoming and accessible as possible for people from all walks of life. • Walking alongside people and building mutually beneficial relationships.

We understand that we are all missionaries and that within the kingdom of God 'everyone gets to play'. Alongside this our leaders know that their primary role is to empower every member to respond obediently to God's call.	• Letting much of the impetus for new projects come from missional communities, rather than from top-down directives. • Encouraging every member of the church to pay attention to the call of God on their lives, wherever this may lead them.
We have nurtured a heart and vision for the whole city, desiring to see broad social transformation.	• Sharing stories and testimonies, providing an exposure and awareness across the whole church for justice and ministry to the marginalised. • Intentionally using language about our call to the whole city and casting vision about social transformation. • Providing training, infrastructure and resources for seven other Sheffield churches, enabling them to serve their own local communities. • Welcoming volunteers to Restore from 20+ churches. • Working with statutory and charity-sector providers in the city to facilitate best outcomes for people experiencing poverty.
We desire to see and serve the whole person.	• Focusing on building community with the marginalised: not just giving them a meal or providing shelter but seeking to disciple them and help them on a spiritual, physical, emotional, relational level. • Making staffing decisions that enable us to channel resources to the places of greatest need; for example, employing an Iranian pastor to serve the Iranian community in Sheffield.

We understand that church buildings and finances are only a means to an end: the extension of God's kingdom in every part of our city.	• Renting/hiring venues in poorer areas so that missional communities can run children's clubs and activities for those neighbourhoods. • Funding a debt-service that has been available for the whole city for nearly 14 years.

THE STORY OF SHIREGREEN

One of the stories that delightfully encapsulates both dimensions is that of Charlotte Codina and the Shiregreen missional community. In August 2004, Charlotte was in South Africa testing a call to foreign missions when she heard the voice of God calling her back to Sheffield with the words, 'My sheep need a shepherd.' This was a divine invitation to put down roots in Shiregreen, one of the most economically challenged areas of the city. Within ten months, God had miraculously provided the means for Charlotte to buy a house in the area. She moved in with three other young adults and they started building a community *with* and *for* the people of Shiregreen. Over the years this missional community has engaged with those in the neighbourhood in many different ways, following God's leading and responding to the opportunities that have opened up. They have run clubs for children, youth and parents. They have hosted a Tuesday evening meal – open to anyone in the area. They have helped the jobless find work, the addicted break free, and the bereaved grieve well. They have advocated for those who struggle to be heard. They have provided a peaceful, joyful presence in a frequently tumultuous neighbourhood. They have seen hearts mended and relationships restored, as well as people's needs met in very practical ways. Charlotte is now married and has children, and together as a family they invited a homeless man to live with them for three years, enabling him to heal emotionally and find employment. One of this missional community's guiding principles is to 'do what they see the Father doing'** and then immerse everything in prayer. In giving their lives to this one corner of Sheffield, they have seen God's *shalom* manifested in countless ways.

LOOKING AHEAD

As a church we are thankful for how the Spirit has led us in pursuit of both dimensions of prophetic culture. But we are conscious of the need to bring the two ever closer. As we look ahead, we are exploring opportunities for the Vertical to serve the Horizontal – for example, by expanding prayer ministry at our foodbanks. We are training people to hear God for social justice issues, and we've recently started a monthly 'Pray for Justice' meeting. We are excited for every opportunity to conform more faithfully to the model of our perfect Prophet and carry his living word to every corner of our city.

** John 5:19

PART 3

CREATING AUTHENTIC PROPHETIC ENVIRONMENTS

INHABITING THE LAND

We have carefully surveyed the prophetic landscape; we now need to know how to successfully inhabit it. Can we do a better job than the earliest European occupants of the Americas? Can the church community realise the full potential of this remarkable terrain without bringing spiritual damage and disease?

Part 3 is about the practicalities of creating an authentic, Jesus-shaped prophetic culture that can stand alongside an equally thriving apostolic, evangelistic, shepherding and teaching culture. We will start by looking at how, as a church, we can learn to listen and respond well to God's voice, and then consider how every one of us can develop prophetic awareness and practice. In chapter thirteen, we will move from a focus on individuals to a focus on the organisation, considering how we activate and develop prophetic intelligence in the body itself.

11

THE PROPHETIC PROCESS

The Sovereign LORD *has given me a well-instructed tongue, to know the word that sustains the weary. He wakens me morning by morning, wakens my ear to listen like one being instructed. The Sovereign* LORD *has opened my ears; I have not been rebellious, I have not turned away.*

ISAIAH 50:4-5

What's the essence of the American landscape? That is a hard question to answer for two substantial continents. For some, it will be the Amazon rainforest; for others, the prairies, or the vast mountain chains of the Rockies and Andes. For others still it might be a scene captured in one of Ansel Adams' iconic photographs of Yosemite National Park.

Similarly, the exploration of the prophetic landscape reveals an array of glorious and diverse features. But we can find its essence. At its heart, the prophetic is about listening to the voice of God: that fundamental posture of receptivity to God's spoken word.

Of the many wonders of our walk with Jesus, one of the greatest is the fact that God speaks to us. The extent of God's communication is far-reaching. He speaks to saint and sinner alike. He speaks personally to individuals about the smallest detail of their lives, and he speaks on a macro level to society and culture. He speaks words of love, identity and comfort, as well as words of warning, correction and challenge. A fundamental aspect of our spiritual inheritance as Christians is that we can learn to hear and identify the voice of God.

For the prophets of old, called to minister in a context where most people couldn't hear God, 'listening' was an all-consuming experience

– something Jeremiah describes as the 'fire in my bones'.[1] God broke into their world irrevocably, and his word – the *dabar-Yahweh* – took hold of them as an overwhelming awareness of divine presence and purpose. For the church today, in the age of the Spirit, God's spoken word is freely and generously available – the sheep of his flock hear his voice.[2] But in this context of abundance, a new *intentionality* is necessary. The church needs a posture of purposeful listening so that we can experience the full impact of what God is saying to us.

Becoming a church that listens well is partly about developing the capacity of each individual to hear and respond to God, but it is also about learning what it means to listen to God *together*. In a world where there is so much distraction, where we find it so hard to be still and to be present to the moment, how does the prophetic church best position itself to hear?

THE PROPHETIC PROCESS

There is a tendency, certainly in charismatic circles, to focus on the delivery of the prophetic word. We get excited about the prophetic *event*, with the prophet coming and telling us whatever it is that God wants to communicate. But a mature prophetic culture requires something much deeper and much more time-consuming: a *process* in which we take seriously Jesus' instruction to 'consider carefully how you listen' (Luke 8:18); a process in which we both hear and obey.

Within the prophetic process there are three distinct elements of listening to God that are required of us. These are applicable to both the Vertical and Horizontal dimensions.

- *Tuning in:* the initial 'hearing' – recognising and receiving God's voice as he shares his heart and his thoughts with us.
- *Discerning:* working out the essence of what God is saying to us – the full meaning behind the prophetic experience.
- *Responding:* determining the application – what it looks like to walk in obedience, and so translating hearing into action.

A holistic listening culture readily embraces each of these elements. When God communicates with us and his reality breaks into our world, we cannot carry on as if nothing much has happened. Rather we need to see this God-moment as an opportunity to learn and change; to walk more closely with Jesus and be more aligned with his kingdom.

Engaging in the prophetic process enables the church to *listen well*. The fundamental prophetic call on the church is to be carriers of the revelation of God – to faithfully hold out his reality so that transformation of hearts and society can take place. To truly embrace this call, we have to be good listeners.

We must not forget that there is something profoundly intentional about God's speaking. His words are never random or accidental. God always communicates for a reason, even if it is for something as simple (and beautiful) as cheering us up on a bad day. Without attention to the prophetic process, we are in danger of wasting the full transformational potential of his spoken word to us.[3]

To allow this process to have the broadest impact, it is useful to employ specific vocabulary in the Vertical and Horizontal dimensions. The words *revelation, interpretation* and *application* can be applied to the Vertical dimension, whereas *holy discontent, clarity of call* and *accountable action* are more useful phrases in the Horizontal.

Revelation
Interpretation
Application

The Prophetic Process:
• Tuning in
• Discerning
• Responding

Holy Discontent
Clarity of Call
Accountable Action

We will examine how this vocabulary fits as we look at each part of the prophetic process in detail. For each part we will also consider:

- The metaphorical *posture* that best positions our hearts and minds before God.
- What has to be *surrendered* at each stage of the prophetic process. There is a necessary reckoning and surrendering if we are going to listen well, and we have to be ruthless in eliminating any resistance in our hearts to the full impact of God's word. To quote Pope Francis, 'Prophecy is born whenever we allow ourselves to be challenged by God, not when we are concerned to keep everything quiet and under control.'[4]
- *Practical steps* for implementation.

TUNING IN

The essence of *tuning in* is recognising and receiving the communication between God's heart and ours. Sometimes this is as quiet as a gentle whisper, a momentary glimpse, or tug on our heart. Sometimes it's an unmistakeable encounter with the *dabar-Yahweh*. But the language of the Spirit is one we can all learn.

This initial part of the prophetic process can look different depending on whether we are listening in the Vertical or Horizontal dimension. It's important to recognise the range of listening that will take place in a healthy prophetic culture.

Vertical: As shown on the axis diagram on page 167, we can use the word *revelation* to describe the experience of connecting with God vertically: we hear the word, see the vision, dream the dream. In this dimension, prophetic listening is largely focused on personal matters: hearing God for ourselves and others, that we all may be strengthened, encouraged and comforted.[5] Sometimes the revelation is for individuals, or it may be for the whole body. Either way, the revelation is designed to bring transformation to our hearts and minds. The prophetic ministry that Paul writes about in his letters mainly refers to this type of 'personal prophecy'.

Handled in a mature way, this is a powerful and necessary ministry with huge potential for good, both inside and outside the church.

Horizontal: In this dimension it is often more helpful to use the language of *holy discontent* as we connect with God's *pathos* and his concerns for justice and righteousness. God gets our attention by stirring our hearts and inviting us to groan with him over particular issues of injustice. There is a deep sense from God that something is wrong – which may manifest as restlessness in our spirits, or grief or passion – as we choose to look properly at the state of the world in which we live. In this dimension, our listening involves hearing God for society and about how we should live justly. We listen so that we may know how to speak to society, and so that, individually and corporately, we know what action we should be taking.

Posture for Tuning In: Sitting

Being a good listener is a skill. When someone really needs us to hear what they are saying, we are wise to stop whatever else we're doing and give them our full attention. Ideally, we sit down with them over a nice cup of tea (if we're English!) and look directly at them.

We choose to be fully present in the moment.

It's exactly the same when we're listening to God. We can't make God speak, but we can ensure that when he does, we are giving him our undivided attention and are wholly receptive.

Learning to tune in isn't a perfunctory exercise, a technical task or a puzzle to be solved; rather it is one part of our ever-deepening relationship with the Father. There is a danger that we can make hearing God task-based, and solely about guidance; that we will treat his voice as a heavenly GPS, simply there to tell us whether to take a left or right and avoid dead ends. But a posture of sitting reminds us that it's always about loving fellowship – and we tune in best when we are fully present and fully expectant, with our faces turned fully towards God. This is why times of gathered worship are often the best context for the prophetic community to tune in to God's communication.

A posture of sitting helps us remember that to tune in we have to slow right down. It's all too easy to rush through the day and ignore the invitation to pause, to linger, to fully engage with God's heart. Whether he's calling us to sit and grieve with him over a particular injustice or sit and receive his words of love and encouragement, there is a necessary *deceleration* of mind and body that frees us to truly abide with him in the moment of unveiling – the moment of making known. In a posture of sitting, we are choosing to dwell with the holy discontent, rather than rushing to try and fix the problem. In a posture of sitting, we are choosing to dwell with the revelation.

The Process of Surrender as We Tune In

Engaging with God's heart and the full weight of emotions he reveals is often costly. Intentionally choosing to expose our own hearts to God's truth – whether truth about ourselves or truth about the society we live in – is not to be taken lightly. Any indifference or complacency has to be surrendered, along with every ungodly distraction. It's not that God requires us to care about every single issue and injustice (whether personal or societal) with the same level of passion; but he wants us to keep our hearts open and malleable, ready for his word.

As we engage with God's heart, we cannot avoid the need to *lament*. The Western church has a strong tendency towards triumphalism, focusing on problem-solving and quick fixes – often with a bit of denial thrown in. This means we don't take the time to properly consider the suffering world, and instead want to jump as quickly as we can to celebration. Our modern worship songs are overwhelmingly centred on praise and celebration, but if we take the time to study the Psalms, we find that over a third of their content comprises lament.[6]

The prophetic church knows that lament is a doorway into hearing from God. As we surrender our attachments to a triumph-and-success mindset and our tendencies to gloss over grief, we are more able to sit in the place of holy discontent and tune into God's heart for justice and righteousness.

This is a time-consuming process. When we lament, we make space to listen to other people's stories and experiences, to see things from their perspective, to feel the deep anguish of their suffering and struggle

– but it's amazing how clear the voice of Jesus can sound as we listen to these narratives.

Lament involves acknowledging the reality of injustice in our neighbourhoods. The church laments when we profess before God the rawness of the distress and pain that is evident around us. In lament, we allow the anguish to be expressed through words, songs and creative arts – through twenty-first-century psalms – as we meet together.

When we lament, we are enabled to recognise the need for transformation, to name the brokenness or sin, and to have our paradigms shifted. Lament reminds us that God is present in all circumstances, even the most difficult. We can offer our lament to him as a sacrificial and prayerful longing that things would change. And lament is never the final prayer; it's the prayer in the waiting, as we anticipate the new word of hope that is just around the corner.

Practical Steps to Tuning In

Expectancy is a vital component of hearing God's voice. If we expect God to speak to us, then we'll probably hear him; if we don't, then we probably won't. If we're going to develop an effective listening culture, we need a well-developed sense of expectation that God will speak to us if we ask him. As we saw in chapter six, there is plenty we can learn from the charismatics about cultivating such a culture – including a sense that whenever we gather together, God is present and active in our midst and the Spirit of revelation is ready to show up with some incredible truth to share with us.

In order to grow in expectancy, we need to recognise the things that can thwart and frustrate it. Disappointment and fear of failure are two of the usual suspects. We have to persevere in our pursuit of God's voice. Developing expectancy is a daily choice and an attitude to cultivate.

The communal cultivation of expectancy involves intentionally creating space to hear God. Brad Jersak describes such a church culture, centred on tuning in to God:

> As with the disciples in Acts 1, we did a lot of waiting. Most of our
> 'business meetings' still involve extended times of worship, silence and

listening prayer … . We listen together, compare notes and act only when we've reached a consensus about what God has said.[7]

A community that is learning to tune in well will also be asking questions such as:

- How is God getting our attention at the moment?
- What *revelation* and *holy discontent* is emerging out of our times of corporate worship and prayer?
- What are we dreaming about?
- How can we ensure that we are reaching a consensus about what God is saying?

A healthy prophetic community will recognise that different people hear God in different ways, and these are often reflected in our varying personalities and character traits. It will also celebrate the fact that we can hear God speak through many spiritual disciplines and practices, rather than one-size-fits-all. For some of us it's the quiet of an empty room; for some it's in the middle of a worship service; for some it's surrounded by nature; for some it's when handing out bags of groceries at the food bank.

DISCERNING

'What on earth do you mean by that?' Have you ever asked that of God?

Discerning is vital and cannot be rushed. Unfortunately, it is usually the part of the prophetic process where most mistakes are made. Often the church has been far too casual in its handling of the prophetic. Divine words designed to heal our cities have slipped through our fingers. Misconstrued prophecies have damaged precious lives. We need to be much more careful in how we bring clarity and understanding to the spoken words of God.

Discerning is where we work out the full meaning of what God is saying to us: the part where we decode and interpret divine communication. And the more we can see this as a *communal* process, the better.

The first step (and one very closely connected to tuning in) is to *discern the source* of the revelation or holy discontent. There are many voices out there, and we need the gift of discernment to recognise God's voice in the midst of our own thoughts, internal chatter and imagination; to be able to separate out God's voice from any demonic interference or deception.

Paul makes this clear in his instruction to the Thessalonians: 'Do not treat prophecies with contempt but test them all; hold onto what is good' (1 Thessalonians 5:20–21). To do this, we need to learn the characteristics of God's voice so that we can distinguish it from all other voices. God's voice always reflects his nature and character, so we need to *listen for the voice that is kind, loving and full of life.*

When I hear God speak to me, the depth of what he says often awes me. His communication is more radical, more pure, more profound than anything I could come up with. And I've learnt to discern through a Jesus-shaped lens, asking, 'Does this look and sound like Jesus?' There is something about the voice of Jesus that is unlike any other. He manages to be tender and challenging at the same time. The more we know him, the more we can recognise his voice. Jesus, as the ultimate and complete Word of God, is the Word through which we discern all other words.

The prophetic community is where this ability to recognise the voice of Jesus is carefully cultivated and where we see people learn good practices in testing prophecy. We test prophecy by checking to see if it

- lines up with Scripture
- ultimately 'strengthens, encourages, and comforts' (1 Corinthians 14:3)
- resonates and brings an awareness of God's presence with it
- finds confirmation in our community of faith
- has a fruitful impact on ourselves and the people around us

Once we are confident that it is God's voice we are hearing, we can seek clarity on the true meaning and full measure of his communication. We are aiming for an elucidation that is crystal clear and razor sharp, so that we can be confident in the specifics of what God is saying to us. This is the very necessary step of translating the 'raw data' into something we fully understand.

In the *Vertical dimension,* this is about accurately *interpreting* the revelation, so that we know how to respond to it. Most problems or controversy associated with prophetic ministry are not because of weak revelation, but because of wrong interpretation. It's all too easy to jump to conclusions and read our own interpretations into what we hear from God.

It's important to recognise that Spirit-breathed revelation is often symbolic. Sometimes prophecy is quite strange and mysterious, and we make assumptions about the meaning of certain images or words. A few years ago, I was listening to God for a prophetic word for a church I was to visit, and God spoke to me through a vision of a rainbow. My initial assumption was that God's word for this church must be 'hope' (in Christian culture we generally associate rainbows with hope or promise), but, as I took the time to seek God for the meaning of this image, I sensed a different message, one that I would have missed had I gone for the most obvious interpretation.

In the *Horizontal dimension,* discerning is about taking the holy discontent and allowing the Spirit to birth a *clarity of call* – so we are clear about what our God-ordained responsibility looks like. As we consider the world around us, and the endemic injustices in every direction, it's easy to get overwhelmed. The need is so great that we can struggle to focus on the one issue that God is highlighting for us. It's important for every Christian and every church to get a clear sense of what God is *specifically* saying to them about social justice. We need the freedom to engage deeply with that one thing rather than pursuing a shallow engagement with lots of things. Without God's specific word, we can end up in a flurry of anxious activity that never leads to lasting change. Individually and corporately, we need a clarity of call: 'Lord, amid all this pain, brokenness and misalignment with your kingdom, what are you calling us to do? What's our responsibility?'

It is helpful here to remember the *twofold listening for social justice* first mentioned in chapter eight. We need clarity about both our message to society and the specifics of what the church should be doing.

The Prophetic Call to Social Justice

Hearing God and speaking prophetically:

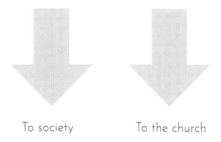

To society   To the church

Perhaps, for example, your church already knows that God is stirring your hearts about the issue of homelessness in your city. You are aware of a holy discontent deep in your spirits, and you are already lamenting over every homeless person on the streets. As a community, you sense you are starting to feel a fraction of what the Father feels as his heart breaks over the misery caused by this issue. You are tuning in well! But what on earth can you do about it? The danger is that this is as far as it goes – you get stuck at holy discontent, or the church responds out of its own strength and understanding instead of waiting on God for his perfect plan. But imagine the kingdom potential if you came together and sought God for a crystal-clear call. Imagine what could happen for the homeless people in your city if you could translate your communal holy discontent into some Spirit-breathed, Jesus-shaped specifics – a clarifying call that encompasses:

- how you should speak prophetically to your city – challenging the status quo so that the root causes of homelessness start to get addressed
- what you should do, practically, to help every homeless person

This twofold discernment process brings clarity about the tangible next step, not just the big picture.

In both dimensions, we need to engage with God's *hope*: hope that God is able to carry out his word and bring the desired transformation;

hope that the promise we are discerning will birth new life. Such hope will energise us and lead us forward to fulfilment.

The Posture for Discerning: Standing

The prophet Jeremiah provides us with the captivating imagery of standing in the council of the Lord. There is something about the concept of standing attentively in God's presence, as we actively wait on him, which helps us properly engage with discernment.

Verses 9–40 of Jeremiah 23 make up a long passage in which false prophets are denounced. And in the midst of this we find verse 18:

> But which of them has stood in the council of the LORD to see or to hear his word? Who has listened and heard his word?

The Hebrew word translated here as 'council' is *sôd*. It's a word that occurs about twenty times in the Old Testament and carries with it the sense of intimacy among a group of people as they share secrets and plans.

Jeremiah makes it clear that no false prophets – those motivated by their own agendas – are permitted to stand in this holy and sacred space. But as members of the prophetic church of Jesus, we can have confidence that we are welcomed in. If we humbly seek after God's heart, we will be taken into his confidence and gain the discernment needed.

This posture of standing attentively before God also reminds us of the importance of *co-discerning* – finding confirmation in the body. The discerning part of the prophetic process is much more effective when we do it together, seeking consensus. We need the input of other people to perceive the full weight and depth of God's word to us – to get a multi-dimensional translation of the prophetic experience into something we clearly understand.

The Process of Surrender as We Discern

Though we are welcomed into the council of the Lord, it is a place where we must ruthlessly lay down our agendas. Before we make any determinations about the meaning of the words we've received from God, we need to enquire of him. And to actively enquire of the Lord requires surrendering all our own reasoning and emptying ourselves of anything that hinders or distorts the godly clarity we're seeking.

It is incredibly easy for our own opinions, perceptions and motives to interfere with the process of discerning, which is why this middle part of the prophetic process is often so hard to navigate. There is a danger of filtering or reshaping the message so that it suits us better. We have to recognise a deep-rooted tendency to want God's word to fit neatly into our world and our priorities; or to put human limitations on its vast possibilities. We need to surrender our own agenda and instead be open to the full measure of his truth.

At its heart, the biblical principle of enquiring of the Lord is about submission. It challenges us to examine our heart posture towards God: our motivations, our focus and our priorities. It requires us to ask ourselves who really is on the throne of our lives.

Practical Steps to Discerning

Those of us with a more activist temperament would rather jump straight from 'tuning in' to 'response'. But the mature prophetic community does all it can to help facilitate the crucial 'discerning' part of the process by creating adequate space and time to bottom out the interpretation and clarity of call. We cannot rush this part of the prophetic process.

As we seek greater clarity, it's important to ask good questions, such as:

- Why has God brought this word to us at this time?
- What are his purposes?
- How does God want to expand our thinking with new truth?
- How does this word speak to our covenant identity and our kingdom responsibility?
- What's the invitation in this word? What's the challenge? How can we ensure we respond well to both?
- What Scripture is relevant?
- What needs to change in us so that we can see the fulfilment of this word?
- What *interpretation* or *clarity of call* is emerging as we reflect together?

The discerning of prophecy is a skill we can all grow in, being confident that the Holy Spirit will faithfully lead us. It's good to remember that we don't have to work everything out by ourselves. We are aiming for a healthy culture of discernment where everyone is confident in their ability to unpack, clarify and interpret God's spoken words to us. Whenever we receive something from the Lord, we shouldn't be afraid to ask him exactly what he means by it.

RESPONDING

Finally, we must respond to what God says to us. In the Gospels we see that Jesus expects his followers to embrace a lifestyle of hearing *and* responding. He endorses those who, with perseverance, allow his words to produce 'a crop' (Luke 8:15). We need to understand true listening as encompassing the whole of the prophetic process.

Unfortunately, *obedience* is often the missing piece in prophetic culture and ministry. There can be a lack of emphasis on the practicalities of our response. In fact, many prophets spend disproportionally little time *doing* compared to the time they spend *hearing*.

As we consider how to remedy this and translate hearing into action, we find ourselves at the place where the *prophetic intersects with discipleship*. In many ways this intersection is at the heart of our relationship with Jesus because, as Christians, we know that the call on our lives is not just to believe in Jesus but to also follow him as disciples. And we can only consistently and effectively follow him if we learn to recognise his voice and then respond with obedience. The following two questions illuminate the fundamental process of discipleship that Jesus presents to us time and again in the Gospels:

- What is God saying to us?
- What are we going to do about it?

These questions are the essence of Jesus' challenge at the end of the Sermon on the Mount: 'Therefore everyone who hears these words of mine and puts them into practice is like a wise man who built his house on the rock' (Matthew 7:24).

It's not enough to simply hear Jesus' words; we also need to align our lives with them. A. W. Tozer reminds us of the danger of a lack of obedience: 'To expose our hearts to truth and consistently refuse or neglect to obey the impulses it arouses is to stymie the motions of life within us and, if persisted in, to grieve the Holy Spirit into silence.'[8]

We can have the most incredible 3D technicolour visions, encounter angels and hear the audible voice of God. However, if we don't *respond* – if we don't allow God's voice to change us and change the world around us – we are like the foolish man who built his house on the sand.[9] We need to be active responders to his revelation.

The Posture for Responding: Walking

We've sat with God and encountered his living word to us; we've stood in his council, carefully attending to the meaning of the message and reflecting deeply on its implications. We now need to walk in obedience to it.

The posture of walking helps the church remember that the prophetic is rarely a quick fix. Fully walking out the word can take time – sometimes years – as we follow Jesus and keep in step with his Spirit, not rushing ahead or lagging behind.

When God speaks into our lives, he wants us to work *with him* to make his words become reality. We could easily think, *well, if it's God, it'll happen* – especially if the word has something to do with God's call on our lives. Prophecies can be amazing offers from God, but are not absolutes, and we need to consider our responsibility to respond to them in faith. We have to learn to cooperate with God to see the outworking and fulfilment of his words to us.

The imagery of walking also reminds us that we respond best to the prophetic when we are travelling together with others – being accountable and well-rooted in community, finding the common pace that will sustain us for the journey.

Different Types of Response

As we seek to walk in obedience, it is helpful to consider the different types of prophetic words we receive. Different types of words from God require different responses:

- *Covenant* words (words of love and affirmation that speak to our identity as God's children) will probably invoke a more *internal* response. These are words that change our inner world, either individually or communally.
- *Kingdom* words (words of calling, purpose and direction) will probably invoke a more *external* response. These are words designed to change our outer world.

Similarly, we can consider the difference between the Vertical and Horizontal dimensions:

- *Vertical* words (words that are wholly focused on God and his presence and heart) will cause us to ask, 'What is the *application* of the revelation that God has brought to us? What change do we make to our lives?'
- *Horizontal* words (words that focus on the social sphere) will cause us to ask, 'What *accountable action* does God require of us? What change do we make to society?'

The Process of Surrender as We Respond

Partnering with God in order to see the fulfilment and fruit he intends will often require radical obedience and perseverance – a long obedience in the same direction.[10] It's worth recognising that once the initial thrill of receiving a word from God fades, we can easily forget our commitment to keep aligned to it.

It's also worth reflecting on how both passivity and a consumer culture can derail us.

Passivity is a potential danger for many prophets, especially in the Vertical dimension. Some hear God easily and receive plenty of revelation, but don't have the discipline of an active and concrete response. To overcome this tendency, they need to count the cost of externalising revelation and embrace accountability. In fact, for all of us, a vital element of listening to God is finding at least one person who will hold us accountable to doing whatever it is that God is calling us to.

In a *consumer culture* the foremost question is, 'What can we get out of it?' So much of the Western church culture is built around satisfying consumers and keeping people happy. We make church life as attractional as possible – which is odd, considering Jesus tells us to take up our cross and follow him. A healthy prophetic culture won't mesh well with a consumer culture. To respond effectively, we have to dismantle the stronghold of consumerism and focus on being disciples. We have to count the cost of obediently following after Jesus.

There are strongholds of passivity and consumerism in many of our churches. Both need naming and repenting of, surrendering any allegiance we may have to them.

One more thing to consider is the need to surrender to the wisdom of the whole body, especially the impetus of the apostles in our midst. Apostles love action and are brilliant at keeping the community moving forward. When the apostolic and prophetic functions are working well together, there is an equilibrium of hearing *and* doing in the church.

Practical Steps to Responding

As I've coached many individuals, churches and organisations over the years, one thing I've noticed is that the ones who are prepared to make *concrete, specific and accountable plans* in response to God's voice are usually the ones who step into the greatest levels of transformation and kingdom impact. When God speaks to us – whether he is speaking deeply into our identity or showing the church how to tackle racial inequality in our city or anything in-between – we need a plan. True discipleship is more than a theoretical acknowledgement of the truth of what God is saying, or vague notions of how we might chew over his words to us. We need to learn to respond intentionally and wholeheartedly every time God speaks into our lives.

Asking good questions will lead to good plans and Holy-Spirit-led action:

- How are we going to nourish the word of life and hope that God has planted in our hearts?
- Can we clearly articulate the right *application* or *accountable action*?

- How do we step into our response in a very practical way over the next few days and weeks?
- What is going to help us overcome any roadblocks?
- Who are we going to be accountable to?
- How are we going to pray on a regular basis for the fulfilment of this word?

Again, the time gap between God's initial word to us and the complete fulfilment could be anything from a few seconds to decades. If we're walking through town and God tells us to 'Give that homeless person your sandwich,' the response will be immediate, and the whole prophetic process will be over very quickly. However, a calling to eradicate homelessness from our city is something that might take a lifetime.

ZERO RESISTANCE

An authentic prophetic culture is one where we have learnt to listen well, both as individuals and as a community. We can summarise the prophetic process using the following diagram:

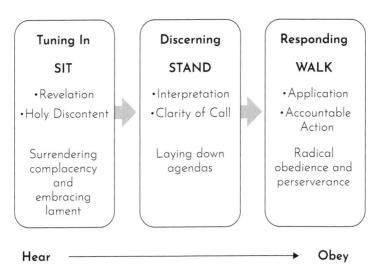

Isaiah 50:4–5 gives us a beautiful picture of the Sovereign Lord awakening the prophet's ears. Isaiah's heart is open, and he is fully committed

to the listening process: 'I have not been rebellious, I have not turned away.' Here there is zero resistance to Yahweh's words.

God's voice initiates God's intended transformation. If we want to follow in Isaiah's footsteps, we have to consider two questions:

- Do we really want to change?
- Do we really want to see the world around us change?

Hearts that are open and committed to God's transformation are hearts that can readily hear his voice. A listening culture is a place where we gladly welcome God's reality, with all its glorious disruptiveness, to come and break into our world and turn us all upside-down.

Heaven is not lacking in transformational power. Change is possible if we take Jesus seriously and learn to become good listeners. We are all made for this – to encounter his living word in the place of perfect love and then be transformed by it.

The mature prophetic community is able to give people an imagination for something better, and then give them the tools to work with the iridescent words that stream unceasingly from the mouth of the Lord. This is how the prophetic church aligns its life with God's heart and intention and speaks into culture, society and the world.

12

PROPHETIC INTELLIGENCE
FOR EVERYONE

I wish that all the LORD's *people were prophets and that the* LORD
would put his Spirit on them!

NUMBERS 11:29

Imagine a church community where a significant percentage of the people
were mature prophets, humbly serving the body to the best of their ability –
taking all the wonderful prophetic intelligence that has been described so far
in this book and applying it skilfully and effectively. Imagine what that would
do for the worship and prayer life of this particular church if one fifth of the
members were fully functioning, Jesus-shaped, Spirit-empowered prophets.
Imagine what it would do for this church's witness in the neighbourhood, as
injustices come crashing down and the marginalised are given a voice. And
then imagine what it would be like if the other four fifths were learning how
to do the things that prophets do.

Every church community, of course, consists of both fivefold prophets and non-prophets. In a church with a mature prophetic culture, *both*
groups of people are growing in prophetic awareness and practice, alongside awareness and practice in the other four functions. Learning how to
think and act like a prophet is one important aspect of everyone's apprenticeship to Jesus.

The focus in this chapter is on how we can all develop our *individual
prophetic capacity*. Some of the content will be particularly relevant to
church leaders, some to fivefold prophets and some to non-prophets. For
all of us, the aim is to contribute towards a community where:

- We welcome the unique role of prophets.
- We know who our prophets are.
- Our prophets are being discipled into mature, Jesus-shaped expressions of the role, so that they can thrive in their calling and serve the church.
- Our prophets are also being discipled into the other four roles (apostle, evangelist, shepherd, teacher), so that they become well-rounded followers of Christ.
- The rest of us are learning prophetic thinking and practice from our prophets.

In chapter four we looked in detail at the wiring and role of fivefold prophets. We can now consider the practicalities of maximising the impact of their role in the body of Christ, exploring each of the points highlighted above.

WELCOMING PROPHETS

In order to develop a thriving prophetic community, we need happy, thriving prophets – individuals who are modelling the prophetic function with grace and maturity, teaching others how to hear God and helping the whole church maintain a passion for justice. We must enable fivefold prophets to flourish in our churches and organisations so that they can use their God-given gifts and talents to equip the whole body to become more Christlike. It's possible for *every* church to do this.

As a reminder, mature prophets are very good at:

- keeping everyone's attention on God
- helping maintain the spiritual health of the body
- speaking covenant identity into people's lives
- strengthening a culture of worship and prayer
- developing a growing community awareness of God's presence and voice
- listening to God on behalf of the community so that we can all keep aligned with God's heart and purposes

- ensuring the downtrodden are protected
- protecting the community from encroaching evil
- cultivating an alternative consciousness
- preparing the church for what God is about to do

As with each of the fivefold roles, it's important to recognise that we're impoverished without persons serving in a prophetic role. Prophets are mission critical. If the prophets are absent, the church is substantially less equipped to fulfil its calling. It's therefore imperative that the prophets' potential for good is fully unleashed upon the church and world.

Eugene Peterson reminds us of the role of prophets in keeping our faith holy and unpolluted:

> The biblical prophets continue to be the most powerful and effective voices ever heard on this earth for keeping religion honest, humble, and compassionate. Prophets sniff out injustice, especially injustice that is dressed up in religious garb. They sniff it out a mile away. Prophets see through hypocrisy, especially hypocrisy that assumes a religious pose. Prophets are not impressed by position or power or authority. They aren't taken in by numbers, size, or the appearance of success ... . A spiritual life that doesn't give a large place to prophet-articulated justice will end up making us worse instead of better, separating us from God's ways instead of drawing us into them.[1]

We need the prophets' unique wisdom, experience, perspective and passion. Our relationship with them is fundamental to defining and shaping the church.

IDENTIFYING PROPHETS

It is vital that those of us in church leadership know who our prophets are, so that we can then disciple and deploy them effectively. But identifying prophets can be surprisingly challenging because many have no clue that they are, in fact, prophets. Those brought up in a church culture where the only association with 'prophet' is the Old Testament stereotype may be reluctant to claim that role. We must be clear in our message that Jesus has given prophets to his church and that it is a legitimate calling for people today. It is also important to communicate that being a prophet does not equate to being weird, wacky or socially awkward.

In addition, we need to develop fivefold understanding and practice throughout the church or organisation, giving people the necessary teaching and vocabulary to properly explore the biblical concepts in Ephesians 4. As people start to get in touch with their own sense of purpose and calling, we can then see who identifies with the role of the prophet.

There are a number of good online surveys that can help individuals get a clearer sense of their fivefold calling. But in my experience the best thing we can do is to facilitate informed discussion and communal discerning. Working out our personal fivefold calling should be a dynamic group process.[2] We can only truly know ourselves in relation to others, in community.

To process this well, it is important to ensure that everyone understands the definitions of each of the fivefold functions and callings – especially what makes each one distinct from the other four, in terms of purpose, competencies, motivation and insights. We need to make sure that, when it comes to 'prophet', we are describing the role using both the Vertical and Horizontal dimensions – and that we don't equate the *gift* of prophecy with the *role*. Remember that the prophetic calling is fundamentally about how someone is wired rather than how often they deliver prophecies.

One useful tool to mention here is the Personal APEST Portrait,[3] which helps each individual develop a profile of their particular fivefold calling by setting out each of the five roles in descending order. This tool provides the unique shape of a person's gifting and calling, which can then be usefully discussed in a group setting.

The beauty of the Personal APEST Portrait is that it not only helps us identify our primary calling but also reminds us that we have differing levels of giftedness across all five callings and that we should develop a basic level of competency in each ministry.

This tool is simple to use. It allows each person to first reflect on which calling is primary or dominant (the one that comes most naturally); then to consider their secondary calling. Each person fills out the diagram below with primary fivefold gifting in the largest circle, secondary in the next largest, and so on.

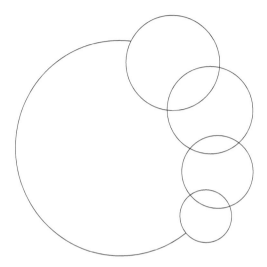

Once individuals have filled in their APEST Portrait, it can be shared – along with their stories, experiences and sense of calling – with a group. Other members of the group then reflect together and give feedback, with an openness to any necessary adjustments. Other people often see strengths and gifts in us that we are not aware of, so it's important that we allow the whole body to help us properly discern our God-given influence and role.

Whatever tool or method is used, the process of working out personal calling is one that cannot be rushed. In my experience it sometimes takes people a long time to settle confidently on the fivefold calling that most resonates for them.

Whereas the roles of teachers, shepherds and evangelists are well understood across most of the contemporary church, many people have had very little teaching and experience of the prophetic and apostolic roles, so it can sometimes take prophets and apostles longer to get to grips with and embrace their callings. This is particularly true of workplace prophets – people whose primary sphere of prophetic influence is the work environment rather than the church. Theirs is a vital calling, but few of them have been given the framework to properly make sense of it.

Whatever tools and processes we use, the aim, as far as the prophetic community is concerned, is to help our prophets self-identify and for the whole church to affirm them in that role.

THRIVING AS A FIVEFOLD PROPHET

If you identify as a fivefold prophet, how can you best flourish in your role? How can you 'prophet' well?

Despite the bad press prophets often get, I know from first-hand experience that if a person finds a church community that welcomes and celebrates prophets, and if they can pursue a humble, servant-hearted outworking of the role, they will be able to fully embrace and thrive in this wonderful calling. And even if individuals are part of a church that doesn't yet understand the prophetic role, they can still find ways to bless and serve the community and walk faithfully with Jesus into maturity.

Because the calling to prophetic ministry is a precious gift from Jesus, it's important to be good stewards of the role. Jesus, by his grace, has given us our particular calling, but it is our responsibility to cultivate it rather than shy away from it. We must grow the gift he has given us, choosing to live according to how God has shaped us, aligned with his purposes for our lives. And one of the most important ways to cultivate this calling is to learn how to thrive in it, not just survive.

To thrive is to be emotionally healthy and spiritually enriched: to prosper, to flourish, to bloom. To thrive is to find the deep joy and satisfaction that comes from knowing how Jesus has perfectly shaped us in his wisdom, so that we can reflect back to him and the world this particular facet of his beauty and glory.

To thrive as a prophet is not to ignore or minimise the costly nature of one's call. There are inherent challenges for each of the fivefold roles, and sooner or later every prophet will come face to face with the particular weight of the prophetic burden. No prophet can escape from the *pathos* of God – that fundamental experience of participation in the feelings of God. How the prophet navigates his or her way through divine anger and anguish will determine whether he or she can still flourish. Prophets also need to learn how to deal with the devastating indifference to evil and injustice that they perceive in so much of humanity. Though their hearts are breaking, and they are acutely aware that God is asking them to act, it may seem as if no one shares their urgency. The question is how to walk this tightrope gracefully – how to avoid being judgemental, how to maintain a soft heart towards the church and the world, and how to keep listening faithfully.

I've learnt that prophets will be better able to carry this burden if they can prioritise discipleship to Jesus, shaping their lives according to his pattern of life and ministry as seen in the Gospels. Prophets need to learn the simplicity of listening as he listened and loving as he loved.

To truly thrive as a prophet, we must learn how to centre our lives around Presence and Justice, the binary star system that all prophetic ministry orbits. We have to slow down sufficiently and carve out ample space so that these two critical themes become our primary focus – our 'essentials'. This is what we are wired to be and to do. We minimise, simplify, prune, disentangle and streamline so that we can maintain a deep hunger for the presence of God and for the establishment of his justice on the earth.

How you do this will be unique to you and will need to be worked out before God with the help of his Spirit. It will look different depending on whether you are a single parent, in full-time education, retired or working two jobs. Your current life stage, personality type and relationship status will all influence the process. But ultimately it is about being apprenticed in the way of Jesus and discovering how he lived out Presence and Justice when he walked this earth.

Many fivefold prophets are unable to fulfil their calling and fail to thrive because they are too hurried and too busy – their lives are too full of 'stuff'. Jesus was never rushed or hurried. He had plenty of time for love, joy and peace. He had plenty of space for Presence and Justice.

Let's consider how this simplification – this holy decluttering – gets worked out in the different dimensions of the life of a disciple.

Intentional Rhythms

The mature Jesus-shaped prophet is one who has developed the necessary patterns, rhythms and habits to grow an ever-deeper relationship with God. Three particular disciplines are worth highlighting:

The discipline of encounter. Mature prophets seek the Father's presence throughout the day, week and year, as they build sustainable patterns into their lives where they can pause, reconnect and listen to his heart. We need to find the habits that create space to *be* – patterns of prayer and worship, of retreat and abiding – that let us hear for ourselves God's words of covenantal love and affirmation. These habits develop in us the heightened awareness that God is always close, present and at work, and that we are continually surrounded by the reality of his light and love.

The discipline of joy. This may sound like a contradiction in terms (at least for those of us who don't like discipline), but there is a clear biblical call to give thanks and be glad, and to orient our spiritual disciplines around the very goodness of God. The prophetic call to lament goes hand in hand with the prophetic call to rejoice. Dallas Willard, in *The Divine Conspiracy*, reminds us that 'God leads a very interesting life and … he is full of joy. Undoubtedly he is the most joyous being in the universe.'[4] In choosing the daily discipline of joy, we are actively becoming more Christlike, reflecting the Father's nature back onto the world as a huge prophetic statement. Jesus makes it clear that his followers will be marked by great joy.[5] Of course, the greatest source of our joy is God's spectacular goodness. The Westminster Catechism gets it right when it states, 'Man's chief end is to glorify God and enjoy him forever.'[6] A key element of how we glorify God is *by* enjoying him. In the face of just how astoundingly glorious he is, if we're not enjoying him, then we are somehow denying or playing down the reality of his nature.

We need to be people who learn how to enjoy God audaciously and relentlessly in the midst of the storms of life. No matter what is going on, he is good, and he is here to be enjoyed. This is so important that Paul makes a point of repeating his exhortation: 'Rejoice in the Lord always. I will say it again: rejoice!' (Philippians 4:4).

The discipline of fullness. The Holy Spirit – sent to us to be our constant friend and companion – is our endless source of peace, power, revelation and wisdom. He is God's very own life shared with us and residing within us, and he is given to us *without limit*.[7] The ongoing command to be 'filled with the Spirit' (Ephesians 5:18) – is consistent with the Father's delight in pouring the Spirit on his covenant people. There is no rationing, no half-measures; we can be filled to the very brim. But this is only possible with a surrendered heart and a willingness to receive. The discipline of fullness is about surrendering our will to him, emptying ourselves, knowing that as we give him our whole selves, he will come and fill us with his glory and presence. We may be jars of clay, but we are made to carry the all-surpassing power of God![8] We are made to be receptacles of his glory, his love, his compassion … his very presence. All he wants is a place to inhabit: an empty vessel, a surrendered soul.

Community

From the simplicity of an ever-deepening relationship with God flows the grace to love the church and to be rooted in community. The healthiest place from which to focus on Presence and Justice is our own church fellowship, with its provision of accountability and prayerful support.

Unfortunately, the local church is often a place of tension for prophets. The way we are wired to challenge the status quo and to see things differently can make church life uncomfortable at times; but when we look at the New Testament model of prophecy, we see that its true home is a healthy, thriving community of God's people. Indeed, according to Ephesians 4, the equipping and maturing of the church is the *point* of prophetic ministry. Community is a crucial lens through which we must view the prophetic experience. It may be uncomfortable, but we have to find a way to make it work.

To thrive as a prophet means loving – truly loving – the church. It means choosing to be embedded at the heart of the community rather than being a critical voice at the edge; choosing to overcome any tendencies towards cynicism. We would do well to observe that, 'Cynics are not prophets. Prophets stand within the community and speak from broken-hearted love. Cynics just stand outside and throw rocks.'[9]

The isolated prophet, disconnected from Christian community, is a dangerous prophet. A historical lack of understanding about their role has led to many prophets either being marginalised and rejected or heavily controlled by church leaders. As a result, they end up a long way from healthy Christian fellowship and accountable relationships, in a place of brokenness, rebellion and judgementalism towards the church. We all have to work hard at overcoming misunderstandings and mistrust and breaking the negative patterns of rejection and isolation. We must prioritise a culture where the ministry of prophets is understood, validated and normalised, and every fivefold prophet has to be intentional about being rooted and grounded in a life-giving community.

Prophets have to find their voice and win permission to speak. Good communication skills are vital. The mature prophet learns to communicate in ways that are less forthright than they might naturally prefer – speaking gently and humbly, perhaps through the medium of poetry or the arts. Prophets must also learn to deal maturely with any frustration or urgency. There is a place for righteous anger, but there is also room for the gentle, graceful word that people will pay attention to.

There is a beautiful simplicity that comes as we choose to be 'speakers of life' within our churches, focused on communicating the goodness of God, and doing so in a manner that people will listen to. We can engage well with both *pathos* and hope, with both critique and love. But ultimately, we want to be people who speak life to the church and the world.

The mature prophet loves the church by cultivating a heart to serve, being a good steward of their prophetic gifts, using every opportunity to strengthen, encourage and comfort their brothers and sisters. The mature prophet loves the church, works well with the other fivefold ministries, learns to minister in a fivefold context, and leverages their strengths for the benefit of the other four.

Love for the World

Prophetic spirituality – far from detachment or retreat from the problems of this world – is having the ears to hear the cry of the lost and the poor. It is a critical awareness of the social and political realities that frame our lives and shape our neighbourhoods. It is the intentionality to perceive the world from God's perspective and to view it through his loving eyes.

When we look closely at the life of Jesus, we see that he shared his time between three relationships: with his heavenly Father; with his close friends and followers; and with the broken, hurting world around him. This is a pattern we too need to follow if we're going to lead fruitful, balanced lives. For many prophets (especially the introverted ones), the idea of engaging missionally and prophetically with the world is challenging. We would rather hunker down in the safety of our prayer closets or in the company of our nice Christian friends. But there is a world out there that is desperate for God's reality, and the mature prophet is someone who is faithful in revealing the true nature of God to those who don't yet know Jesus.

To genuinely thrive as a prophet, we need to maintain a healthy outward dimension to our lives and ministry, keeping in step with the Spirit as we discern the harvest fields and remain on the lookout for people of peace.[10] There is much we can learn from the evangelists – those great social connectors, with their gifts for communicating the good news persuasively. Every prophet needs to have at least one evangelist in his or her close network of friends; someone who can challenge and provoke us towards a greater missional engagement.

It is very easy for prophets to judge the world instead of loving it. We can be overtaken by rage against the unrelenting darkness that we are so sensitive to, to the endemic evil that our eyes are drawn to time and again. The words of Hosea make perfect sense to us: 'There is no faithfulness, no love, no acknowledgment of God in the land. There is only cursing, lying and murder, stealing and adultery; they break all bounds, and bloodshed follows bloodshed' (Hosea 4:1–2).

The world may be a very dark place at times, but we are to be people of radical love and mercy, who are able to turn judgement into reconciliation in the light of the cross and offer hope instead of condemnation. Loving the world may mean we lament with Jesus over the brokenness, but it also means a willingness to listen for his words of restoration and to help create a community of radical welcome and healing.

Simplifying our lives around Presence and Justice will enable us to keep one foot planted firmly in the world. We can pray for our cities. We can walk the streets and look around through the eyes of Jesus. We can stay abreast of current events. We can read the newspapers while sitting with the Father. Let us be people who nurture a deep love for whatever corner of the globe God in his wisdom has placed us in; people who slow down sufficiently to notice, to care and to be part of mending whatever is broken.

EMBRACING YOUR GIFT MIX

One particular element of learning to thrive as a prophet is to recognise that there are many different expressions of the role. Prophets come in all different shapes and sizes. Studying the lives of the biblical prophets indicates a rich variety of personalities and ministry styles. We can appreciate their different voices and differing concerns without losing sight of their overarching call to the prophetic role. When it comes to fivefold prophets today, there is an equally rich distribution of styles and emphases.

Many prophets will have a particular leaning towards either the Vertical dimension or Horizontal dimension, with the Vertical prophet being more drawn to the message of covenant faithfulness and the Horizontal prophet more concerned with the message of social justice. As long as we are mindful of the need for balance between the two dimensions, and don't end up siloed in one camp or the other, we can accept the particular direction we lean and where our core passions lie.

We can also consider how our primary calling to the prophetic sits alongside our other fivefold preferences, especially our secondary calling. This is where the Personal APEST Portrait comes in handy. Using APEST lettering, we can describe these four sub-sets of prophets:

- **PAs**: prophets with an *apostolic* bent, who love to pioneer and start new projects.
- **PEs**: prophets with a passion for *evangelism*, who love sharing the good news with others.
- **PSs**: prophets who love using their prophetic gifts to *pastor* and care for people.
- **PTs**: prophets who are strong in biblical wisdom and understanding, and who are gifted in *teaching* others about prophecy.

Knowing and appreciating our own particular gift-mix can go a long way towards ensuring that we have clarity, focus and fulfilment regarding our specific role and purpose in the kingdom of God.

FIVEFOLD DEVELOPMENT

I want to reiterate that holistic fivefold development is for everyone. A key aspect of maturity for any disciple of Jesus comes through not only welcoming our own particular fivefold calling but also allowing ourselves to be refined and formed by the other four roles – growing our *whole* fivefold awareness and aptitude. Because each fivefold gift is an expression of Jesus, we all should be seeking to attain a level of maturity across all five ministries, especially those we are weakest in.

Regardless of what our personal fivefold gifting is, each of us needs to be

- developing in our own fivefold role and calling (for example, apostles learning how to be better apostles)
- equipping others in our own role (for example, teachers helping non-teachers grow in their teaching ability)
- maturing in the other four (for example, shepherds growing in evangelistic understanding and aptitude)

There is a twofold benefit to developing our 'other four'. First, *we become mature, well-rounded disciples* who look more like Jesus. Teachers need to know how to evangelise; shepherds need to know how to strategise. As we explored in chapter two, the Son of God functioned perfectly in all five. Character and maturity are developed by being prepared to move away from our natural strengths and preferences and being stretched into areas where we feel a little uncomfortable. Second, *our main calling is strengthened*. If, for example, your primary fivefold calling is that of an evangelist – that's wonderful! But think how much your evangelist's ministry would be enhanced by walking with prophets for a season and being discipled by them into a deeper prophetic aptitude and ministry. Prophetic gifts are powerful tools in the hands of evangelists as they share their faith and connect with those outside the church.

By intentionally experiencing and developing all five roles – these five ministries that are perfected in the life of Christ – we will grow more into his likeness and be well equipped to extend his kingdom.

I'm a fivefold prophet, but I've spent years working alongside apostles. I have been discipled in apostolic thinking and practice and am deeply appreciative of their unique contribution to the body of Christ. Crucially, my time with apostles has made my prophetic ministry much more effective because I've learnt to bring an active *application* to the prophetic – sharpening and refining prophetic vision so that it can become a reality; turning all my lovely, fluffy prophetic dreams into something concrete and useful.

The mature prophetic community is a place where our prophets are being discipled in the other four roles. We need to create a culture where it is easy for prophets to come alongside and learn from the apostles, evangelists, shepherds and teachers. The last thing we want is a holy huddle of prophets who can only usefully function inside the prophetic bubble and have no idea how to successfully start things, share their faith, care for people and study the Bible. A mature (and useful) prophet is one who is actively working on developing their whole fivefold.

THINK LIKE A PROPHET, ACT LIKE A PROPHET

Having spent some time looking at how prophets can embrace their calling, we now need to consider how the whole church can learn from the prophetic role. The mature prophetic community is one where our prophets are thriving and the rest of us are learning prophetic thinking and practice from them. To do this, it is beneficial to recognise both the *internal* and *external* aspects of what it means to be a prophet.

Each of the fivefold roles has its own unique perspective – a particular bias or worldview, an internal processing style, an instinctive tendency, a way of seeing things (in terms of people, possibilities or problems) that others cannot see.[11] To engage with the *internal* world of the prophet, we can reflect on prophetic

- consciousness
- thinking
- intelligence
- sensibility
- awareness

And we can then go on to consider the more *external* side of prophetic

- practice
- habits
- ministry
- aptitude

We want to learn to both *think* like a prophet and *act* like a prophet.

Even if 'prophet' comes at the bottom of our personal APEST list, we can still discover opportunities for prophetic growth and flourishing, as long as we are curious and courageous enough to step out and learn. The Holy Spirit, who has the very DNA of Christ, dwells within to make us as Jesus-like as possible, and God's good purpose is to conform each of us to the image of his Son[12] – and that includes the prophetic part of Christ's image.

When one of my friends took a fivefold survey, she discovered that 'prophet' came last for her, but she was so determined to grow her prophetic competency that she committed to two years of coaching with Accessible Prophecy.[13] She has learnt to love the way of prophets, and her growing prophetic ministry has had a significant impact on her church.

In considering how *everyone* can actively participate in the world of the prophet and emulate Jesus the perfect Prophet, here are four practical ways in which we can both think our way into a new way of acting and act our way into a new way of thinking.

Learn the Prophet's Perspective

The aim here is to explore something of the heart and consciousness of a prophet – to learn to look at the world through their eyes.

We can start by investigating the many great books, blogs and podcasts that dig deep into both the Vertical and Horizontal dimensions of the prophetic. But one way in which we can begin to learn the prophet's perspective is to spend time reflecting on the words and concepts that tend to get prophets' hearts racing. We can take a list like the one below and slowly and meditatively make our way through it, ideally journaling about or discussing each word in turn. What might these words mean for the prophet? How do prophets seek to live these things out? How do these words reflect the theological roots of the prophetic?

- Truth
- Integrity
- Depth
- Mysticism
- Holiness
- Beauty
- Dream
- Justice
- Prefigure
- Reimagine
- Intuition
- Alternative
- Pioneer

These words don't belong exclusively to the prophets, but they deeply resonate with every prophet's soul. As we take time to prayerfully muse over each one, we will be learning to think like a prophet.

Of the fivefold, the prophetic function is the one that often asks the most questions. So, another way of gaining a prophetic perspective is to consider the type of questions a prophet asks – and then practise asking them:

- 'What is God saying in this situation?'
- 'Are we being obedient to God's call on our lives?'
- 'Are we being faithful?'
- 'What spiritual influences or powers are at work here?'
- 'What assumptions need challenging or shaking up?'
- 'Where is repentance required of us?'
- 'Where have we compromised our core values?'
- 'What is an alternative way of approaching this issue?'

Practical Listening Exercises

Prophets are good at hearing God's voice – they are particularly attuned to his heart – but that vital ability to discern the still small voice of God amidst all the other voices competing for our attention is one we can all learn.

The best way to grow in prophetic listening is regular practice – engaging daily or weekly in simple exercises that open up the door to revelation. We can practise listening to God for ourselves and for others; for covenantal words that draw us deeper into relationship with him; as well as for kingdom words that equip us to fulfil the call on our lives.

The use of regular listening exercises doesn't negate the profoundly relational and spontaneous aspect of hearing God's voice, but it reminds us that the language of the Spirit is a language to be learnt and developed. God's generosity in pouring out his revelation to us needs to be honoured as we make regular space to pay attention and refine our listening skills.

As an example, here is a simple exercise adapted from my book *My Sheep Have Ears*:[14]

Step 1: Start in a place of thanksgiving. Psalm 100 tells us that we enter into the Lord's presence through thanksgiving and praise. Spend some time giving thanks for all the blessings God has poured into your life, and then engage in praising him for who he is. Rejoice in his steadfast goodness.

Step 2: Spend some time simply resting in the Father's love. Remind yourself of your covenant identity as his beloved child. Enjoy being still in his presence, receiving his peace and knowing that the Father delights to speak to you.

Step 3: Read Psalm 23:1–3 slowly and meditatively. Think about Jesus, the Good Shepherd, leading you to the green pastures and still waters. Picture yourself and Jesus in that tranquil scene.

Step 4: Ask God this question: 'Lord, how are you refreshing my soul today?'

Step 5: Listen for the answer. Remember that God speaks in many different ways. You may find that a fleeting image pops into your head, or some words, or a verse from the Bible. It may be something as simple as a sense of peace or love. Just go with it; don't dismiss it. Write it down and give thanks.

Apprenticeship and Immersion

If we are serious about developing our prophetic thinking and action, then sooner or later we will want to be apprenticed by a mature prophet. Intentionally spending time with someone who can authentically model prophetic mindset and behaviour, and who can disciple us in both of these, can be incredibly beneficial. I'm aware that not everyone has access to people like this, but if we are in a church with recognised prophets, we can ask them for mentorship.

We can also look for environments where the prophetic function is overtly expressed – particular places, ministries and organisations where prophetic awareness and action is prominent – and consider how we can immerse ourselves in such a culture for a period of time.

With both apprenticeship and immersion, we can observe how mature prophets shape the culture around them, both inside and outside the church. We can watch how they provide vision, nurture hope, bring discernment, and prioritise authentic spirituality to create a culture that is ethical, radical and prefigurative.

Prophetic Seasons

Every so often God, in his wisdom, will allow us to spend time operating out of our weaknesses rather than our strengths. To mature us as disciples, he will take us through particular seasons where we are significantly less comfortable; periods of time where we need to stretch and grow in a fivefold ministry that isn't our primary calling.[15]

One sure-fire way of developing our prophetic intelligence is to spend time operating prophetically – having a season of life when the circumstances require us to function as a prophet. Whereas the previous three learning opportunities described above require intentional investment, this fourth one we have little control over. God will determine the timing and nature of a prophetic season in our lives. But if we are brave enough, we could pray for one to come along at the right time.

My husband is a workplace apostle – called to make our city's health-care system a better place for all. He loves applying apostolic vision and strategy in the secular context in which he works. But he has recently gone through a period where he had to function much more as a prophet – standing up for justice and righteousness and speaking truth to power. It wasn't an easy time for him. He didn't actively choose it, but under-standing it from the perspective of the fivefold was very beneficial, and this prophetic season has undoubtedly strengthened him in his apostolic calling.

THE WAY OF THE PROPHETS

Prophetic sensibility and practice are available for all to learn. As we follow in the footsteps of our perfect Prophet, we can gain much satisfaction, as well as maturity, from apprenticing in the way of the prophets. A growing proficiency in prophetic ministry and action is something to be faithfully praying for, and individuals can grow in the prophetic function in a healthy learning environment that is effective in identifying, disci-pling and deploying prophets.

13

DEVELOPING PROPHETIC CULTURE

In all my prayers for all of you, I always pray with joy ... being
confident of this, that he who began a good work in you will carry
it on to completion until the day of Christ Jesus.

PHILIPPIANS 1:4-6

My husband has significantly influenced the culture of our local neighbourhood. He was the driving force behind the launch of our summer street party – a day full of food, conversation, music and fun – which now takes place every year. The street party, in turn, has led to our family hosting a monthly meal for our neighbours. Alongside this, the pandemic-induced lockdown prompted most residents to join our street WhatsApp group, which provides a regular source of advice, support and humour. Our little neighbourhood in suburban Sheffield has, over the last ten years, become a friendlier and more welcoming community. The culture has changed. The place 'feels' different.

When we talk about the culture of a church, a business, or indeed a Sheffield street, we are talking about shared characteristics within a social group or organisation; characteristics such as perspectives, values and behaviours. Organisational culture is 'the way we do things around here'.[1] But therein lies the rub. If we are used to a certain way of doing things, culture *change* can be very challenging. It requires the people in the organisation to adapt their thinking and their habits. And to see meaningful change happen across an entire church, movement or social group necessitates a significant level of strategic implementation and perseverance from leaders.

Changing a church's culture to one of healthy and impactful engage-ment with the prophetic will mean a change to 'the way we do things around here'. Thinking and habits will be different. Things will 'feel' differ-ent. It may seem a daunting task, but it's possible for any church to develop a mature prophetic culture – we simply need to know where we are going and how to get there. We have to be able to turn theory into practice, to bridge the gap between rhetoric and reality.

In this chapter I suggest some practical steps for growing and sustain-ing a healthy prophetic culture so that *together* we can express the full extent of the prophetic function and thus reflect an important part of the complete image of Christ. (See the appendix for an overview of how we can use the description of Jesus the perfect Prophet from chapter one to capture a snapshot of what the mature prophetic church looks like.)

LET'S BE HONEST

To reshape culture requires us to start with an honest assessment of the current reality and then to confront the facts. So, what is really going on in many of our churches today?

We know from Ephesians 4 that Jesus has given five specific roles and functions to the church, in order that the body of Christ can be built up to maturity and equipped to display his fullness to the world. But as mentioned back in chapter two, large sections of the church have histori-cally excluded the apostolic, prophetic and evangelistic functions. As we look across the many expressions of the body today, we tend to find that only two – the shepherds and teachers – are validated and normalised. The majority of church leadership and culture has been shaped from a shepherding and teaching framework, and the influence of the APEs (apostles, prophets and evangelists) has been largely missing from the local church. It's not that Jesus has stopped giving these people-gifts to his body, but if these people find church a hostile environment, they will go elsewhere – whether that's the overseas mission field, the business world, or (as is the case for many prophets) the parachurch organisation.

The overwhelming emphasis on the shepherding and teaching func-tions, to the detriment of the other three, results in a church that fails to live up to its vast potential. We become a shadow of what was intended: an immature, half-formed, ineffective church, unable to pioneer and to oppose tyranny, and incapable of missional movement. We have to find a way to activate the missing 60 per cent so that we can mobilise the whole of the fivefold ministry. We must develop methodology to reintegrate the apostolic, prophetic and evangelistic ministries with that of the shepherds and teachers.

To grow the kind of prophetic culture Jesus intends, we need to be aware of the scale of the problem we are facing. Fortunately, many people are waking up to this huge gap and the necessity of rediscovering and reactivating the fivefold ministry in the church. The APEs are coming in from the cold. This is good news for the prophets. Many churches are starting to ask how they can begin to grow an authentic prophetic spirituality. This is something to be celebrated, as long as we recognise that the solution won't come from focusing exclusively on the prophetic.

As we keep in mind the need to raise the *whole* fivefold, we can now look at the particular issues around the prophetic.

We start by being honest about the realities of our current situation and identifying any dysfunction. As noted in chapter ten, dysfunction arises when the Vertical and Horizontal dimensions are disconnected from each other. Here, I want to highlight two further manifestations of prophetic dysfunction. One, that we have just described, is *avoidance* – when the prophetic function is all but missing from the church or organisation. The other (the opposite) is *precociousness* – when the prophetic function is overly dominant.

Two types of prophetic dysfunction

AVOIDANCE	PRECOCIOUSNESS
APEST	APEST

Avoidance. Prophetic avoidance can manifest in the following ways:

- *Ignorance:* No attention is paid to the prophetic because it is not on the radar.

- *Suppression:* Deliberate evasion or repression of the prophetic.
- *Inexperience:* Awareness of the prophetic and its benefits but little knowledge of how to nurture it.

When avoidance is the issue, churches are desperately lacking in prophetic understanding and ministry. I talk to many church leaders who are wary of any kind of engagement with the prophetic, whether Vertical or Horizontal. Perhaps they have seen too many problems arising from immature prophets and badly handled prophetic ministry. They may be nervous of the way the prophetic threatens to bring disruption and challenge the status quo. It often seems easiest just to shut it down. But if we eliminate the prophetic role and function, we are eliminating a significant percentage of Christ's ministry from the church and will ultimately lack long-term sustainability as an organisation.

Precociousness. The other type of dysfunction is caused by *too much* emphasis on the prophetic. As hard as this may be for some prophets to grasp, if the prophetic function is excessively dominant, it will have a detrimental effect on the church as a whole. A strong bias towards the prophetic will not create a balanced fivefold culture. If the prophetic is seen as the answer to everything, we end up with disengagement from the rest of the fivefold ministries and all sorts of unhealthy and ugly expressions of church. Unsurprisingly, the church that is most vulnerable to prophetic precociousness is the one led by a prophet. I'm sure we can all think of churches that have become over-reliant on the prophetic, to the extent that such ministry monopolises all others, and we end up with a self-absorbed parody of Jesus' own prophetic ministry. A precocious prophetic culture is probably an indication that the prophetic is being implemented badly despite its prevalence, so work will be needed to establish a healthier expression. Maturity comes from both quantitative and qualitative development.

If our problem is a low or non-existent prophetic function, then we need to find ways to raise it. If our problem is that of precociousness, then we need to raise the other four functions.

One key point we will consider further in the next section, is that a weakness or lack in the other four ministries will put a cap on how far we can grow the prophetic.

INTERDEPENDENCE

As we have already explored, an authentic church is a Jesus-shaped church – a manifestation of Jesus' living and healing presence. To express the whole measure of the fullness of Christ, we need all five ministries on board. The mature church is about the *interdependence* of the fivefold, with each function meaningfully integrated into the whole, so that the entire community can learn from each one. Each of the five brings its own unique wisdom, experience, strength and passion that is perfectly designed to grow the body, as long as the other four are actively present. Each role contributes something that the others cannot.

As much as we want to promote the prophetic function, it should never dominate or separate out from the other four. For too long prophetic ministry has been contaminated by an attitude of superiority and independence, with many prophets turning their backs on the rest of the church. A healthy and mature prophetic culture is only ultimately possible within a balanced fivefold culture. To grow the prophetic, we always need to maintain this holistic approach.

This is where *systems thinking* can be beneficial – seeing the five-fold ministries as an interconnected, cross-pollinating whole, where we are only as strong as our weakest part. We cannot simply focus on our strengths and ignore our weaknesses; we need to attend to all five. If one or more of the other four are weak or lagging, it will limit how much the prophetic can flourish. We want to see high expression and compe-tency in all five. Fivefold maturity is all five functions working together for the sake of the kingdom and the good of the organisation, with each one recognised and celebrated for its contribution. Jesus has designed his church so that the combined effect is greater than the sum of the parts. The *synergy* of all five operating together with strength and power is how we get the glorious presence of Christ truly visible in his church.

FIVEFOLD ASSESSMENT

As long as we ensure that we are not ignoring the full fivefold perspec-tive, we can go on to work out the best way to activate and develop the prophetic function. A great first step is to do an assessment of the church or organisation's current fivefold profile.[2] In the same way that an individual can assess his or her own personal APEST portrait, so a church or organisation can evaluate its current understanding and expression of the fivefold ministries. When we assess a whole church, rather than an individual, we are of course hoping to find a balanced, symmetrical fivefold profile, because this will indicate the fullness of Christ. In reality we are likely to find some kind of imbalance. Knowing where this imbalance lies enables us to target training and resources where they are most needed.

Such an evaluation will give us an indication of how strong or weak, growing or struggling, the prophetic is in comparison to the other four functions, and how we might be able to leverage our strengths to address our weaknesses. With a clear picture attained, we can go on to develop a contextually relevant strategy for improvement.

HOW TO GROW A PROPHETIC CULTURE

I have worked with churches of all shapes and sizes from a wide range of denominations and streams, and I believe that – with intentional investment, prayer and practice – a healthy, mature prophetic culture can be grown almost anywhere. Such a culture will produce all sorts of kingdom fruit, as discipleship and mission are significantly empowered. But intentionality is vital. We have to be deliberate in the plans we make and in the way we use our resources. We also have to be intentional in our long-term commitment to the process. Culture change does not happen overnight! It takes longer than we think, with many bumps in the road and obstacles to overcome. One of the best things we can do is to keep in step with the Spirit, letting him set the pace. He is the very best mentor when it comes to facilitating culture change. We would be wise to let his voice speak into our leadership decisions and strategic development at all stages of the process.

It's important to point out that developing prophetic culture is not just for the local church. We can apply the idea of a prophetic community to a variety of faith organisations beyond the local congregation. Once we have worked out the necessary principles and tactics for culture change, we can then implement them contextually in our teams, ministries, denominations or movements. Healthy prophetic culture is relevant in gatherings ranging from a discipleship group or ministry team to a large parachurch organisation. The questions we are asking in this chapter are applicable to any expression of Christian community.

A Holistic Perspective

A holistic prophetic culture also extends beyond the walls of the Christian organisation and into the workplace. When we talk about growing prophetic culture, we need to have the big-picture perspective of a culture that influences many aspects of society. The prophetic function is designed to operate in any setting in which God's people are present.

Not all of us spend our days in the church. In fact, most of us spend a large proportion of the week in a secular environment, in whatever workplace or sphere of influence God has led us to. Any place where disciples of Jesus are called to serve – including business, the public sector and the arts – can be places where prophetic ministry can flourish. Prophetic consciousness and ministry are equally relevant in the corporate world as they are in the church, and understanding how the prophetic function contributes to the health and productivity of the non-church organisation will enable us to properly support all expressions of prophetic ministry represented by our church community.

Prophetic intelligence can be a positive contribution to any organisation and bring a wide range of benefits, especially at the strategic and culture-setting level. It's easy enough to take any of the elements of the prophetic function and translate them into a secular setting, whether that is passion for purpose, foresight and insight, creativity, useful questioning, quality control, integrity, advocacy, authenticity, or the impulse for change. A wise organisation would do well to ensure the prophetic voice is heard in the boardroom and on every committee.

As the church seeks to strengthen and develop prophetic culture and ministry, it may need a paradigm shift in order to understand that a significant proportion of this ministry is going to take place outside *ecclesia*. We need to carefully consider what the prophetic function looks and feels like in the workplace, and how we can value and promote it. There will be prophets in workplaces who need celebrating and empowering; but more than that, there will be many members of the church community who are called to extend prophetic culture into their secular area of influence. These are people who are prepared to stand up for truth and justice; people promoting kingdom ethics; people ready to question dubious practices and policies. Developing prophetic culture in the workplace is simply an extension of the church's prophetic ministry – a very important extension, and one that sadly is rarely recognised for what it is.

I would love to see many more people being prayed for in church on Sunday, ready to be sent out as prophetic witnesses to their workplace on Monday. I would love to see fivefold prophets training and equipping the rest of the body in prophetic thinking and lifestyle, *specifically for the workplace*. I would love to see those church members who sense the Holy Spirit calling them to whistleblowing and the exposure of unjust systems, supported on all sides by their church community. I would love to see every local church on the lookout for the prophetic voices in secular society and the business world that they can support and champion.

Growing a prophetic culture is learning to see that the work of the church is as much in the Monday to Friday of the workplace as it is in the sanctuary on a Sunday. So, the church member speaking truth to power in a business context is part of the church's prophetic ministry; the church member advocating for the vulnerable in the city's public services is part of the church's prophetic ministry.

To do this – to develop a truly holistic prophetic culture – the church will need to repent of old ways of thinking and develop a mindset that no longer sees the secular-sacred divide. Just as is the case in the church setting, we need new paradigms and practices so that we can support people in the workplace to be a prophetic voice and witness.

Awareness and Application

A prophetic culture is developed as we equip the church with both awareness and application. This means combining a thorough, biblical *understanding* of the prophetic with plenty of opportunities to *apply* this knowledge. Maturity, as indicated on this diagram, is when both are attended to.[3]

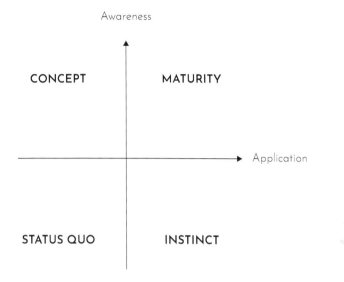

As already noted, discipleship to Jesus is essentially a twofold process of hearing and obeying – of *knowing* and *living*. We hear his voice, change our way of thinking, and then actively step out in obedience. If we are going to successfully disciple the church in prophetic culture, we certainly need to increase the collective *understanding* of the fivefold ministry and the prophetic function. People need to comprehend and value the prophetic, and there is much to learn. But we also want to give ample opportunity for people to *live* the prophetic – to step out, practice and experiment; to apply their knowledge in a real-world context. If we don't provide a safe environment where people can learn to listen to God, engage with his heart, and practically respond, then involvement with the prophetic will remain at a conceptual level. It is not enough just to know about the prophetic function; we have to experience it.

Markers: Inside and Outside the Church

One important part of growing a mature prophetic culture is ensuring that all the different aspects of such a culture are attended to. As we've seen throughout this book, the prophetic function is much more than simply delivering prophecies, as valuable as these are. There are many facets to prophetic ministry, and maturity is ensuring a balance between them all.

We certainly need a balance between the Vertical and Horizontal dimensions. Below is a list of key questions drawn from the four elements of a healthy Vertical culture and the four elements of a healthy Horizontal culture (see chapters seven and nine). These questions can be answered using a numbered scale, with 1 being low and 10 being high. The answers will help the church community to highlight any gaps or areas of vulnerability.

Faithfulness culture
To what extent

- do we love God wholeheartedly?
- are we satisfied with him alone?
- are we vigilantly guarding the covenant relationship?
- is it easy for people to develop a life of intimacy with God?

Presence culture
To what extent

- do our patterns and practices cultivate an awareness of God's presence?
- are we expectant for an encounter with God?
- are we actively choosing to be in his presence?
- are we surrendered to the work of the Spirit in our lives?

Revelatory culture
To what extent

- are we hearing and recognising the voice of God?
- are we able to discern where God is leading us?
- are we strengthening, encouraging and comforting each other through prophetic gifts?
- are we hearing God's words of life for our neighbourhoods and people of peace?

Holiness culture

To what extent

- are we committed to personal transformation through ongoing repentance?
- do we have an authentic and effective discipleship culture?
- do we allow God to speak into every area of our lives?
- are we responding with obedience when God speaks?

Alternative culture

To what extent

- do we, as a community, surrender our established thought patterns to the lordship of Christ?
- are we becoming aware of our cultural blind spots?
- do we nurture an alternative consciousness to that of the dominant culture?
- do we give people permission to lament over injustice?

Advocacy culture

To what extent

- are we brave enough to speak truth to power and support whistleblowers?
- are we speaking on behalf of the poor and marginalised?
- can we effectively critique the status quo?
- are we asking the right questions of the society we are in?

Incarnational culture

To what extent

- are we ready for God to incarnate his word in us?
- can we be a prefigurative community?
- are we using the arts to express God's superior reality?
- do we as a community embody the *shalom* of the kingdom?

Activist culture

To what extent

- can we hear God clearly for what action we should take?
- are we sufficiently informed and mobilised to make society better?
- are our activists prayed for and supported?
- are we living justly?

Intentional questioning like this enables us to collectively work towards a big-picture mindset and a truly holistic environment.

Strategies for Development

Over the years, as I've worked with churches on culture change, the following strategies have been crucial in building a mature prophetic culture:

Ensure everyone is confident in hearing God for themselves. A fundamental building block for any prophetic culture is to equip *everybody* to recognise how the Good Shepherd speaks to him or her on a personal level. Jesus promised that his sheep would know his voice (John 10), and hearing his voice is the birthright of every child of God. This is the starting point, and it flows out of a deep covenantal relationship with the Father. We can hear his voice because of our identity as his beloved children.

In a healthy prophetic culture, there is a good level of confidence across the church; people know how to hear and are actively listening. They may not consider themselves as especially prophetic, but they know how to seek God's heart and hear him for themselves. They can recognise the particular ways in which the Spirit communicates to them. They are hearing God speak to them for affirmation, encouragement and guidance.

Strategic questions we can be asking about our overall confidence:

- What teaching or training do we need to offer in order to build this confidence across all sectors of our church community?
- Are we telling the everyday stories of lives impacted through the voice of God?

Work out what language is needed in your culture to normalise and demystify the prophetic. Language is very influential in creating culture. A careful and intentional use of language will do much to shape the prophetic culture in our churches or organisations. Prophets are often guilty of using flowery, long-winded and super-spiritual language to talk about their experiences and explain their perspective. This usually has the effect of alienating (and frustrating) the rest of the church. There is much work to be done in normalising and demystifying prophetic experiences and gifts, and a key part of growing a healthy prophetic culture is being intentional about the language we are using.

Part of our role as leaders is to establish the type of culture we want to see grow through the language we use. If our aim is normalisation and accessibility, then we need to be on the lookout for any unhelpful language that is creating barriers to the whole community engaging with the prophetic. We need to employ normal and everyday vocabulary to describe the strange and mystifying nature of much of the prophetic experience, and be wise to the specific nature of the context in which we are ministering. In some churches I work with, particularly the more conservative ones, it is much more pragmatic to use the phrase 'listening prayer' than 'prophecy', because the latter raises too many issues or alarm bells.

Language is also important in establishing the particular ethos and value system we want to see developed around prophetic ministry. So, a strategic step forward is to be clear about our key values (see later point below) and then develop a vocabulary based on these.

It's worth remembering that the Holy Spirit can help us find the specific language that can unlock difficult situations and smooth a path for everyone to enjoy the riches of prophetic engagement.

Strategic questions we can be asking about our language:

- What vocabulary should we be actively using whenever we talk about the prophetic?
- Which words or phrases should we avoid in our context?

Identify your prophets, then disciple and deploy them to build up the body. For prophets to be the amazing blessing Jesus has designed them to be, we need to find them, disciple them, and help them embrace their role. As we saw in chapter twelve, we can develop strategies to help us with this process. We can be in conversation with our small group leaders, youth leaders, student workers and others on the leadership team, asking them to be on the lookout for anyone who they think may be demonstrating the shape and wiring of a fivefold prophet.

Following on from the strategic use of language, we may well need to be sensitive in utilising the word *prophet* and recognise that it has a lot of baggage for some people. When encouraging potential prophets to embrace their role, we might be wise to phrase it something like this:

> It seems that God has wired you in a particular way, and with a particular role to play – in that you have a passion for God's heart/you find it easy to hear his voice and help others tune in/you have a passion for social justice. It would be great to explore together what it might look like for you to grow more into this role in our church and how God might want you to equip others.

As well as being strategic in identifying prophets, we need to become skilled in discipling them, so that we can lead them to a place of maturity. Prophets are disciples first; discipleship and accountability are key for their development. In fact, healthy prophetic culture can only be established in a culture of discipleship. Without an emphasis on discipleship, the prophet is highly vulnerable to all sorts of pitfalls and hazards, such as lack of accountability, isolation and judgmentalism. When we emphasise discipleship (rather than gifting), it downplays any sense of spiritual hierarchy and helps people embrace wholeness and maturity.

We also need to be strategic in finding the best ways to deploy our prophets. Any church will have many opportunities for prophets to serve the community and build up the body, for example inviting them to listen to God for words of encouragement for members of the congregation. (See the case study at the end of chapter ten for practical examples of how we have done this at my church in Sheffield.) We can look for opportunities for our prophets to serve the other fivefold ministries. Intentional use of language will help prophets see their role as *equippers* of others. It's not just about their own ability to hear God, but it is also about them multiplying their prophetic intelligence into others. This sometimes requires a major shift of mindset, since it challenges many prophets who would rather go it alone and focus on their own prophetic ministry rather than invest in others.

Strategic questions we can be asking about developing prophets:

- What language will enable our church to understand and embrace prophets?
- What processes are in place to ensure our prophets are being discipled?

Ensure that the Vertical and Horizontal are both developed and work well together. This should be obvious by now. But it takes more than just knowing the theory; it has to be worked out in practice. To hold the middle ground in our local churches is going to require a high degree of strategic planning and implementation. Vertical and Horizontal prophets need to be talking together, praying for each other and ministering together. Our community needs to have a depth of understanding around the theology of 'covenant and kingdom'. We will have to ensure that our prophetic ministry has a strong outward dimension; and we will need to cultivate the right sort of language that pulls the two dimensions together.

Strategic questions we can be asking about balancing the Vertical and the Horizontal:

- Do we have a strong enough vision for being a community of both dimensions?
- What opportunities are there for our Vertical and Horizontal prophets to work together on a project?

Work towards a leadership team that reflects the whole fivefold ministry. A healthy senior leadership team ought to reflect the whole fivefold ministry so that it can better represent the ministry of Jesus. In an ideal situation, we would have each fivefold calling represented by a mature leader with that calling. Even if that is not our current reality, we can still be strategic in ensuring the five different voices are at least *heard* at a senior level.

We need to carefully consider how we welcome prophets to the table, and how we empower them as they offer their unique gifts and contributions. It's all very well having a prophet on the team, but if we sidetrack them with other responsibilities rather than releasing them to fully express their prophetic calling, we are wasting a valuable opportunity. One aspect of this is recognising that they bring a voice that otherwise would not be heard. If the whole team has a high level of fivefold awareness, we are more likely to seek out and value the prophetic perspective.

If it's not possible to invite a mature prophet to the leadership team from *within* a church or organisation, then perhaps the next step is to consider how to work with prophetic leaders in the city or region.

Strategic questions we can be asking about our leadership team:

- Is the fivefold ministry adequately represented at the executive level of our organisation?
- Who could bring a mature prophetic voice into our senior team?
- Are we welcoming the prophetic voice into our decision-making?

Consider whether you need a prophetic team. A great way to develop prophetic culture in many church contexts is to gather a team of people with the right heart and vision to specifically focus on raising this culture, building both awareness and application of the prophetic. Such a team doesn't have to be filled solely with prophets; in fact, it will be a much more successful team if it isn't. But it will need to be made up of people who desire to see the whole of their church or organisation equipped in prophetic gifts and ministry.

Recruitment for the team can be based around the early adopters – those people who are open to new ideas and are aware of the need for culture change. They will be the ones able to grasp the vision and run with it, and who are also positive role models for the rest of the community.

The list of questions laid out on pages 214–216 could form the basis of a team's objectives and provide a framework for making and implementing some great plans. But in many ways the number one goal for a prophetic team is to pray – to soak the initiatives in prayer and to stand guard around the young shoots of a prophetic culture.

Strategic questions we can be asking about a prophetic team:

- How could a prophetic team lead to more effective and sustainable culture change?
- Who should be on this team?

Establish your key values and principles. Effective culture change needs to be rooted and grounded in godly values and principles. We will need to invest time in discussions that allow these values and principles to emerge with consensus from the heart of the community.

Values and principles may well be contextualised depending on the shape and nature of our church or organisation, but here are some essential ones I believe every community needs to consider:

Values

- ***Love.*** Our primary motivation for every facet of prophetic ministry is love; love for God and love for his people.
- ***Humility.*** We lay aside our own agendas so we can serve God with a pure heart. We recognise the corrosive nature pride brings to prophetic ministry.
- ***Servant-hearted.*** Our emphasis is on serving the church and world through our prophetic gifts and calling. Authentic prophetic lifestyle is always marked by a heart to serve.
- ***Accountable.*** Accountability is vital for any healthy engagement with the prophetic, so we build discipleship-based accountability into the heart of our ministry.
- ***Bible-based.*** Every expression of prophetic ministry and culture must be grounded in Scripture, so we cultivate a passion for biblical understanding alongside our pursuit of prophetic spirituality.

Principles

- *Accessibility.* A prophetic culture is one where prophetic aware-ness and practice is accessible to all.
- *Multiplication.* A prophetic culture is one that is reproducible with a focus on investing in others.
- *Expectancy.* A prophetic culture cultivates a confidence that God will speak if we ask him to.
- *Community.* A prophetic culture operates out of love for the body of Christ and ensures that prophets are firmly embedded in the church community, with a heart to edify and encourage the whole church.

Once we are clear on our values and principles, we can go on to ensure they are shaping our language. Here are some strategic questions we can be asking about our values and principles:

- How are we going to determine our key values and principles?
- Does our language reflect our values?

Taking a Lead

A word of encouragement for leaders: you don't have to be a prophet your-self to lead prophets and release a healthy prophetic culture. For many, the prospect of leading and discipling prophets can seem quite daunting. The prophetic personality doesn't always come with a reputation for being easy to work with; and there are plenty of immature prophets who strug-gle to submit to leadership. But if our priority is building a healthy five-fold culture, we will be able to find the tools and tactics we need to lead our church or organisation into areas that we are not naturally strong in ourselves. Over the years, many of the healthiest expressions of prophetic culture I've observed have been led by non-prophets.

Leaders need to be confident in being a living example – to embody the culture we want to see grow. It's no good just *teaching* it; we have to do it. We can only lead others where we have gone ourselves, so we have to be prepared to step out and model a healthy engagement with the prophetic function. This means talking about our mistakes and failures as much as our successes. It also means conveying the message we value and actively live out both Vertical and Horizontal dimensions. Allowing imitation – letting others get close enough to us so they can see how this awareness and application works in our lives on a day-to-day basis – is a powerful factor in multiplying the type of culture we desire.

PRACTICAL EXERCISES

We become what we repeatedly do. To develop into a community that naturally flows in prophetic consciousness and lifestyle, we have to start with intentionality around praxis. We need to work out which particular prophetic practices we want to express regularly as a community and what habits we want to embed in our communal rhythms.

Below are some simple practices for any church or organisation to consider – three with a Vertical emphasis and three with a Horizontal emphasis. These can be applied in any communal setting, including a staff team, small group or ministry team. They may not feel easy or instinctive at first and will bring a level of vulnerability, but if they are practised on a regular basis, they will in time start to feel a natural part of community life.

- Organise a team retreat day that includes silence and contemplative exercises. Mediate on Psalm 23 and the image of Jesus as the Good Shepherd.
- Set aside some quality time to exercise the gift of prophecy. Get into pairs and practise listening to God for each other, asking God for words that will strengthen and lead forward.
- Create a notice board where people are welcome to post words, pictures and verses that encourage the whole community.
- Choose a social justice issue that resonates with the group. Spend some time expressing your lament together and then write a 'holy discontent' psalm about it.
- Select a local issue (for example, illiteracy or food poverty) and spend some time researching how it is impacting your local

neighbourhood. Then commit as a group to meet weekly for an hour to pray, spending the first half listening to God, and then the second half in intercession. Discern together how to practically respond.

- Investigate who in your church community or relational network is being called by God to speak truth to power in the workplace. Work out a plan to support them through prayer and prophetic encouragement.

MAKING THE CHANGE

Culture change is possible because we have God on our side. We can take heart from Paul's words to the Philippians – God has started this good work in us, and he will complete it.[4] The potential for becoming the mature multi-faceted church of Jesus Christ is planted deep in our spiritual DNA. We can partner with him to see this potential realised. We can have hope for the church.

CONCLUSION

CARRYING THE REVELATION OF GOD

*That which was from the beginning, which we have heard,
which we have seen with our eyes, which we have looked at
and our hands have touched – this we proclaim concerning
the Word of life.*

1 JOHN 1:1

The church of Jesus Christ needs to reclaim its prophetic identity and rediscover its prophetic voice. A voice that speaks hope to the hopeless, that calls for transformation across all spheres of human experience, and that is more than capable of standing up to tyranny and oppression. A voice that originates in the heart of our utterly free, powerful and compassionate God – the Father who chooses to reach out to a humanity craftcd in his image and make himself known. A voice that is carried on the winds of the Spirit to every corner of the globe, ready to be perceived by all who take the time to listen. This earth-shattering, paradigm-shifting, yet tender voice cannot be appropriated for human agendas and ideologies. The prophets of old were overwhelmed by it, as they allowed the word of Yahweh to be wholly incarnated in their lives. Prophets today can learn to thrive in the profound depths of this voice as they teach the church to discern and carry it.

The voice to be rediscovered is the voice of love. The prophetic is the love language of the God of relationship and revelation; the love language of the Father who grieves over a broken world and who longs to restore, mend, heal and make new. It's the language we are given in order to love the world and call it back to its true home. Whether we are standing in front of presidents, protesting on the streets, or on our knees in the prayer closet, our prophetic words and actions must speak a language of love, radiating from the depths of God's heart.

As we seek to learn this language, we cannot look anywhere other than the Word of Life himself: Jesus, our Lord. He is the greatest expression of this love language. He is the ultimate communication, the definitive revelation. He is the very essence of prophecy and the Word through which all other words are judged.[1] Jesus speaks to all of creation through the language of self-giving, radical, redemptive love. A love that will always call us to be the best version of ourselves; a love that will always be heard by the lost sheep, the prodigals and the marginalised. The prophetic voice of the church today is simply an echo of this greatest of all Words, expressing the greatest love we have ever seen.

If Jesus is the greatest prophecy, then we as his church need to create enough space for him so that the world can see him and be captivated by him. Our greatest prophetic task is to let Jesus be Jesus in our midst. The mature prophetic church is one that can hold out and demonstrate God's Jesus-shaped reality with such clarity that every false voice is silenced and every false god exposed for what it is.

TWO CONFESSIONS

There is much joy for the body of Christ in the process of rediscovering our prophetic identity and voice. As we near the end of this book, I want to frame this rediscovery by gently reminding the church of two confessions we can make together.

The first confession is that *we tend to stay in our comfort zone*, as illustrated by the Sinai story. At the mountain of God, Yahweh established the covenant between himself and his chosen people, holding out the promise that they would be a 'kingdom of priests and a holy nation' (Exodus 19:6). This was an invitation to draw close, to hear his voice and hold out the revelation of Yahweh to all other peoples on earth. But at this crucial moment, the people chose to keep their distance.

When the people saw the thunder and lightning and heard the trumpet
and saw the mountain in smoke, they trembled with fear. They stayed
at a distance and said to Moses, 'Speak to us yourself and we will listen.
But do not let God speak to us or we will die.'

Exodus 20:18–19

The people placed Moses – the intermediary – between themselves and
God. The Israelites chose a secondary form of communication. Their
prophetic role was henceforth subcontracted out to individual prophets
and priests.

This scene at Sinai resonates for us as we take seriously the call to be a
prophetic church. The story reveals the common tension between human
nature's tendency to draw back from God and the prophetic impulse to
draw close. The hesitancy the Israelites expressed is the same reluctance
we wrestle with today, because his voice demands much of us. The Sinai
narrative highlights the temptation to stay at a safe distance and keep the
volume turned down low.

There is a world out there that desperately needs to hear the voice of
God through his prophetic church. But it will cost us something as we
relentlessly pursue his presence and boldly speak from his heart. Are we
willing to stand before the fire of his glory and listen to his voice? Are we
prepared for an encounter with the very heart of God, knowing what it
may demand of us? Will we give up our cosy and settled existence and be
ready for the glories of his holy disruption?

Jesus' prophetic purposes for his body are vast. We are not created for
the comfort zone; rather, we are created for the ultimate adventure of a life
lived with God. We will only become the fully formed prophetic church
God intends us to be by laying aside our desire for worldly security and
running expectantly towards him. Initial hesitancy can be transformed
into eager pursuit once we've caught a vision of the absolute goodness of
God.

The second confession is that *we are reluctant to seek common ground*.
Much of this book has been an exploration of the two wonderful dimensions of the prophetic: the Vertical and Horizontal. We cannot afford to
neglect either one. We have to find a way to reach across the divide, and

love that which is different from us. I've already delivered a call for bringing the two together in chapter ten. This union will be strengthened when we see that Jesus is not only the greatest prophecy and perfect Prophet, but he is also the very place where the Vertical and Horizontal meet – the *focal point* of the Vertical and Horizontal dimensions. Beyond bringing the two dimensions together, we allow them to meet in Jesus. Like separate beams of light converging to create an optical image, so Presence and Justice must come together to produce the clear image of Christ in our midst; and they are designed to come together through the convex lens of the prophetic church.

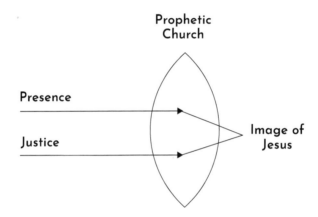

If we keep our eyes fixed on Jesus and allow both dimensions to merge in our midst, we will be able to offer the world a clearer, fuller image of Christ, and be authentic carriers of God's revelation.

COMBATTING DISTRACTION AND INDIFFERENCE

As we prioritise the convergence of the Vertical and Horizontal, we will also have the necessary weapons to confront the twin evils of *distraction* and *indifference*. We need to wage war on distraction because it insidiously eats away at our devotion to God. We need to wage war on indifference because it steals our compassion for others. Both keep us from paying attention, whether to God or to God's concerns. Both stop us from fully engaging with God's reality. Both prevent the flourishing of holiness.

Distraction is at the root of much prophetic malady and has been named as a barrier to authentic spirituality from the early church onwards. In the great fourth-century work on the desert fathers, the *Conferences of the Fathers*, John Cassian notes how the root of all difficulties in prayer is distraction.[2] Much more recently Ronald Rolheiser writes, 'We, for every kind of reason, good and bad, are distracting ourselves into spiritual oblivion.'[3]

In many ways, distraction is the principal doorway to idolatry in the twenty-first century. It quenches the work of the Holy Spirit in our lives, deadens our effectiveness and stifles our ability to be fully present to God. There is no limit to the amount of revelation God has for us, but we are distracted away from so much of it.

Social media, smartphones and multiple streaming services are playing havoc with our attention spans. We have assimilated into a culture of hurry and busyness that leaves us looking anxiously at the immediate future, or guiltily at the past, with no ability to be fully present in the moment with God. We rush from one activity to another, with little margin for praying, waiting and discerning. Millennials are considered to be the most over-stimulated and distracted generation,[4] but we all have our work cut out to focus on one thing for any length of time. We've been left with little ability to truly rest in God's presence and gaze on his beauty. Rather than asking *God* to show up – the God who is always with us and closer than we could possibly imagine – it is *we* who actually need to show up to the present moment.

Indifference is anathema to God's heart for justice, righteousness and *shalom*. In his Lenten message of 2015, Pope Francis wrote that this 'selfish attitude of indifference has taken on global proportions to the extent that we can speak of a globalisation of indifference. It is a problem which we as Christians need to confront.'[5] How can we be indifferent in the face of so much injustice? We've believed the lie that we can live a faithful life without caring for the poor and marginalised. We have become blasé about the pain and suffering of others. We are not prepared to sit and listen to the cries of the oppressed, choosing instead to switch channels, turn to the next page of the newspaper, or cross to the other side of the street. We find it easier to remain ignorant about the plight of the asylum seekers and trafficking victims in the parts of the city we rarely visit.

Commenting on indifference, Abraham Heschel says:

> There is an evil which most of us condone and are even guilty of: indifference to evil. We remain neutral, impartial, and not easily moved by the wrongs done unto other people. Indifference to evil is more insidious than evil itself; it is more universal, more contagious, more dangerous. A silent justification, it makes possible an evil erupting as an exception becoming the rule and being in turn accepted ... . The great contribution [of the prophets] to humanity was their discovery of the evil of indifference.[6]

The mature prophetic function is truly vital in combating these two present-day evils. The prophetic church refuses to be distracted away from our love of God and refuses to remain indifferent to the needs of our neighbour. The battle will be won as we joyfully hold both dimensions together through the power and grace of the Holy Spirit and by cultivating a thriving prophetic culture.

AN ANCIENT INVITATION

In the end, two challenges face the prophetic church: the challenge of *stepping out of our comfort zone* and the challenge of *finding common ground*. In the first is a call to relentlessly pursue the voice and heart of God, whatever it may cost us. In the second is a call to be the unblemished lens that holds Presence and Justice together and thus forms the perfect image of Jesus. My prayer is that every expression of the glorious body of Christ will be able to embrace these challenges and become a mature prophetic community.

But alongside the challenges, I want you to hear the invitation, that ancient invitation that has always been offered to the people of God: the joy of being carriers of the revelation of the Triune God. Whatever church we belong to, whatever background or tradition we are familiar with, it is possible for every Christian community to delight in this call and to grasp that our very identity is to be a people through whom God's reality is seen, heard, felt and encountered – the reality that is both consuming fire and endless love.

APPENDIX

THE PROPHETIC FUNCTION: JESUS AND HIS CHURCH

We can cultivate an imagination for a genuinely prophetic culture by focusing our attention on Christ's multi-faceted prophetic ministry. By taking the description of Jesus the perfect prophet from chapter one, we can see how the well-developed prophetic function can edify the body and help bring about the type of maturity described in Ephesians 4:12–16.

This is something worth working for. A church with a mature prophetic culture will have depth and integrity, will be countercultural and radical, and will be spiritually robust. It is possible for any church – big or small – to grow a thriving prophetic ministry.

Jesus the Perfect Prophet	The Mature Prophetic Church
Revelation of the Father	Carries the revelation of the Triune God to the world; holds out God's reality for all to see
Word of God made flesh	Hears and speaks God's true word to the world and the body in love
Mediator of the new covenant	Keeps the church true to its covenantal relationship with God
Only does what he sees the Father doing	Discerns and obeys the will of the Father, and maintains a passion for our God-given purpose
Is led by the Spirit	Is attuned to the voice of the Spirit, and committed to following where he leads

Jesus the Perfect prophet	The Mature Prophetic Church
Prioritises prayer and worship	Maintains a culture of authentic prayer and worship; cultivates devotion to God
Discerns the hearts and minds of people	Walks powerfully in the gift of discernment, attentive to the needs of all; can read cultural mindsets
Calls people to repentance	Makes spiritual health a priority; calls for the transformation of hearts and society
Confronts evil	Engages effectively in spiritual warfare, pulling down the strongholds that keep people in captivity
Speaks truth to power	Asks questions of decision-makers; is prepared to be countercultural in confronting oppressive institutions
Challenges injustice and unrighteousness	Cultivates a commitment to social justice and mobilises the community to take effective action
Demonstrates solidarity with marginalised people	Provides a voice for the voiceless
Speaks prophetically of the future	Can read the times and operate with profound foresight; can see the big picture of where God is leading his people
Exposes ungodly religion	Protects the body from idolatry, compromise, hypocrisy and pseudo-spirituality

ACKNOWLEDGEMENTS

Thank you to St.John for your endless support and encouragement over the last three years. I could not have written this book without you. And thank you to Joanna, Matt, Kate and Izzy for cheering me on and being the best family I could possibly imagine.

Thank you to Anna Robinson for being a wonderful editor (and a good friend).

Thank you to Alan Hirsch for writing the foreword and introducing me to Balthasar.

Thank you to Brandon Kelly, Mimika Garesché, Hannah Montgomery, Ellie Sanderson, Julie Dirkse, Norm Dyck, Peter Ibison, Nike Adebajo, Mike Rutter, Rich Robinson, Vanessa Chamberlin, Jayne Franklin and Charlotte Codina for your valuable contributions and feedback.

Finally, thank you to the Accessible Prophecy family around the world. I love being on this adventure with you.

NOTES

FOREWORD

1   See, for example, Julia Duin, 'Charismatics Issue "Prophetic Standards" To Address False Trump Prophecies', *Religion Unplugged*, 29 April 2021, https://religionunplugged.com/news/2021/4/28/charismatics-issue-prophetic-standards-to-address-false-trump-prophecies.

2   Joseph Mattera, 'The Need for Prophetic Standards in the Church', 4 May 2021, https://josephmattera.org/need-prophetic-church/. See also Joseph Mattera, *The Purpose, Power, and Process of Prophetic Ministry* (New York: eGen Co, 2021). Mattera himself is a prominent leader of the influential network USCAL.

3   Alan Hirsch, *5Q: Reactivating the Original Intelligence and Capacity of the Body of Christ* (Atlanta: 100 Movements Publishing, 2017), 102–105.

4   See https://bobekblad.com/resources-2/books-articles/.

INTRODUCTION: OFF THE MAP?

1   Ezekiel 43:2; Revelation 1:15.

2   1 Kings 19:12.

3   See, for example, Hosea 2:19–20 and Hosea 11.

4   Exodus 34:14.

5   Exodus 3:5; Psalm 24:3; Isaiah 8:13.

6   Exodus 19:6, 22:31; Leviticus 11:45, 20:26; Deuteronomy 7:6; Romans 1:7; Ephesians 1:4.

7   Exodus 3:15; Isaiah 6:8–9; Jeremiah 1:7.

8   Exodus 3; 1 Kings 19:11–13; Ezekiel 1.

9   Isaiah 6; Jeremiah 23:18; Amos 3:7.

10   Aaron Chalmers, *Interpreting the Prophets: Reading, Understanding and Preaching from the Worlds of the Prophets* (Downers Grove IL: InterVarsity Press, 2015), 6–7.

11   See, for example, the last few chapters of Isaiah, and Ezekiel 38–39.

12   John 14:9.

13   Acts 2:17.

14   1 Corinthians 2:10–12.

15   Interviewed in the *Financial Times*, Eliot Higgins, founder of Bellingcat, says 'We're

on the precipice of the misinformation age', Henry Mance, *Financial Times*, 30 January 2021, https://www.ft.com/content/0f31590f-74cf-4cfa-b0d6-92e8f27d6d34. See also Sinan Aral's TED talk, 'How we can protect truth in the age of misinformation', TED, 16 January 2020, https://www.youtube.com/watch?v=-7ORAKULel4.

16 John 14:26.
17 John 16:13.
18 John 16:8.
19 John 10:1–5.
20 John 3:8.

1 THE BIGGER PICTURE

1 We will come back to the concept of prophetic intelligence throughout the book.
2 'The Guardian's 1986 "Points of view" advert', *The Guardian*, YouTube channel, https://www.youtube.com/watch?v=_SsccRkLLzU.
3 The biblical foundations of these two approaches are explored in chapters six and eight.
4 Colossians 1:15.
5 See John 14:8–9.
6 John 17:3, 26.
7 For example, Exodus 3:6,14–15.
8 For example, Exodus 34:6-7; Isaiah 43:10–13.
9 For example, Jeremiah 31:3; Ezekiel 5:13.
10 Jeremiah 29:13.
11 John 17:21–23.
12 Luke 15:20.
13 Genesis 1:27–28.
14 See, for example, 1 Samuel 3:21, 1 Kings 18:1, Jeremiah 1:4-5.
15 Isaiah 9:6–7 (the Hebrew word translated as 'peace' in these verses is *shalom*).
16 Walter Brueggemann, *The Prophetic Imagination* (Minneapolis: Fortress Press, 2018), 36.
17 Abraham J. Heschel, *The Prophets* (New York: HarperCollins, 1962), xxvii.
18 Heschel, *The Prophets*, 6.
19 See C. S. Lewis, *The Lion, the Witch and the Wardrobe* (The Chronicles of Narnia) (London: HarperCollins, 2002).
20 Brueggemann, *The Prophetic Imagination*, 9.
21 C. S. Lewis, *A Grief Observed* (London: Faber and Faber, 1961), 52.
22 Exodus 3:4.
23 Exodus 3:10.
24 Brueggemann's *The Prophetic Imagination* speaks powerfully of the role of prophetic ministry in generating an alternative consciousness. We will return to this theme in chapter nine.
25 Exodus 19:6.

26 John 14:9.

27 John 1:18; Colossians 1:15.

28 John 1:1, 14, 3:34; 1 John 1:1.

29 Luke 22:20; Hebrews 9:15.

30 John 5:19.

31 Matthew 4:1; 12:28; Luke 4:1, 14, 18.

32 Luke 6:12.

33 Matthew 9:4; 12:25; Luke 6:8; 9:47.

34 John 4:17–18, 29; Luke 19:5.

35 Matthew 4:17; 15:7.

36 Luke 7:21; Romans 8:1–4; Hebrews 2:14–15.

37 See Jesus' confrontations with the Pharisees and with Pilate; John chapter 18.

38 A good example of this is John 8:1–11; see also Luke 4:18–19; Matthew 10:26–27.

39 Brueggemann, *The Prophetic Imagination*, 88–89.

40 For example, Matthew 9:10; John 4:1–26.

41 For example, Matthew 24; Mark 13:2.

42 Matthew 23:1–12; Luke 13:10–17.

43 For example, Matthew 21:11; Mark 6:15; Luke 24:19.

44 John 14:12.

2 A JESUS-SHAPED CHURCH

1 Sir Walter Raleigh was also a spy, coloniser of Ireland and prime marketer of tobacco.

2 See, for example, Charles C. Mann, 'How the Potato Changed the World', *Smithsonian*, November 2011, https://www.smithsonianmag.com/history/how-the-potato-changed-the-world-108470605/.

3 Our beloved fish and chips.

4 Ephesians 1:4, 11.

5 Ephesians 1:5.

6 Ephesians 2:10.

7 Ephesians 2:19.

8 Ephesians 2:6.

9 Ephesians 2:14.

10 Ephesians 2:21.

11 To keep things simple, I am using the term *fivefold ministry* throughout the book to refer to the five ministries listed in Ephesians 4:11. Other authors or practitioners may refer to the acronym APEST, to 5Q (Alan Hirsch), or to the Pentagon (Mike Breen).

12 The Greek word in Ephesians 4:11 is *poimen,* and while some English Bibles translate it as *pastor*, it is frequently translated as *shepherd* throughout the New Testament.

13 Alan Hirsch and Jessie Cruickshank, *Activating 5Q: A User's Guide* (Atlanta, GA: 100 Movements, 2018), 15.

14 Alan Hirsch, *5Q: Reactivating the Original Intelligence and Capacity of the Body of Christ* (Atlanta, GA: 100 Movements, 2017), 87.
15 We will explore this further in chapter twelve.
16 This is the central message of Hirsch's *5Q.*

3 THE OLD TESTAMENT TRADITION

1 Rembrandt van Rijn, *Jeremiah Lamenting the Destruction of Jerusalem*, 1630. The painting can be viewed online at the Rijks Museum website, https://www.rijks-museum.nl/en/collection/SK-A-3276.
2 I first heard it phrased like this by my friend Ceri Harris, leader of Burlington Baptist Church, Ipswich.
3 Alan Hirsch frequently uses the idea of reactivating latent gifts in *5Q.*
4 I'm grateful to Paul Maconochie who originally shared this with me.
5 1 Kings 17:2, 8; 18:1; 19:9; 21:17.
6 1 Kings 17:1; 21:19.
7 The term 'literary prophets' refers to the four major prophets (Isaiah, Jeremiah, Ezekiel and Daniel) and the twelve minor prophets (Hosea to Malachi). It should be noted that we cannot be certain who was responsible for composing their prophetic words in written form, or the process by which these books came to bear their names. For further discussion, see Chalmers, *Interpreting the Prophets*, 22ff.
8 For example, Matthew 2:6; Luke 3:4–6; Romans 9:33.
9 Mark 2:22.
10 Heschel, *The Prophets*, Introduction xxi and following.
11 See, for example, Jeremiah 1:7–10.
12 Deuteronomy 18:20.
13 For example, the prophet Nathan was an advisor to King David.
14 For example, see Jeremiah 26.
15 1 Samuel 9:9.
16 1 Peter 1:2, Galatians 5:22–23.
17 John 16:8
18 Exodus 33:11.
19 For more on this see Brueggemann, *The Prophetic Imagination*, 6ff.
20 Exodus 3:14.
21 Exodus 33:11.
22 Isaiah 3:8.
23 In his sixth volume on the glory of the Lord, Hans Urs von Balthasar writes brilliantly about how, from the perspective of the covenant, we can essentially understand sin as infidelity. 'Evil arises precisely at the point where this God seems insufficient to Israel, which therefore turns away from him to look for other gods. Evil *is* this very act of turning away.' Hans Urs von Balthasar, *The Glory of the Lord VI* (Edinburgh: T&T Clark, 1991) 201–205.
24 For more on this see Heschel, *The Prophets*, 29–31.

25 Jeremiah 7.

26 Ezekiel 3:1–2.

27 Jeremiah 13:1.

28 Hosea 1:2–3.

29 Balthasar, *The Glory of the Lord VI*, 219.

4 NEW COVENANT PROPHETS

1   Though he might have had an inkling of this. See Jeremiah 31:33–34.

2   Revelation 1:9-20.

3   Here I'm using the title *Apostle* in the traditional sense of referring to one of Jesus' twelve disciples.

4   1 John 1:1–3.

5   Matthew 11:3.

6   Adrienne von Speyr, *John: The Word Becomes Flesh – Meditations on John 1-5* (San Francisco, CA: Ignatius Press, 1994), 24.

7   John 14:16–17.

8   2 Corinthians 5:18–19.

9   Heschel, *The Prophets*, xxi.

10 It's interesting that it is John's Gospel that adopts the most dualistic, black-and-white perspective; throughout, people are either 'of God' or 'of the world,' and it contains many contrasts between light and darkness, truth and falsehood, life and death. etc.

11 Evelyn Underhill, *The Mystics of the Church* (Eugene, OR: Wipf and Stock, 2002), 12.

12 I really like Shawn Bolz's phrase 'translating God'. For more on this concept, see Shawn Bolz, *Translating God: Hearing God's Voice for Yourself and the World Around You* (Newtype, 2015), 166–167.

13 We see Judas and Silas doing this in Acts 15:32.

14 Heschel brilliantly described the experience of being immersed in the words of the prophets as 'being exposed to a ceaseless shattering of indifference.' Heschel, *The Prophets*, xxv.

15 *Kairos* is the Greek word for *time* that is used in Mark 1:15. This is not a chronological, sequential time but rather a significant moment when something notable happens. In *Building a Discipling Culture*, Mike Breen writes about how we can understand a *kairos* moment as a time when 'God breaks into our reality and really gets our attention.' Breen, *Building a Discipling Culture* (3DM Publishing, 2016), 76–78.

16 I'm aware that this term is problematic because it is not gender-neutral; but the English language doesn't yet provide a sufficient alternative.

17 There is a good chapter titled 'Prophetic Watchmen in the Church' in Greg Haslam's book *Moving in the Prophetic: a Biblical Guide to Effective Prophetic Ministry Today* (Oxford: Monarch Books, 2009).

18 Walter Brueggemann puts it like this: 'The alternative consciousness to be nurtured serves to energise persons and communities by its promise of another time and

situation toward which the community of faith may move. To that extent, it attempts to … live in fervent anticipation of the newness that God has promised and will surely give.' *The Prophetic Imagination*, 3.

19   Dietrich Bonhoeffer, Confirmation sermon, Germany, April 9, 1938.

5   THE PROPHETIC COMMUNITY

1   Romans 8:15; Ephesians 1:5.

2   2 Corinthians 5:17.

3   John 1:12; 1 John 3:1.

4   Henri Nouwen, *Love, Henri: Letters on the Spiritual Life* (London: Convergent Books, 2016), 340.

5   Mark 1:11.

6   See, for example, social psychologist Sherry Turkle's *Alone Together: Why We Expect More from Technology and Less from Each Other* (New York: Basic Books, 2017).

7   Oxford Review, 'Collective Intelligence', https://oxford-review.com/oxford-review-encyclopaedia-terms/collective-intelligence/.

8   Prerna Chikersal, et al., 'Deep Structures of Collaboration: Physiological Correlates of Collective Intelligence and Group Satisfaction', 2017, https://doi.org/10.1145/2998181.2998250.

9   Alan Hirsch, among others, uses this framework of Vertical and Horizontal. See *5Q*, 102.

10   Exodus 33:11; Luke 6:12; 2 Corinthians 12:2.

11   This is not about judging others. We have to learn how to name societal sin in a mature, loving, culturally appropriate manner.

12   JR Woodward, *Creating a Missional Culture: Equipping the Church for the Sake of the World*, (Downers Grove, IL: InterVarsity Press, 2012), 95.

13   Luke 10:27.

6   THE MOUNTAIN

1   Exodus 3:1, 3:12, 18:5, 24:13, 1 Kings 19:8.

2   1 Kings 19.

3   Though scholars are not agreed, this likely took place on Mount Tabor, north of Mount Horeb.

4   Richard Foster, *Streams of Living Water: Celebrating the Great Traditions of Christian Faith* (London: HarperCollins, 1998), 49.

5   Luke 10:38–42.

6   Psalm 46:10.

7   Quoted by Martin Laird, *Into the Silent Land: The Practice of Contemplation* (London: Darton, Longman and Todd, 2006), 23.

8   Richard Foster, *Celebration of Discipline: The Path to Spiritual Growth* (London: Hodder, 1980), 13.

9   See Graham Cooke 'Permission Has Been Granted', *Brilliant Perspectives*, 7 January 2021, https://brilliantperspectives.com/permission-granted/.

10 Henri Nouwen, *Bread for the Journey: A Daybook of Wisdom and Faith* (New York: HarperCollins, 1997), 13.

11 John 13:23.

12 John 15:2; Hebrews 12:1.

13 John 14:16 NKJV.

14 John 10:10.

15 Ephesians 5:18.

16 1 Corinthians 12:4–11.

17 John 14:18.

18 John 16:7.

19 John 14:20.

20 Acts 2:17–18.

21 1 Corinthians 2:9–11.

22 1 Corinthians 12:7.

23 Mark 1:15 NKJV.

24 Luke 3:22, 4:1, 4:14.

25 I really like The Bible Project's video on the theology of the temple; see https://bibleproject.com/explore/video/temple.

26 Exodus 40:34–38; 1 Kings 8:10–11.

7 CLIMBING THE MOUNTAIN TOGETHER

1   Revelation 2:4 NKJV.

2   Exodus 13:21–22.

3   Genesis 1:2.

4   Matthew 28:20.

5   John 15:5.

6   John 17:23.

7   Colossians 3:3.

8   Laird, *Into the Silent Land*, 15.

9   Brother Lawrence, *The Practice of the Presence of God*, trans E. M. Blaiklock (London: Hodder & Stoughton), 44.

10 1 Corinthians 14:3.

11 Romans 8:29.

12 Travis Kroeker and Bruce Ward, *Remembering the End: Dostoevsky as Prophet to Modernity* (New York: Routledge, 2001), 23.

8   THE ROAD

1   Harvard's Michael Sandel explores three contrasting subcultures, each with their own claim on the word, in his book *Justice: What's the Right Thing To Do?* (London: Penguin Books, 2010).

2   Micah 6:8.

3   See, for example, Genesis 39:21; Exodus 15:13; 2 Chronicles 7:3; Psalm 13:5, 17:7, 23:6, 36:7; Isaiah 54:10 NRSV.

4   Exodus 3:4–15.

5   Exodus 2:11-15.

6   Heschel, *The Prophets*, 288–289.

7   For example, Romans 8:26, 12:15.

8   For a good summary on this see 'Justice: Hiding in Translation', *God Loves Justice*, 13 December 2018; https://www.godlovesjustice.com/blog/2018/10/30/rmmrdqb6aureh1cekjqw4iw4s42a.

9   See for example Psalm 82:3; Proverbs 21:3; Micah 6:8; Zechariah 7:8–9.

10   Psalm 33:5.

11   Psalm 89:14, 97:2.

12   Isaiah 9:7.

13   Leviticus 25:8–55, 19:9–10.

14   Psalm 85:1, 10.

15   Isaiah 32:16–18

16   Adam L Gustine, *Becoming a Just Church: Cultivating Communities of God's Shalom* (Downers Grove, IL: InterVarsity Press, 2019), 21.

17   Lisa Sharon Harper, *The Very Good Gospel: How Everything Wrong Can Be Made Right* (New York: WaterBrook, 2016), 14.

18   Heschel, *The Prophets*, 250.

19   Amos 7:14.

20   Amos 3:8.

21   His first words as recorded in Mark's gospel are a declaration that the kingdom of God has come near (Mark 1:15).

22   Luke 6:17–36.

9   ON THE ROAD TOGETHER

1   Brueggemann, *The Prophetic Imagination*, 3.

2   Jenny and Justin Duckworth, *Against the Tide, Towards the Kingdom* (Eugene, OR: Cascade Books, 2011), 39.

3   Heschel, *The Prophets*, 5–6.

4   See https://www.tearfund.org/.

5   Cited (in the original Portuguese) in Zildo Rocha, *Helder, O Dom: uma vida que marcou os rumos da Igreja no Brasil* (Helder, the Gift: A Life that Marked the Course of the Church in Brazil), (Petrópolis: Editora Vozes, 2000), 53.

6   Brueggemann, *The Prophetic Imagination*, 3.

7   Gustine, *Becoming a Just Church*, 74.

8   Ibid., 63.

9   Ibid., 71.

10 Ibid., 59.

11 Romans 12:2.

12 Quoted by Jay Milbrandt, *Go and Do: Daring to Change the World One Story at a Time* (Illinois: Tyndale House, 2012), 117.

13 Rabbi and therapist Edwin H. Friedman developed the concept of non-anxious presence in his book *A Failure of Nerve: Leadership in the Age of the Quick Fix* (New York: Seabury Books, 2007).

14 Foster, *Streams of Living Water*, 175.

15 *The Oxford English Dictionary*, s.v. 'politics'.

16 Balthasar, *The Glory of the Lord VI*, 213.

17 Galatians 4:3, Colossians 2:8.

18 2 Corinthians 10:4.

19 Matthew 6:10.

10   BRINGING THE TWO DIMENSIONS TOGETHER

1   Gustine, *Becoming a Just Church*, 45.

2   Luke 1:35, 41, 67; 2:25; 3:16; 4:1, 14.

3   Luke is the only Gospel writer who mentions that Jesus was praying at the time of his baptism (Luke 3:21). See also Luke 5:16; 6:12; 9:18, 28–29; 11:1; 22:32, 41.

4   For example, the parables of the Rich Fool in Luke 12:13–21 and the Rich Man and Lazarus in Luke 16:19–31.

5   Luke 4:18–19.

6   Brad Jersac, *Can You Hear Me? Tuning in to the God Who Speaks* (Oxford: Monarch Books, 2006), 229.

7   Neil Cole, *Primal Fire: Reigniting the Church with the Five Gifts of Jesus* (Carol Stream, IL: Tyndale House, 2014), 156.

8   Brueggemann, *The Prophetic Imagination*, 3.

9   Ibid., 81.

10 Shane Claiborne, *The Irresistible Revolution: Living as an Ordinary Radical* (Grand Rapids: Zondervan, 2006), 309.

11 For a comprehensive overview, see Mike Breen, *Covenant and Kingdom: The DNA of the Bible* (3DM, 2010).

12 Adapted from Hirsch, *5Q*, 160.

11   THE PROPHETIC PROCESS

1   Jeremiah 20:9.

2   John 10:27.
3   Isaiah 55:10–11 is a great reminder of the potential transformative power that comes with God's spoken word.
4   Pope Francis (@Pontifex), Twitter, 22 July 2020.
5   1 Corinthians 14:3.
6   See Craig Greenfield, 'Worship Music is Broken. Here's What We Can Do About It', 17 September 2021, https://www.craiggreenfield.com/blog/worship-music-is-broken. See also Michael J. Rhodes, 'Why Don't We Sing Justice Songs in Worship?', *Christianity Today*, 30 September 2021, https://www.christianitytoday.com/ct/2021/september-web-only/rhodes-ccli-top-25-worship-songs-singing-justice-songs.html.
7   Jersak, *Can You Hear Me?*, 195.
8   A. W. Tozer, *That Incredible Christian* (Harrisburg, PA: Christian Publications, 1964), 49.
9   Matthew 7:26–27.
10 Originally quoted by Nietzsche but popularised in recent years through Eugene H. Peterson's book of the same title. Eugene H. Peterson, *A Long Obedience in the Same Direction: Discipleship in an Instant Society* (Illinois: InterVarsity Press, 2000).

12   PROPHETIC INTELLIGENCE FOR EVERYONE

1   Eugene Peterson, 'Introduction to Amos' in *The Message Devotional Bible: Featuring Notes and Reflections from Eugene H. Peterson* (Colorado Springs, CO: NavPress, 2018), 1009.
2   See Hirsch, *5Q*, 150–151.
3   Ibid., 150.
4   Dallas Willard, *The Divine Conspiracy: Rediscovering Our Hidden Life In God* (London: Harper Collins, 1998), 62.
5   John 15:11, 16:24, 17:13.
6   For further information, see http://www.epcew.org.uk/wsc/wsc-html.
7   John 3:34.
8   2 Corinthians 4:7.
9   Brian Zahnd (@BrianZahnd), Twitter, 30 July 2019.
10 In Luke 10, Jesus' missional strategy is focused on finding the person of peace (Luke 10:5–7).
11 In *5Q*, Hirsch is explicit in taking the concept of 'intelligence quotient' (IQ) and applying it to the fivefold ministry. Thus he talks about the five intelligences (or aptitudes) of APEST: AQ (apostolic intelligence), PQ (prophetic intelligence), etc. *5Q*, 44.
12 Romans 8:29.
13 You can find details of Accessible Prophecy coaching at https://www.accessibleprophecy.com/.
14 Cath Livesey, *My Sheep Have Ears: Prophecy Within Discipleship and Mission* (2015), 33–34.
15 Mike Breen uses the language of 'base and phase'. Your 'base' ministry refers to your

primary fivefold ministry; your 'phase' ministry refers to a particular period when God gives you opportunity to stretch into one of the other four. See Breen, *Building a Discipling Culture*, 167–171.

13 DEVELOPING PROPHETIC CULTURE

1   See M. Jason Martin, "'That's the Way We Do Things Around Here'": An Overview of Organizational Culture', *The Electronic Journal of Academic and Special Librarianship*, *Vol 7., No. 1* (Spring 2006) http://southernlibrarianship.icaap.org/content/v07n01/martin_m01.htm.

2   The 5Q Collective now has a number of tests to diagnose a church or organisation's fivefold profile; see https://5qcentral.com/.

3   Concept and diagram developed by Rich Robinson, Movement Leaders Collective (https://movementleaderscollective.com/) and is used in the 5QCollective training (https://5qcentral.com/5q-collective/).

4   Philippians 1:6.

CONCLUSION: CARRYING THE REVELATION OF GOD

1   I like how Balthasar expresses it in his book on prayer: 'He gathers up all the words of God scattered throughout the world and concentrates them in himself, the intense focus of revelation.' Hans Urs van Balthasar, *Prayer* (San Francisco: Ignatius Press, 1986), 19.

2   John Cassian's Tenth Conference; see Rowan Williams, *Silence and Honey Cakes* (Oxford: Lion Hudson, 2003), 12.

3   Ronald Rolheiser, *The Holy Longing: The Search for a Christian Spirituality* (New York: Random House, 2014), 33.

4   See, for example, *Udemy In Depth: 2018 Workplace Distraction Report*, https://research.udemy.com/wp-content/uploads/2018/03/Workplace-Distraction-Report-2018-2021-Rebrand-v3-gs.pdf.

5   Message of his Holiness Pope Francis for Lent 2015, 4 October 2014, https://www.vatican.va/content/francesco/en/messages/lent/documents/papa-francesco_20141004_messaggio-quaresima2015.html.

6   From the speech 'Religion and Race' January 14, 1963.

Accessible Prophecy is a ministry that trains people and churches around the world in healthy and mature prophetic culture and ministry. Our vision is to make prophecy normal and accessible for every follower of Jesus. We provide strategic training, coaching and resources.

Our training opportunities include:

- Online cohort-based coaching for discipleship in prophetic life-style and ministry
- Training in the prophetic call to social justice
- Leadership coaching for developing prophetic culture
- Mentoring in prophetic art

For more information, please visit our website:
www.accessibleprophecy.com

or contact us at:
connect@accessibleprophecy.com

Printed in Great Britain
by Amazon

29580269R00153